The Which? Guide to Insurance

About the author

Virginia Wallis is a freelance writer and editor who has worked with a large insurance company as a member of a project writing and designing its consumer literature and forms. Formerly a financial writer in the Which? Money Group, editor of *Which?* magazine's annual *Tax Saving Guide* and an editor on *Which?* magazine, she is a regular contributor to *Which? Way to Save Tax* (also published annually by Which? Books).

Acknowledgements

The author and publishers would like to thank the following for their help in the preparation of this book: Sophie Gumpel, Phil Telford, Neil Walkling and Teresa Fritz of the Services Research Group at *Which?* magazine; Jonquil Lowe, author of *Be Your Own Financial Adviser* (published by Which? Books); and Alison Lindley of the Legal Affairs department at Consumers' Association.

The Which? Guide to Insurance

Virginia Wallis

 CONSUMERS' ASSOCIATION

Which? Books are commissioned and researched by
Consumers' Association and published by
Which? Ltd, 2 Marylebone Road, London NW1 4DF
Email address: books@which.net

Distributed by The Penguin Group:
Penguin Books Ltd, 27 Wrights Lane, London W8 5TZ

First edition June 1998

Copyright © 1998 Which? Ltd

British Library Cataloguing in Publication Data
A catalogue record for this book is available from the British Library

ISBN 0 85202 725 7

For a full list of *Which?* books, please write to Which? Books, Castlemead, Gascoyne Way,
Hertford X, SG14 1LH or access our web site at www.which.net

Cover and text design by Kyzen Creative Consultants

Typeset by Saxon Graphics Ltd, Derby
Printed and bound in England by Clays Ltd, Bungay, Suffolk

Contents

★An asterisk next to the name of an organisation in the text indicates that the address can be found in this section

Introduction

Every year, we spend billions of pounds on that elusive commodity, 'peace of mind'. To the person who has just had an insurance claim settled in full and with no fuss, it is money well spent; to the many thousands of people who find that their insurance does not deliver what it seemed to promise, it is money down the drain.

Part of the problem is that it is often only when you come to make a claim that you discover that the peace of mind you have paid for evaporates just when you need it: nearly half the complaints dealt with by the Insurance Ombudsman Bureau concern the mismatch between consumer expectation and the cover actually provided by a policy. This is particularly true of insurance sold on the back of another product, such as travel insurance, loan payment protection insurance and insurance for domestic appliances. A consumer may be pressured into buying the policy on offer, but hard-pressed to discover precisely what is and what is not covered, or indeed whether the policy duplicates cover already bought (a common problem with travel insurance). This situation is not helped by the fact that a lot of these types of insurance is sold by people who know little about the product they are selling but a great deal more about the commission earned when they sell it.

Commission is no doubt what is attracting major retailers and the privatised utilities to offer insurance to their customers; and the *absence* of commission is what the newer direct insurers like to stress in their promotional material. Mortgage lenders have known for years that the commission they get from selling insurance makes it a profitable sideline, and this has been the main reason for their over-selling of endowment mortgages. Commission also had a large part to play in the mis-selling of personal pensions – the review of which is set to continue until the year 2000.

And when the year 2000 arrives, do not expect your insurance to pay out for any problems you have with equipment as a result of the 'millennium bug'. The Association of British Insurers has made it clear that because the year 2000 problem is an avoidable one, insurance will not cover it.

It is clear that private insurance provision is in future going to play a larger part in our lives: according to the government's Green Paper on Welfare Reform (published in March 1998), insurance will deliver a substantial share of welfare provision by the year 2020; investment-type insurance will be sold as part of the new Individual Savings Account (due to replace PEPs and TESSAs in April 1999); and insurance will be a key element in the reform of the civil legal aid system. However, what is not yet clear is the exact form that private insurance provision will take and how far the government will be successful in getting the insurance industry to address the failings of its current products.

The government, the Insurance Ombudsman and Consumers' Association have all criticised loan payment protection insurance for not providing the kind of protection you might expect it to provide and – according to the Ombudsman – for its being mis-sold to people who have no hope of the insurance ever paying out because it does not cover their personal circumstances. Consumers' Association and others have attacked personal pensions for being expensive and overly complicated, criticisms which the government hopes will not be levelled at its proposed 'stakeholder pension' (currently envisaged as a cheaper and simpler type of personal pension). The regulator has already expressed concern at the way in which some types of long-term care insurance are being sold – an issue that needs to be addressed by the Royal Commission on the funding of long-term care, due to report in early 1999.

As the pressure to buy insurance increases, *The Which? Guide to Insurance* – which deals both with general insurance and with insurance as an investment – will help you to make an accurate assessment of your needs. It explains alternatives to insurance (where these might be appropriate), and pinpoints which sorts of insurance are really worth buying and which are of questionable value. You will find detailed information on what policies do and do not cover, together with advice on judging how suitable each type of insurance is for your own personal circumstances. There is help on how to compare policies and how to get the cover you need without paying over the odds for it. If you have to make a claim, there is guidance to ensure that your claim is settled in full and without delay. But if things do go wrong, you will find information on taking matters further if you think your insurer is trying to wriggle out of its obligations.

The best defence against being mis-sold inappropriate insurance or having a claim rejected is to know what you are buying and to ask the right questions. *The Which? Guide to Insurance* will help you to do just that.

Chapter 1

Insurance basics

If the financial consequences of losing your home, belongings, good health or income are too dire to contemplate, you need insurance. If you could find some other way of coping financially, at least in part, insurance is not a necessity; but you do need it if you want to know that someone else will foot the bill if disaster strikes. One exception is car insurance: if you want to drive a car on a public road, you are legally required to have insurance.

Insurance is intended to put you back to where you were before something unexpected or unpredictable happens that results in your suffering financially. With the exception of investment-linked insurance (see page 11), you are not supposed to profit from it, which explains why you do not have to pay tax on any payments made to you under most insurance policies.

Whether you choose to take out insurance depends on three main factors: the likelihood of loss occurring, the severity of the financial consequences if it does, and what you have to pay for the insurance. For example: the likelihood of your house being burned to the ground is slight but the financial consequences are extremely severe and the rebuilding costs will be far more than you would pay in insurance premiums. It is more likely that your washing machine will break down than that your home will be destroyed, but if it does break down you would face a £50 repair bill at best and at worst you would have to replace it – and both of these scenarios could turn out to be a lot cheaper than paying for insurance. Whether you need to buy insurance also depends on how keen you are to maintain the status quo in the face of financial loss (such as losing your job) and what other resources you have available to help you cope.

Do you need insurance?

As with any other financial product, which particular type of insurance you need to buy depends on your personal circumstances. The table below gives an overview of the types of insurance available (which are discussed in more detail in the following chapters) and the circumstances in which you might want to consider buying.

Your insurance choices

Your personal circumstances	Type of insurance to consider first	Other insurance you could consider
you own your own home	• buildings insurance	
you have belongings that you could not afford to replace	• contents insurance	• appliance insurance
you drive a car (or other motor vehicle)	• car insurance	• mechanical breakdown insurance
you want the option of paying for private medical treatment	• private medical insurance	• dental insurance
you will be travelling abroad	• travel insurance	
there are people who are financially dependent on you	• term insurance • mortgage protection insurance	
you would not have enough to live on if you were unable to work because of illness	• permanent health insurance	• critical illness insurance • accident and sickness insurance
you would be hard-pressed to pay off your debts if you became unemployed	• mortgage payment protection insurance	• insurance for personal loans and credit cards
you would not want to sell your home to pay for long-term care in your old age	• long-term care insurance	
you work for yourself	• business insurance	
you want to be able to go to law but you don't qualify for legal aid	• legal expenses insurance	
you have unusual requirements	• specialist insurance	

> **Insurance as an investment**
>
> This chapter, and most of this book, deals with general insurance – i.e. straight insurance which pays out if you have a valid claim but which gives you nothing back if you don't. Some insurance products mix straight insurance with an investment element so that – on the face of it – you get something back even if you don't claim. The most common example of this is investment-type life insurance where part of what you pay in premiums buys a modest amount of life insurance while the rest is invested. (See Part 5.)
>
> However, as a general rule, if you want to buy insurance – i.e. you are anxious to protect yourself against potential financial loss – it is better to buy straight insurance and to keep your investments separate. The exceptions to this rule are personal pensions (see Chapter 18), annuities (see Chapter 19) and some investment-type life insurance linked to an interest-only mortgage (see Chapters 20 and 21), all of which can be worth considering in some specific circumstances. The rules relating to the selling of investment-linked insurance are dealt with in Chapter 22.

What insurance covers

One of the main reasons that insurance claims are rejected is that the insurance did not cover the cause of the claim. It is therefore very important that you read your policy, which contains the terms of the contract that you and the insurer entered into when you bought the insurance. The policy tells you what the insurance covers, sets out the circumstances in which the insurer will – and will not – pay out and explains your rights as a policyholder. There is no doubt that some policies can be hard going; however most policies these days are reasonably clear and a distinct improvement on the gobbledegook found ten years ago. If you are having problems understanding what your policy says, do not hesitate to contact your insurer.

Warning

Don't rely on the honeyed words and warm assurances of the friendly marketing bumph: if you want to find out precisely what your insurance covers – and so reduce the risk of having a claim rejected – it is vital that you read the policy.

As well as giving details of what the insurance covers, the policy will also explain the 'conditions' – if any – attached to the insurance cover. It is a condition of most buildings insurance, for example, that you keep your home in a good state of repair. You also need to check for 'endorsements' which tell you about extra conditions and exclusions (see below) that particularly apply to you. If you live in a high-risk area, for example, you may be covered for theft under your contents insurance only if you have fitted certain types of door or window locks.

What insurance does not cover

When you buy insurance, the person selling it to you should point out the most important 'exclusions' – i.e. the circumstances in which the insurance will *not* pay out. However, that does not mean that you will be told about every last detail of what the insurance does not cover.

Tip

Ideally, you should read the policy *before* you buy any form of insurance but in practice it is unlikely that you will be given the opportunity. This is particularly true of insurance sold on the back of something else, for example travel insurance with a holiday, loan payment protection insurance with a loan, appliance insurance when you buy appliances and other electrical goods. However, you can get a good idea of the kind of cover you can expect each type of insurance to give you by referring to the sections 'What is covered' and 'What is not covered' in the chapters which follow.

Choosing the right policy

There can be a yawning chasm between what the promotional literature for an insurance product promises and what it will actually deliver, which is why it is so important to get a realistic view of what you are insured for by reading the policy and/or asking detailed questions before you buy. However, as well as checking the *circumstances* in which the policy will pay out, you should also check *how much* the policy will pay out. This includes checking whether:

- there are limits on what you can claim – a lot of insurance has different limits applying to different parts of the policy and there may be limits for certain individual items
- you have to pay the first part of any claim – i.e. if there is a 'compulsory excess' of £50 or £100, for example
- a claim will be paid only after a certain amount of time has elapsed – which is common for insurance designed to replace income
- there is a limit on the length of time during which money will be paid to you (on insurance such as loan payment protection insurance).

If, having checked the detail, you find that the insurance fails to meet your expectations or you cannot get a sensible explanation from the person selling you the policy, ask yourself if it is really worth paying for. At this point, it is a good idea to compare the cost of the insurance with the financial consequences of not buying it at all. For example, if you discover that the insurance you thought would pay off your credit card bills in full if you lost your job turns out to meet only a small proportion of the payment and then only for a year, you may decide that using your savings to pay off your debts would be a better alternative.

How much cover?

The guiding principle of insurance is that you can claim for what you lost and no more. This means that there is absolutely no point insuring for more than you need to because it will be a waste of money. 'Over-insuring' does not mean that you can claim for more than you stand to lose as a way of making money. If your insurer suspects that your claim has left you better off than before (this is called 'betterment' in the insurance industry's jargon), your claim will be reduced. For example, if your portable television is stolen and you claim to replace it with a state-of-the-art model with a huge screen, your claim will be reduced to the amount you would need to buy another portable.

Another more general principle is that you get what you pay for. If you insure for less than you need to – i.e. you are 'under-insured' – payment of any claim will usually take into account the fact that the premiums you paid were for a lower amount of cover. If, for example, you insure the contents of your home for £15,000 but the cost of replacing them is £20,000, any claim you have to make will be reduced in line with your under-insurance (i.e. only 75 per cent of your claim will be met). Similarly, if you make a claim to replace something as new – your three-year-old camera, for example – but the insurance you bought gives only 'indemnity' cover (where the insurance will pay the value of the item at the time you lost it), your claim will be reduced to the figure you would need to buy a three-year-old camera.

Warning

Don't assume that 'new-for-old' means that you will always be able to claim the cost of replacing something with a brand new item. Your insurer can insist that you have the item repaired if this is a practical solution. Some things – clothes, for example – are never covered on a new-for-old basis.

Life insurance works differently because you agree what will be paid out – the 'sum assured' – when you take out the policy. If you die, the agreed lump sum is what will be paid to your dependants. Whether this is enough or too much is a question of getting your sums right at the outset (see Chapter 10).

Don't duplicate

With the exception of life insurance, the principle that you should not profit from insurance also comes into play if you are covered for the same thing under two different policies: you cannot claim twice. Instead, when you claim you are obliged to tell the insurer about any other insurance you have that might also pay out. The insurers then agree how much of your claim each will pay. To avoid paying two sets of premiums for the same cover, check what your current policies cover you for before you buy other insurance. We highlight the particular instances in the chapters which follow.

You will also find that insurance will not pay out if there is some other way to compensate you for your loss – for example, you could sue your builder for the shoddy workmanship that contributed to damage to your home, or you can claim state benefits to replace at least part of your income lost as a result of sickness.

What insurance costs

What you pay for insurance depends on a number of factors, the most influential of which is the risk to the insurer that you will claim and that the insurer will have to pay out. Armies of actuaries and statisticians are employed to assess the probability of the things that trigger a claim actually happening. They will also look at the number of people who want to insure against the same risk: the more people there are paying into the pot from which claims are paid, the less it will cost each individual policyholder.

However, this does not mean that all policyholders always pay the same amount for their insurance. As you would expect, the higher the level of cover you want, the more you pay. Your personal circumstances – and how they affect the likelihood that the insurer will have to pay out – are also usually taken into account and reflected in the price you pay. For example, if you live in a high-crime area, you will pay more for contents insurance; if you are a young driver or you have a history of accidents, you will pay more for car insurance; the older you are, the more you will pay for life insurance.

If insurers think that you represent too high a risk, they can decide not to insure you or they can load the premiums. What they cannot do is offer you different terms or refuse you cover on grounds of your sex, race or disability. They can, however, alter the terms or refuse you cover if their decision is based on information or data which is accurate and relevant to the assessment of the risk. This includes actuarial or statistical data, medical or scientific research and individual medical reports.

Insurance, disability and health problems

If you are disabled or if you suffer long-term ill health, you may experience problems getting any type of insurance that requires evidence of your health. Some health-related charities – for example the British Diabetic Association* and the British Epilepsy Association* – may be able to recommend sympathetic insurers and intermediaries that offer specialist schemes. These claim they can often offer a better deal because experience enables them to assess the risks of an individual case more accurately. Some generalist insurers are appointing specialist health underwriters and setting up medical health lines to advise on individual circumstances.

Note that under the Disability Discrimination Act 1995, insurers can offer different terms to or refuse disabled applicants only if the decision is based on information or data which is accurate and relevant to the assessment of the risk. If you fall within the scope of the Act and you think the insurer has treated you unfairly – for example, your premiums are higher than normal or you have been refused insurance – challenge the insurers to produce evidence to justify their assessment.

Cutting the cost

When buying insurance, getting the cover you need should be your first priority but price comes a close second. Competition in the insurance market means that the most effective way of cutting the cost of your insurance is to get quotes from several different sources (see 'Where to buy' opposite) before you buy. You can also cut your costs in other ways – although these vary according to the type of insurance you are buying. In general, you will find that you can pay less in premiums by:

- paying more than the compulsory excess towards any claim
- waiting longer before claiming (e.g. in the case of permanent health insurance)
- not claiming

- asking about discounts which may be available to certain groups of people or for taking certain steps to reduce the insurer's risk of having to pay out
- limiting the circumstances in which you can claim.

Where to buy

There are two main providers of insurance: insurance companies and Lloyd's underwriters, both of which 'underwrite' insurance policies – this means that they take on the risk of insuring you and pay your claims. You can buy insurance from insurance companies either direct or through a broker (see below) but you cannot buy a policy direct from Lloyd's: you have to use a broker. Conversely, the newer direct insurers will deal only with their customers, not with brokers – i.e. you can buy *only* directly from these sorts of insurance companies.

The insurance middlemen

While there are only two sorts of insurer, there is no shortage of people willing to sell you insurance. As well as buying direct from an insurance company, you can buy through an intermediary, which could be your bank, building society or another financial institution, or one of the many insurance brokers, advisers and consultants who advertise in the press and in *Yellow Pages*. The advantage of using an insurance intermediary is that they should do some of the donkey work of comparing policies for you – although how widely they cast their net when seeking out suitable policies depends on the type of intermediary they are.

Insurance brokers

The only intermediaries entitled to call themselves brokers are those who are registered under the Insurance Brokers (Registration) Act 1977. Among other things, brokers must have at least three years' experience in the insurance industry, must take out professional indemnity insurance (which covers them against your losing money if they are negligent or fraudulent), and should give independent advice based on a wide range of policies on the market, including Lloyd's policies if they are Lloyd's brokers or if they have an arrangement with a Lloyd's broker. Lloyd's brokers are the only brokers entitled to do business at Lloyd's but they can also sell the policies of insurance companies.

All insurance brokers must abide by a statutory code of conduct for which the Insurance Brokers Registration Council★ (IBRC) is responsible. The IBRC also deals with any complaints about the way a broker sold you insurance. You can obtain a list of brokers in your area by contacting the British Insurance and Investment Brokers' Association★ (BIIBA).

Independent intermediaries

These people often call themselves insurance advisers or consultants, and should give you independent advice about general insurance policies offered by any number of companies. They should have the same level of professional indemnity insurance as a broker but they do not have to follow a statutory code of conduct. Instead they agree to abide by a code of practice drawn up by the Association of British Insurers★ (ABI). If you have a complaint about the way insurance was sold to you, you have to take the matter up with the insurer if you cannot resolve it with the intermediary. You can check that an independent intermediary has the necessary professional indemnity insurance by contacting the ABI.

Company agents

These are not independent: they may be employees of the insurance company or an agent who can offer insurance from a maximum of six insurance companies. The insurance company (or companies) they represent takes responsibility for the advice they give you and requires its agents to follow the ABI Code of Practice.

Commission

Both brokers and independent intermediaries have to tell you how much commission they will be paid by the insurer whose policy they are selling you; company agents do not have to tell you. Any intermediary who is not a broker is also required by the ABI Code of Practice to tell you at the outset the capacity in which he or she is selling – i.e. whether he or she is independent or a company agent.

Warning

The rules for selling general insurance are different from the rules for selling investment-linked insurance. Some brokers registered with the IBRC are allowed to sell investment-linked insurance. Other intermediaries and companies cannot sell or give advice on investment-linked insurance unless they are authorised to do so by the Personal Investment Authority* (currently part of the Financial Services Authority*). For more details of what should happen when you buy investment-linked insurance, see Chapter 22.

Tip

A broker or other intermediary can be particularly useful if you have unusual or difficult insurance needs – if you want life cover, for example, but your health is poor, or you are considered to be high-risk because you have made a lot of claims in the past, or you want to buy specialist insurance.

Getting the best deal

No single broker, intermediary or insurance company will cover the whole insurance market. To stand the best chance of getting the cover you want and the cheapest quote, contact several brokers (including at least one with access to Lloyd's policies) or independent intermediaries, a couple of direct insurers (which do not sell their products through intermediaries) and a couple of Best Buy companies picked out in the regular reports on insurance published by *Which?*★ magazine. Make sure that whoever you are dealing with:

- tells you which insurer is offering the policy being recommended
- explains why the policy is suitable for you
- gives clear answers to any questions you have and contacts the insurer if he or she cannot answer them immediately
- goes through what is covered and what is not covered by the insurance

- tells you about any conditions you have to fulfil
- gives clear information about the procedures for claims and complaints – including telling you which dispute-settling scheme the insurer belongs to (see Chapter 23)
- makes it clear that the insurance may not pay out if you give inaccurate information or if you withhold information when applying for the insurance
- points out that you are responsible for all the information given on the insurance application form.

Warning

Be very careful if a broker or other intermediary fills in a proposal form on your behalf. Read what has been written before you sign it and make sure all the facts are exactly as you stated. It is always preferable to fill in any form yourself.

Buying insurance

Once you have decided which insurer offers you the best deal, you will need to fill in a proposal form. If you buy over the telephone, the questions you are asked will be the same as those on the form. You will receive a copy of the filled-in form to check and sign. It goes without saying that when asked a question either on the proposal form or when applying over the telephone, you should tell the truth. You also have a duty to 'disclose material facts' which means that you have to tell the insurer about anything that may affect the insurer's view of the risks involved in insuring you. In practice, you should not have to guess what the insurer considers to be 'material' because the person selling you the insurance should ask specific questions about the things that matter.

Once the insurer has accepted your application and you have made arrangements to pay the premium, you will receive your policy. Read this very carefully to check that you have the cover you wanted and that there are no conditions or endorsements of which you were unaware. If everything is fine, you are covered. If there is anything you are not clear about, go back to the person who sold you the policy and ask questions until you are satisfied. If you are not satisfied, you can cancel the policy, but do this as quickly as possible.

Fighting fraud

In 1997, according to the Association of British Insurers, the insurance industry paid out £595 million in fraudulent claims. In an attempt to tackle this problem, which pushes up the price of insurance for honest policyholders, the ABI announced action on two anti-fraud databases. One gives insurers access to the names of people convicted of insurance fraud. The other – the Claims and Underwriting Exchange Register – gives insurers shared information taken from application and claim forms. This has already helped to reduce the number of fraudulent claims.

Keeping your insurance up to date

Your duty to disclose does not end once you have bought the insurance: you also have to keep the insurer informed about any changes to the information you gave when you bought the policy.

In general, the main things insurers need to know about are whether you have changed your job or if you or anyone covered by the policy has been convicted of an offence. The other things they need to know depend on the type of insurance you have: if you have health insurance, the insurer will want to know if you have started to participate in an activity – hang-gliding, for example – which could increase the risk of your making a claim; if you have buildings or contents insurance for your home, it will be relevant to inform them of any changes to its state of repair or its use (you are now running a business from home or you are letting it, for example).

It can also be in your interests to tell the insurer about anything that will *reduce* the risk of your claiming, such as – in the case of contents insurance – having window locks installed or – in the case of health insurance – the fact that you have not smoked for at least three years.

You will find further information on the kind of things that are relevant to particular types of insurance in the chapters which follow.

How to claim

The key to making a successful claim is making sure that you buy the right cover and that you keep to any conditions and endorsements detailed in your policy. You should also follow the insurer's own claims procedure to the letter and supply all the supporting evidence requested – this will vary according to the type of insurance you have bought. If you used a broker or other intermediary to buy your insurance, they can help you with your claim, although there may be a charge for doing this. If your policy is with Lloyd's, any claim has to be made through the broker, from whom you will also receive payment in settlement of the claim. If you experience problems with getting your claim paid, you should complain – see Chapter 23.

Part 1

Insuring your home and possessions

Chapter 2

Buildings insurance

If your home were burned to the ground, could you afford to rebuild it? That is an extreme case, but if the answer is no, then you need buildings insurance. If you have a mortgage to buy your home, your lender will insist on it but it makes sense even if you do not have a mortgage. If you live in a block of flats or a tenement property, your insurance responsibilities will be explained in your lease. You may also need buildings insurance if you are a tenant and your rental agreement states that insuring the fabric of the property and/or any fixtures and fittings is your responsibility.

What is covered

Buildings insurance covers the fabric of your home (the bricks and mortar, windows, roof and other integral parts) as well as fixtures and fittings (such as kitchen units and central heating boilers). In this chapter, 'house' generally means either house or flat. Buildings insurance is not a maintenance contract: it is intended to provide cover for *specific* damage or loss as a result of *specific* occurrences, not to pay for your running repairs. A condition of buildings insurance is that you keep your property in a good state of repair and take reasonable steps to prevent damage to it.

Buildings insurance will cover you against damage caused to your home (but not to your possessions) by:

- fire and smoke (but not smoke damage on its own)
- lightning
- explosion

- earthquakes (these do happen in the UK but you will need proof that there has been a tremor strong enough to cause damage to your property)
- storms or flooding (but not if the damage is to a hedge or fence)
- subsidence, heave or landslip (though you usually have to pay the first £1,000 of any claim)
- any sort of vehicle or animal crashing into your home
- aircraft or things falling from them
- falling trees, lampposts, telegraph poles or parts of them
- breaking and collapsing of satellite dishes, television and radio aerials (but not damage to the dishes and aerials themselves)
- theft or attempted theft (the cover is for repairing the damage, as a result of a forced entry for example, not for replacing any items stolen, which is covered by contents insurance: see page 43)
- riot (for which there is an exact meaning in law and a time limit of seven days for making a claim)
- vandals and what the insurance industry calls 'malicious persons'
- water overflowing or escaping from water tanks and pipes
- leaking oil escaping from heating systems.

What might be covered

If your home is damaged by any of the causes listed above, your policy should pay out. A good policy – though not all – will also cover you for:

- accidental damage to underground pipes and cables within the boundaries of your property (but not wear and tear)
- frost damage or the freezing of water in pipes
- accidental damage to fixed glass and sanitary fixtures, such as windows, glazed doors, baths and basins (but see 'What is not covered' opposite)
- the costs involved in removing debris or clearing the site after damage has occurred
- professional fees (for architects, surveyors and others) incurred because of having to repair or rebuild your home as a result of the causes of damage listed above
- the cost of rebuilding or repairing the building to meet statutory regulations or local by-laws

- the cost (up to certain limits) of alternative accommodation – or loss of rent from tenants – if the damage means that you cannot live in the house
- your legal liability as owner of the property – usually up to a maximum of £1 million. Note that if you live in your home, your contents insurance covers you against legal claims (see page 43): for example, if a tile falls off your roof and hits a passer-by. Your buildings insurance pays out for legal claims if you do not live in the home (for example, if it is let to tenants), but you are still responsible for maintenance and repairs.

Cover for accidental damage

If you want the policy to pay out for accidental damage (if your drill slips while you are putting up a shelf, for example, or brown stains appear on your newly painted bedroom ceiling because you caused the hot-water tank to overflow), you will have to ask for accidental damage cover but you have to pay extra for this.

Renting and letting

If you intend to let your home to tenants, you will need to tell your insurer that the property is to be let: standard policies are often invalid for let property. It is also worth taking out extra insurance that is available specifically for landlords, for example to cover lost rental income and legal expenses. If you are renting a property from a landlord, check what your insurance responsibilities are; the details should be given in your rental agreement. Although your landlord may take responsibility for the fabric of the building, you may be responsible for damage to fixtures and fittings.

What is not covered

The things you will not be able to claim for are listed in the 'exclusions' section of a policy document. In the case of buildings insurance the following exclusions will almost certainly be listed, and excluded:

- damage as a result of bad maintenance (you have a responsibility to keep your property in a good state of repair, so if your roof is blown off in a storm because you have not kept it in good condition, the insurance company will not pay out)
- routine repairs for normal wear and tear on the property (you will not be able to claim for getting your house repainted just because it is time it was done)
- wilful damage (e.g. a fire you start yourself)
- accidental damage, unless you have asked for this to be specifically included in the cover
- gradual damage caused by processes like rot, woodworm, mildew and rust
- smoke damage where there have been no flames or burning (if you want smoke damage to be covered you will have to ask for the policy to be extended to cover it – and pay more)
- flood or storm damage to a fence or hedge
- damage to underground pipes and cables outside the boundaries of your property (which are the responsibility of the gas, electricity or water company)
- damage caused by sonic bangs, radioactive contamination or war
- the full cost of damage as a result of subsidence, heave or landslip (there is always an excess to pay)
- damage caused by domestic pets
- certain causes of damage – such as theft and burst pipes – if your property is left unoccupied or unfurnished for a specified period (often 30 days)
- damage as a result of subsidence, heave or landslip to boundary and garden walls, gates, hedges, fences, paths, drives, patios and swimming-pools, unless the main building, garage or other outbuildings are damaged at the same time
- damage as a result of normal settlement, shrinkage and expansion
- damage to solid floor slabs or damage resulting from the movement of solid floor slabs, unless the external walls of the building are damaged at the same time
- damage as a result of faulty workmanship (in that case you should sue the workman) or defective materials
- damage during demolition, structural alteration or repairs
- damage from coastal or river erosion

- damage caused by the settling of newly made-up ground (the industry jargon for this is 'compaction of infill')
- any damage for which you could claim compensation under legislation.

Most policies will exclude cover for matching sets (a bathroom suite, for example) if only one item is damaged but no matching, suitable replacement is available. Some policies may also exclude or restrict claims for:

- damage caused by vandalism or riot in Northern Ireland – and some insurers will not insure property in Northern Ireland at all
- homes built before a certain date (generally 1900 or 1850).

Insurance for new houses

If you buy a newly built home, you may have trouble getting a mortgage unless it has a ten-year warranty such as the Buildmark Warranty from the National House Building Council (NHBC) or a warranty from Zurich Municipal. These sorts of warranties provide insurance cover against the builder going bust while the house is being built, most defects for the first two years after the house is built, and, until the house is ten years old, major structural faults (such as foundation failure, distortion or collapse of roof structures and chemical failure of materials that affect load-bearing structures). Warranties can be transferred into the names of the new owners if you sell before the warranty has expired. However, although this type of insurance does provide some useful cover, it will not cover all defects that may arise with a new house, and it is certainly not a substitute for buildings insurance.

Choosing the right policy

The right policy is the one that will give you the best cover from what is on offer, at the best price. There are basically two types of policy to choose from: sum-insured policies and bedroom-rated policies.

29

Whichever type of policy you go for, you should make sure that you get new-for-old cover. The alternative is indemnity cover, which is cheaper than new-for-old cover but any claim you make for repairs or rebuilding will be reduced for wear and tear.

Sum-insured policies

These are likely to be the cheapest type of buildings insurance for most people. With this type of policy, you insure for the amount it would cost to rebuild your home (which is not necessarily the same as what it would cost to buy). What this figure – the 'sum insured' – should be depends on what the property is built of, how big it is and where in the UK it is situated. The premium you pay is based on the size of the sum insured – usually expressed as a cost per £1,000. For more details on how the 'sum insured' is calculated, see 'How much cover?', opposite.

Bedroom-rated policies

These base the amount you are insured for on the number of bedrooms in your house (including bedrooms that you use for another purpose: as an office, for example). The more bedrooms you have, the higher your insurer will assume the rebuilding cost to be. This is convenient because you do not have to work out the precise amount of cover that you need. The drawback is that the actual cost of rebuilding your house may be lower or higher than the figure assumed by the insurer. This means that you could be paying over the odds for your policy or be under-insured; although if there is no limit on what the rebuilding cost can be, you will be covered.

Combined policies

If your home is broken into and your television is stolen, you claim on your buildings insurance for the damage to your house but on your contents insurance for the theft of your television. Some insurers will offer you a discount if you take out both your buildings and contents insurance with them. This may simplify things when you come to claim, but you will not necessarily be getting the best deal either in money terms or in terms of getting the cover you require. To find out if any combined policy deal is worthwhile, you need to get quotes and details of cover for separate policies.

How much cover?

You need to insure your property for the amount it would cost to rebuild it, which includes not just labour and materials but also the cost of removing rubble, fees for professionals such as architects and surveyors, and other rebuilding costs. The rebuilding cost can be quite different from the likely resale value of your home, or its council tax valuation, which could be much more or much less. This is not as bizarre as it sounds if you bear in mind that the market value of your home, unlike the rebuilding cost, takes into account many factors unrelated to the cost of building. For example, two identical houses at opposite ends of a road may have very different market values because of their immediate surroundings.

If you are buying buildings insurance because you are getting a mortgage, your mortgage valuation should say how much the property should be insured for. If you are not getting a mortgage, you will either have to work out the rebuilding cost yourself or you can get a professional insurance valuation done by a qualified surveyor. (The Royal Institution of Chartered Surveyors★ can provide a list of its members.) You should always seek a professional surveyor's advice if you live in one of the following types of property:

- a house built of stone or other materials which are not brick
- a house with basements and cellars or more than three storeys
- a flat (because types of construction vary, as do responsibilities for the insurance of shared areas)
- a house with special design features
- a particularly large house
- a house which is of historic interest or which is a listed building, since it will almost certainly have to be rebuilt to its original design using appropriately authentic materials
- a house containing hazardous materials – asbestos, for example – likely to require special precaution or treatment following damage or demolition
- a house or flat in Northern Ireland or the Channel Islands.

If none of the above applies to you and you do not want to pay for professional help, you can get advice on how to calculate the rebuilding cost of your home from the Association of British Insurers:★ ask for the information sheet called 'Buildings insurance for homeowners'. This tells you how to measure the floor area of your home, how to do the calculations using building cost tables produced by the Royal Institution of Chartered Surveyors and which extras – such as the cost of double glazing or a burglar alarm – to add in.

On the face of it, there are no complicated sums to do if you choose a bedroom-rated policy because all you need to do is count the number of bedrooms. However, if you do not calculate the rebuilding cost, you will not be able to work out if a sum-insured policy would be better value and you will not be able to check if the cover offered by the bedroom-rated policy is sufficient. You may also find that a bedroom-rated policy is not on offer if your house has more than a certain number of bedrooms.

Buildings insurance when you move

It becomes your responsibility to insure your new house or flat the day that you exchange contracts to buy the property. However, you should keep your buildings insurance cover on your existing home until completion, in case the buyer defaults. Let your insurer know in writing, beforehand, that you want an overlap. The cost of insurance varies depending on where you live so you may be charged a higher or lower premium. The move might provide a good opportunity to change insurer, in which case you should cancel your old policy if you pay monthly or, if you paid a year's worth of premiums, you should ask for a refund for the unexpired portion of your existing policy.

Over- and under-insurance

If you insure for substantially more than the cost of rebuilding you will be over-insured, which is a waste of money. However, if you insure for less than the rebuilding cost of your home (i.e. you are under-insured) your claims can be refused or, more likely, they will be made 'subject to average'. This means that the insurer will calculate what you *should* have been insured for, then look at what proportion of that sum you are *actually* insured for, and then pay out the same proportion of *any* claims you make. So if you should be insured for £100,000 but you are actually insured for £75,000, the insurance company may pay only 75 per cent of any claim.

Cutting the cost

It is a false economy to insure your home for less than the rebuilding cost but you can cut costs in other ways:

- **Change your insurer** It may seem obvious, but you do not have to stay with the same insurer just because you are living in the same property. Unless you are tied into an insurance policy because of a special mortgage package, you can change your insurer as often as you like – although it makes most sense to review your policy annually when it comes up for renewal.
- **Pay more towards each claim** Most buildings policies have a 'compulsory excess' (the amount you *have* to pay towards any claim you make) of £50, although it can be as high as £100. If you agree to pay more (called a 'voluntary excess'), you should get a reduction in your premium. Note that subsidence claims usually have their own excess of around £1,000.
- **Avoid 'all-risks' policies** All policies cover you against 'specific perils' (those listed under 'What is covered' on page 25), which are generally things over which you have no control, such as storm damage or damage caused by fire or theft. 'All risks' cover means that you can also claim for accidental damage (such as putting your foot through the ceiling), but since there is a greater chance that you will make a claim, 'all risks' cover pushes the price up.
- **Check for discounts** Some insurers offer discounts to certain groups of people – for example, people over 50, teetotallers, or people in certain professions or trades unions. You may get a discount for measures you take to make your home more secure, although this is more common with contents insurance (see page 55).
- **Stay loyal** Some insurers will reward loyalty and/or a clean claims record with a reduction in your premium. However, you should compare quotes from other insurers to make sure that the loyalty bonus or no-claims discount is really worth having.
- **Haggle** You may not get much joy from a direct insurer, but intermediaries may be open to negotiation on price, especially if

they suspect that they might be about to lose your custom; unless, of course, you are a serial claimer in which case they may be glad to see the back of you.

Special cases

If there is something special (or different) about your home – for example, it has a thatched roof, it is a house-boat or caravan or of particular historic interest; or if you own an unoccupied property, a property you let, an estate, a farm, a block of flats, a holiday home or a very 'high-value' home; or if you live in living quarters as a member of HM Forces – it may be worth asking a broker to get you quotes for specialist insurance that is tailored to your situation.

Buying your policy

To be sure of getting the best deal, you should get quotes from several different insurers, but before you get quotes, you will need to know:

- what the rebuilding cost of your home is
- when your house was built
- what kind of cover you want: for example, whether you want to be insured for accidental damage
- how much you are prepared to pay towards each claim (bearing in mind that the excess for subsidence claims is usually ten times more than the excess for other sorts of claim).

It can also be useful to know when you last claimed on your buildings insurance in case a no-claims discount is on offer.

Where to buy

You can get quotes and buy buildings insurance either direct from an insurer or through a broker or other intermediary; most will deal by phone. When getting quotes, check that they include insurance premium tax.

You do not have to stick with your mortgage lender's chosen insurance policy

If you are getting a mortgage, your lender will make it a condition that the property is insured and will probably be keen to arrange cover: lenders get commission for doing so. Most lenders will allow you to arrange your own insurance, but they will want proof that the policy provides adequate cover for their security, and will often charge a fee of around £25 for the administrative costs of checking this. If you have a special mortgage deal which commits you to buying your lender's insurance, you have no choice in the matter, although you may be free to switch insurers after a few years.

The price you pay for a sum-insured policy is based on the rebuilding cost of your home, which in turn depends on where you live and the type of house or flat you live in. If you live in an area prone to subsidence, you will be classed as 'high risk'. Scotland and Northern Ireland are less prone to subsidence than other areas of the UK and are rated as 'low risk' by most insurers. For a three-bedroomed, semi-detached house, typical amounts per £1,000 of the cost of rebuilding range from under £1 in a low-risk area to nearly £3 in a high-risk area.

Once you have filled in your application form or given your agreement over the phone, you should receive your policy documents, together with details of how to pay. Check these documents

The cost of convenience

If you are given the option of paying for your buildings insurance by adding the premium to the amount you owe on your mortgage, do not take it. It may sound convenient but not only will you pay interest on the insurance premium for the full life of the mortgage (usually 25 years), you will also have an extra loan (made up of the insurance premiums) to repay when you pay off the mortgage.

very carefully to make sure that you are buying the cover you asked for. If anything is not clear, ask for an explanation.

How to pay

You can pay in full straight away or in monthly instalments – usually by direct debit. If you decide to spread the cost over the whole year by paying monthly, check that there is no additional credit charge for doing this.

Keeping your insurance up to date

To avoid policyholders being under-insured as a result of inflation, insurers 'index-link' the sum insured to keep pace with rising (or falling) rebuilding costs as measured by the House Rebuilding Cost Index. The sum insured moves in line with the index during the year but does not affect how much you pay in premiums until the renewal date, when the premium is recalculated to take account of the effect of inflation on the sum insured.

Although index-linking should guard against the insured rebuilding cost not keeping pace with inflation, it will not take into account any increases in the rebuilding costs as a result of improvements you make to your home such as building an extension or installing double glazing. Nor will it take into account price increases for non-standard building materials such as stone. If you have made major alterations which could affect the rebuilding cost,

A case of under-insurance

When George took out an index-linked buildings insurance policy, he felt reasonably sure that he would not become under-insured. He had just had a survey done which put the rebuilding cost of his house at £91,000. Six years later, he remortgaged his house and was surprised to find that while his index-linked insurance had risen to £118,000, the rebuilding cost had more than doubled to £210,000. This was partly because George had carried out improvements to his house and had not adjusted the sum insured to compensate, and partly because his house is made of stone which had risen in price much more quickly than standard building materials.

tell your insurer, otherwise you may find that you are under-insured. You should also tell your insurer about anything that might reduce the building cost of your home, for example if you have knocked down a redundant garage. Whatever you do to your home, it makes sense to review the cost of rebuilding it every few years.

How to claim

Disaster strikes: what should you do? If the damage done to your property is as a result of theft or vandalism, first call the police. It may well be a condition of your policy that you do this and the insurer will ask you for the crime number that the police will give you.

Emergency measures

After a break-in, the next step is to get emergency temporary repairs done to secure your home, make it weatherproof or to prevent further damage being done. If your insurer runs a 24-hour helpline, ring that, since your insurer will either be able to organise the repair for you or will give you the telephone numbers of its preferred repairers. It may even agree to meet the costs of emergency repairs directly.

It is better to get the insurer's consent for emergency work to be done, but if this is not possible (for example, there is not a helpline to phone), organise the repairs yourself, making sure that you keep copies of all paperwork. While you are waiting for the emergency repairer to turn up, do what you can to limit further damage and, if possible, take photographs of the damage.

At this stage, do not throw anything away because your insurer may wish to have the damage inspected. If you have suffered very serious damage – a fire, for example – salvage anything you can and keep any remains.

Filling in the claim form

If you have not already done so (by phoning the helpline), contact your insurance company or broker and ask for a claim form. The form will ask you when, where and how the damage occurred, and how much you are claiming. You should send back the completed form within 30 days of the loss occurring (or from when you first noticed it). If you are not yet able to get an estimate for part of your claim (cleaning and redecorating after a fire, for example), tell your insurers that you intend to submit a further claim later on.

Do not bother to fill in a claim form if the amount you are claiming is less than the amount you have agreed to pay towards any claim or if the damage is not covered by your policy.

Repairing the damage

Do not get any permanent repairs done – or replace damaged fixtures and fittings – until you have your insurer's agreement. Your insurer will expect to see several competitively priced estimates for repairs to be done or for the costs of replacements. Your insurer may also ask for receipts for fixed items that you want to replace. Do not assume that you will automatically get a replacement for something: even with a new-for-old policy, your insurer can insist on having an item repaired or cleaned rather than replacing it.

If you are claiming for damage to part of a matching set – a bathroom basin, for example – the insurer will not necessarily agree to replace the whole set if you cannot find a matching replacement. They should, however, agree to pay for 'colour matching', if appropriate.

Washbasin blues

After failing to find a matching replacement for the washbasin that had been accidentally damaged, Muhammed wrote to his insurer claiming the cost of replacing the whole bathroom suite. The insurer wrote back saying that it was liable only to pay for the cost of replacing the washbasin and not for the rest of the bathroom suite which was undamaged. It did send Muhammed a list of firms which produced similar suites but since the basin that had been damaged was over 18 years old, none of them could supply a match. Muhammed went back to his insurer to ask if it would pay to have a white basin painted by a specialist firm to match the blue of the existing suite. In reply, the insurer offered to pay half the cost of replacing the other undamaged items as well as the full cost of replacing the basin. Muhammed decided that this was a reasonable offer and accepted.

Providing proof

Before your insurer is prepared to settle, you may have to supply proof of the validity of your claim. If your home is damaged by bad weather, you may need to convince your insurer that your house was in a good state of repair by getting a builder's opinion as to what caused the damage, or by providing a recent invoice to show that you had just had work done on your house. To succeed with a claim for severe-weather damage, you may also need to provide expert proof, which you can get – for a small charge – by phoning the Met Office Insurance Consultancy★ (for England and Wales), the Scottish Climate Office★ (for Scotland and parts of England on the Scottish border), or the Belfast Climate Office★ (for Northern Ireland). If the damage to your home was as a result of an earth tremor (not unknown in the UK), you can get expert proof from the Global Seismology and Geomagnetism Group of the British Geological Survey.★

Bad maintenance invalidates claim

One rainy night, the flat roof over a dormer window in Alice's loft collapsed. Alice contacted her insurer who told her to go ahead with repairs to prevent further damage. Afterwards, the insurer contacted the builder who had done the repair work. He said that the damage was due to the poor construction of the roof and general wear and tear, so the insurer refused to pay Alice's claim.

Checks on your claim

The alternative to your providing proof is for your insurer to send a claims inspector round to check the details of your claim (which is why it is important to hang on to damaged items); and to advise you on ways of avoiding similar claims in the future. The inspector will also be checking that the damage was not caused as a result of bad maintenance; if it was, your claim will be rejected.

Loss adjusters

If your claim is very large or complex, your insurer may appoint a loss adjuster to investigate it. A loss adjuster checks that the claim is genuine, that it is within the terms and conditions of your policy and that the amount you have claimed is reasonable. Loss adjusters are not normally employees of the insurance company but their job is to act in the interests of the insurance company rather than in your interests. However, they can also be helpful in pointing out things that you had not realised you could claim for.

Loss assessors

Regardless of whether your insurer appoints a loss adjuster, you can appoint a loss assessor to act for you in settling your claim (contact the Institute of Public Loss Assessors★). A loss assessor should help you to prepare and submit the claim and ensure that settlement is reasonable. However, think carefully before instructing a loss assessor. You cannot add his or her fees to your claim – and these could be as much as 30 per cent of the value of your claim, whatever the outcome.

Help is at hand

When Arthur's house was badly damaged by fire, he could not face the work involved in preparing his claim: finding out if he was adequately insured, getting estimates from three builders, getting plans of the house drawn up, getting a rebuilding and restoration schedule prepared and submitting it to the council for planning permission, and then negotiating with the insurance company's representative. So he hired a loss assessor who dealt with the claim for him and, after lengthy negotiation, reached an excellent settlement with the insurers.

When the claim is paid

It may take a while, but most claims are settled without the need for further negotiation. When you get the cheque, you may be asked to sign a dated 'discharge receipt' or 'satisfaction note'. If it says that the payment is 'in full and final settlement' of your claim, add the words 'so far'. Then you will be able to make a further claim if you discover more damage (from the same cause) later.

Getting problems sorted out

If the payment is less than you expected or if your claim is rejected, find out why. In a survey of subscribers to *Which?*★ magazine (conducted in May 1996), common reasons for a claim being rejected or reduced were:

- the insurer had deducted an amount for wear and tear
- estimates for repairs were too high (in the insurer's view)
- the policy did not cover the particular cause of damage
- the person claiming had not fulfilled the policy conditions (keeping your home in a good state of repair, for example)
- the claim was scaled down because of under-insurance (see page 32).

If the explanation you get is reasonable, and if, after reading your policy, you can see that the insurer has a point, you will have to accept what the insurer offers. However, if you think that the insurer is simply trying to wriggle out of its obligations, you should complain (see Chapter 23). You can also complain if you think that your claim is being dealt with inefficiently or if you think that the insurer is deliberately taking longer to process your claim than is necessary. Contact the Insurance Ombudsman Bureau.★

When is a hedge not a hedge?

When Roger's hedge burned down, he claimed on his buildings insurance. However, his insurer rejected his claim on the ground that because the hedge was over eight feet tall it was not a hedge but a series of trees. Conveniently for the insurance company, trees were not covered by Roger's policy. After reaching impasse with his complaint to the company, Roger took his claim to the Insurance Ombudsman, who decided that as the destroyed trees had been planted specifically to form a boundary, they formed a hedge and the insurance company would have to pay the claim.

Chapter 3

Contents insurance

If you would not bat an eyelid at the prospect of having to pay to replace any or all of your possessions out of your own pocket, you probably do not need contents insurance. If, on the other hand, you would prefer to pay someone else to foot most of the bill if your things are damaged or stolen, then you do. Even if you do not own your home, it is extremely unlikely that your landlord's insurance will cover the possessions you bring with you as a tenant – and it may be a requirement of your rental agreement that you insure against damage to some of your landlord's belongings.

What is covered

Whereas buildings insurance covers the fabric of your home (including certain fixtures and fittings such as kitchen and bathroom units), contents insurance covers the moveable things in your home – including money – which belong to you and the members of your family who live with you. Contents insurance policies cover your belongings either on an indemnity basis or, more commonly these days, on a new-for-old basis.

Indemnity cover means that your claims will have something knocked off for wear and tear. If you choose this type of cover (rare these days), you should be prepared to replace items with second-hand goods or make up the difference between the new and second-hand price out of your own pocket.

New-for-old cover means that stolen or destroyed items can be replaced with brand-new ones, so your claims should be met in full unless the insurer insists on repair rather than replacement, if this is a feasible solution. However, some items – such as clothes and bed linen – are automatically covered on an indemnity basis, even though all your other possessions may have new-for-old cover.

Most standard policies will cover your belongings *while they are in your home* against damage or loss caused by:

- fire and smoke (but not smoke damage on its own)
- lightning
- explosion
- earthquakes (e.g. a tremor could cause an expensive ornament to fall off the mantelpiece)
- storms or flooding
- subsidence, heave or landslip
- any sort of vehicle or animal crashing into your home
- aircraft or things falling from them
- falling trees, lampposts or telegraph poles, or parts of them
- theft or attempted theft – cover is for replacing stolen items, not repairing damage as a result of forced entry (included in your buildings policy, page 26)
- riot – for which there is an exact meaning in law and a time limit of seven days for making a claim
- actions by vandals and other 'malicious persons' (in the industry jargon)
- water overflowing or escaping from water tanks and pipes
- leaking oil escaping from heating systems.

As part of the standard package on many policies, you will usually find that, up to specified limits, you will be covered for:

- your legal liability as occupier of your home (e.g. if a tile falls off your roof and injures a passer-by). Damage or injury that your pets cause will not be covered unless you specifically ask for this – in which case the premium may go up, depending on your type of cover.
- damage to satellite dishes, and television and radio aerials. Any damage caused to your home by these items (say a falling dish wrecks your front porch) is covered by your buildings policy.

No loss on legal liability

A few years ago, Susan employed a local builder to replace some loose roof slates. Unfortunately, he used an inappropriate ladder and slipped off the roof, suffering very serious back injuries. The builder was not covered by personal accident insurance and sued Susan for damages. Because Susan's contents policy covered her legal liability as owner of the property, her insurer managed and paid for what turned out to be a prolonged legal battle which finally ended in court, where Susan was cleared of any liability or negligence.

What might be covered

Insurers are constantly updating the type of cover offered by their standard packages, which affects what is included in the price of the basic premium. If the following are not 'automatically included' in or 'built-in' to the standard package, and you need them, you will either have to buy a different policy or buy the cover as an extension to the standard policy – and pay extra:

- replacement keys and locks if your keys are lost or stolen
- accidental damage to televisions, hi-fi equipment, computers and videos
- accidental damage to mirrors, glass-top tables and other furniture containing glass
- theft of, or damage to, belongings temporarily removed from your home (e.g. things you take with you when visiting friends, or items that your student children take to college)
- theft of bicycles from your home
- cover for office equipment (e.g. a computer or fax machine) if you work from home
- theft of things you usually leave out in the open, such as garden furniture
- cover for the contents of your freezer if made unfit for human consumption (e.g. following a power cut) – you will not necessarily be covered if you switch the freezer off by accident

- the cost of temporary accommodation if disaster strikes and you are unable to live in your home (which may duplicate cover included in your buildings policy – see page 27)
- a cash payment if an adult member of your household dies as a result of fire or burglary at your home – not really worth having if all the adult members of your household are covered by life insurance (see Chapter 10)
- compensation for metered oil and water (e.g. if a pipe was damaged and large amounts of metered water escaped, you would have to pay the water company for the loss)
- loss or damage to possessions in storage while you move house (if you are not planning to move, this kind of cover is an unnecessary frill and it may duplicate insurance you take out when using a professional removal firm)
- cover for legal expenses if you are involved in a lawsuit; this may also include access to a legal advice helpline. For more on legal expenses insurance, see Chapter 16.

Plants and gardens

As part of your possessions, house plants and their pots should be covered by a contents policy. However, it is very unlikely that plants growing in the garden, unsecured window boxes and other plant life outside the house will be covered by a standard policy. If you want to insure things left out in the open – including expensive terracotta pots, garden furniture and other garden ornaments – check whether your insurance covers you and ask your insurer to extend your cover if necessary.

What is not covered

A standard contents insurance package may include limited accidental damage for some of your belongings, but unless you pay extra you will not be covered for all accidental damage, nor will your belongings be covered outside the home – see 'Optional extras', page 47. No contents policy will cover you for:

- your buildings – unless you buy a combined contents and buildings policy
- theft of or damage to your car, whether or not it is covered by car insurance (see Chapter 5)
- normal wear and tear
- electrical or mechanical breakdown (see Chapter 4)
- gradual damage caused by processes like rot, woodworm, mildew and rust
- most day-to-day pet-related damage (e.g. your cat clawing away at the upholstery)
- catastrophes such as sonic bangs, radioactive contamination and war
- theft and damage if your home is left unoccupied for a certain period of time (usually 30 days but sometimes longer)
- matching items (so if one chair from a three-piece suite is damaged beyond repair, you cannot claim to replace the whole suite)
- theft of your belongings, if you let or sub-let your property.

Theft of pets is not covered, but you can ask for this to be included. However, if your pet is particularly valuable (financially rather than emotionally), you can either ask for your contents insurance to provide cover, or you can take out specialist pet insurance (see pages 49 and 233).

Renting and letting

If you are a tenant, you may find that a standard contents policy will not give you the cover you need against damage both to your own possessions and those of your landlord. If you are a landlord, you are likely to find that your contents policy will specifically exclude theft or damage of your possessions in the property that you let. In both cases, it would be worthwhile asking a broker for a specialist policy.

Limits on cover for high-risk items

Most policies put limits on what will be paid out for 'high-risk' or valuable items – those which are most likely to get stolen and cost a lot to replace, such as televisions, hi-fi and camera equipment, jewellery, works of art, clocks, watches and stamp and coin collections. There may be a 'single article' limit of £1,000, for example, and also an overall limit of around £10,000 for the total of your high-risk possessions. Alternatively, the limits may be worked out as a percentage of the total value of the belongings that you are insuring. These limits represent the most that will be paid out for these sorts of items in the event of a claim, even if the cost of replacing them is higher than the limits given in the policy. If your valuables are worth more than the insurer's limits, you will either have to make up the difference between what the item costs to replace and what the insurer will pay out, or pay more for a higher limit.

Optional extras

No policy will include cover for all your belongings all the time – unless you pay for it. 'All-risks' cover is the industry term for an extension to your policy designed to cover other eventualities: for example, accidental damage to your belongings while they are in the home, or loss, theft or damage to your possessions when you take them out and about – or both. The two types of cover can be sold separately, although 'all risks' usually means cover for your possessions outside the home as well as inside it – you should check what is included with your insurer.

A standard policy may pay a claim for accidental damage to certain specific items in the home environment (see 'What might be covered', page 44), but will not pay out if you spill wine on the carpet or break an expensive ornament. If you want your policy to pay out in all sorts of situations, you should buy additional 'accidental damage cover'. This costs more because there is a greater chance of you making a claim. However, if most of your possessions would cost less to clean, repair or replace than the amount you have to pay towards any claim (typically the first £50), or have purely sentimental rather than monetary value, then accidental damage cover is not worth buying.

Cover for one but not the other

While they were decorating, Mr and Mrs Ginelli spilt wood stain on the sofa of their three-piece suite. They knew they could submit a claim because – with two young children in the house – they had taken the precaution of buying accidental damage cover. They could not find a replacement sofa which matched their chairs, so they claimed for the whole suite. The insurance company told them (quite correctly) that the sofa and chairs were insured as separate items and that they could claim only for replacing the sofa. When the Ginellis complained that this would leave them with a non-matching suite, the insurer agreed to pay to have the whole suite recovered.

Home and away

Because most standard policies cover your belongings only while they are in the home, if you want cover against loss, theft or damage when you take them outside the building – including taking them abroad – you will need to buy an all-risks extension to your policy, which may be referred to as 'contents cover away from the home' or 'personal possessions cover'. This is useful if you have an expensive handbag, briefcase or other luggage, or you regularly take the following sort of items out of the house:

- jewellery
- cameras and camcorders
- expensive sports equipment
- a mobile phone (but you will not be covered for breakdown or unauthorised use)
- a bicycle (although a standard policy might cover theft of your bicycle from your home, it might not be covered elsewhere)
- a personal organiser or lap-top computer
- an expensive fountain pen
- a musical instrument (if it is very valuable you may need specialist insurance)
- glasses or contact lenses (tell your insurer that you specifically want cover for your contact lenses to avoid their exclusion)

- special equipment that you take out of the house (e.g. if you take your sewing machine or DIY tools to an evening class).

You have to pay extra for this type of cover – and there is likely to be an overall limit on what will be paid out for an all-risks claim, as well as a limit for each individual item covered – but it can save you money on your travel insurance (see Chapter 9), since your belongings will typically be covered for 60 days anywhere in the world (though different insurers have different limits). An all-risks extension to your contents policy can also be cheaper than buying separate insurance for a mobile phone or contact lenses, for example. All-risks cover will also give better cover than your car insurance (see Chapter 5) for theft of items from your car – provided theft was as a result of forced entry, you had kept the objects stolen out of sight and the car was locked.

Purchase protection insurance

Some credit cards provide free insurance against the damage, loss or theft of goods you buy with the card. Cover typically lasts for 90 or 100 days from the date of purchase. The level of cover varies according to the card issuer. If you already have 'all-risks' cover (see 'Home and away', opposite) under your contents policy, this cover is of limited value, but if not it could be a useful perk.

Special cases

Although you can buy separate insurance policies to cover special belongings such as mobile phones, contact lenses, musical instruments, sports equipment, small boats and caravans, it can be cheaper to ask your insurer to extend your contents policy to cover these sorts of items at extra cost. Your contents insurance can also be extended to cover theft of your pets and damage they do to other people and their property, but if you want insurance against the expense of certain veterinary bills (not all treatments can be covered) you will need to take out special pet insurance (see Chapter 17).

However, a specialist policy may be a better deal if you have 'non-standard' belongings – your house is furnished with a lot of valuable antiques, for example, or you are a hi-fi fanatic who has just splashed out on the latest kit. You should also contact an insurance broker to enquire about specialist policies if the property which houses your possessions is unusual in some way (e.g. it has a thatched roof, or is living accommodation provided to you as a member of the armed forces).

Contents insurance when you move

When you move, your belongings need to be insured while *en route* from your old home to your new one. If you use a removal firm, you may be offered their insurance. Before you accept, however, check your current contents policy – many policies include this cover as part of the standard package. If your policy does not cover your belongings while they are in transit, compare the cost of the removers' insurance with the cost of paying your insurer to extend your policy. If you are *not* using a removal firm and your contents policy fails to cover the transfer of your possessions, you should definitely ask for an extension to your policy. Even if you already have an all-risks extension, it is unlikely to cover all your belongings.

Choosing the right policy

There is no point in buying contents insurance that does not pay out when you make a claim. To avoid having claims rejected or reduced, make sure that:

- you have new-for-old cover if you want most of your belongings to be replaced as new (see 'What is covered', page 42)
- the insurance covers your belongings for what you want them to be covered for (see 'Optional extras', page 47)
- you are insured for the right amount.

How much cover?

Making sure that you are insured for the right amount depends in part on which of the two types of policy you choose.

Sum-insured policies base what you pay for your insurance on what it would cost you to replace *all* your possessions (for new-for-old cover) or what they are currently worth (for indemnity cover). This figure is the 'sum insured'. Unless you have your insurer's specific agreement to exclude some of your possessions, the sum insured should include everything you own – see 'Valuing your possessions' (below) for how to work this out. It is your responsibility to get the sum insured right. If the figure is too low, it will not reflect the true replacement value of your belongings and you will be under-insured – meaning that any claims you make will not be paid in full. If it is too high, you will be over-insured and paying above the odds for your policy: over-valuing your possessions does not mean that you will be able to claim for higher-specification items as the insurer will verify their cost before paying out.

Bedroom-rated policies base what you pay for your insurance on the number of bedrooms in your house. This sort of insurance may not be available if your house has more than a certain number of bedrooms (including those that you do not use as bedrooms – a sewing room at the top of the house, for example).

- If a bedroom-rated policy offers unlimited cover, you do not need to know the total value of your possessions and there is no risk of you being under-insured. However, you may still need to calculate the replacement cost of high-risk items – see 'Valuing your possessions', below.
- If a bedroom-rated policy puts a limit on the amount you are insured for – e.g. £35,000 – you will still need to work out the total value of your possessions to see whether the policy's limit will provide sufficient cover.

Valuing your possessions

Guarding against under-insurance of your belongings is time-consuming and tedious, but essential if you want to ensure that any claims you make are paid in full. Even if you have decided to buy a bedroom-rated policy with unlimited cover, you will still need to give the insurer a figure for the cost of replacing high-risk items.

High-risk items

The following advice relates to new-for-old cover. For indemnity cover, see page 54.

The checklist below lists things that are typically considered to be high-risk or high-value items and are usually subject to limits on what will be paid out in the event of a claim. To work out the total value of all your high-risk items, fill in what it would cost to buy replacements for everything applicable. If you do not keep abreast of the prices of electrical goods, find out up-to-date prices for the

Checklist for high-risk items

Item	Cost of replacing as new (£)
television(s)	} 490.
video recorder	
tuner	
amplifier	
speakers	
radio(s)	
portable tape/CD player(s)	
personal stereo	
personal CD player	
camcorder	
camera (including separate lenses, flash guns)	100
binoculars	50
computer	
computer printer	
fax machine	
clocks	30
watches	30
jewellery	
other items made of precious metal	
fur coats	
valuable pictures	
works of art	
curios and collections (e.g. stamps, coins)	
antiques	
expensive sports equipment (e.g. golf clubs, skis)	
other valuable items	
Total	

Tip

It is likely that if you ever have to claim for any high-risk items, your insurer will want to see proof that you owned the items before agreeing to pay for a replacement. It could be worth tracking down the receipts for everything you list or, if you threw the receipts away, taking a photograph or digging out some other form of proof (e.g. a repair bill or any document giving details of the item plus your name and address). You should also note down details of the make, model and serial numbers of items such as videos and cameras.

---

nearest equivalent of each item on your list, either from advertisements or by going round the shops.

Getting a valuation

For items that you cannot replace as new – antiques and valuable paintings, for example – you may be asked to supply a professional valuation. Contact the Incorporated Society of Valuers and Auctioneers* for a list of valuers who will undertake insurance valuations. It is also a good idea to keep photographs (taken from different aspects) of distinctive valuable items. A valuation for insurance purposes represents what you would have to pay to replace lost or stolen items. With antiques, this normally means replacement with another item of a similar style and in a similar condition. Because the insurance value is what you would have to pay to replace your goods, rather than what you could sell them for, the amount will be higher than a sale valuation to take account of dealer margins. For easy-to-replace antiques, collectables and fine art items the insurance valuation is generally at least double the sale value. For rarer or more intricate items, it could be two to four times as much as the sale valuation.

The rest of your belongings

Once you have valued your high-risk belongings, you have a choice: you can give up on the valuing process and buy a bedroom-rated policy with unlimited cover, or you can guess at the value of your possessions and risk being under-insured or you can go through every room in your home – not forgetting the loft, cellar, garage and garden shed – making a list of all your other belongings (including furniture, carpets, rugs, curtains, lamps, ornaments, plants, books, videos, CDs, LPs, tools, kitchen equipment, glass-ware, china, cutlery, iron, ironing board and so on) in order to work out what it would cost to replace them; you should do this the same way as for high-risk items (page 52). The Association of British Insurers★ provides a free information sheet entitled *Home Contents Insurance* which includes a room-by-room checklist.

Indemnity cover

Even if you buy new-for-old cover, your clothes and household linen – towels, sheets and so on – will always be covered on an indemnity basis which means that, as well as finding out their replacement value, you need to make a deduction for wear and tear using the following calculation:

$$\frac{\text{current replacement value} \times \text{current age of item (in years)}}{\text{estimated total life}}$$

Not enough cover

When Tom was burgled he had items worth £2,265 stolen. After he claimed for them on his insurance, a loss adjuster (see page 40) was sent from the insurance company to examine the evidence. He added up the total value of Tom's possessions and arrived at a figure of £15,755 – but Tom had only had his contents insured for £10,068, so was clearly under-insured. Since Tom had insured for only 60 per cent of the true value of his possessions, he received only 60 per cent of the amount claimed.

The sum insured

With a sum-insured policy, to arrive at the total amount you should be insured for add together the total of your high-risk items and the total for the rest of your belongings (after making a deduction for wear and tear for clothes and linen, as above) and round this figure up to the nearest thousand pounds. You must insure *all* your contents for the right amount – if the total sum is too low, whatever amount the insurer pays out will be scaled down proportionately.

Cutting the cost

Sum-insured policies base what you pay on the sum insured – so the bigger this is, the more you pay – while with bedroom-rated policies the insured amount is based on the number of bedrooms. With both types of policy, the amount you have to pay varies according to where you live – it is usually based on your insurer's record of claims for your postal district: the more high-risk the area, the more you will pay. Short of moving to a low-risk area, there is not much you can do about this – but you can cut costs in other ways.

- **Reduce the sum insured** If you own things that you would not necessarily want to replace – e.g. LPs, shelves full of paperbacks you are never going to read again, white-elephant wedding presents – you may be tempted not to include them in your calculations. This is not a good idea since the sum insured must represent the *total* value of your possessions, irrespective of whether you would replace every last item. However, some insurers may be willing to specifically exclude certain items provided that you both agree to this (preferably in writing) when you take out the policy. There is no guarantee that your insurer will agree to your own personal exclusions, but it is worth a try – especially if you own a lot of things which are of little value second-hand but which would cost a lot to replace as new.
- **Take security precautions** Fitting secure door and window locks is a sensible precaution against burglary wherever you live and many insurers will reward you with discounts for being security conscious, maintaining a regularly serviced burglar alarm or belonging to a Neighbourhood Watch scheme. If you live in a high-risk area, your insurer may insist that you install five-lever mortise locks on external doors and key-operated win-

dow locks on vulnerable windows before it will agree to cover you against theft. If taking security measures is a condition of insuring you, the discount may not be on offer.

- **Act your age** One of the advantages of growing older is that you can pay less for contents insurance (insurers believe that the older you are, the greater care you take of your possessions). Many insurers will give discounts to people over 50 and some award discounts to the over-45s. On the other hand, some insurers penalise people under 30 by charging them more.

- **Pay more towards your claim** Most insurers require you to pay the first £50 of any claim – called a 'compulsory excess'. If you offer to pay more towards each claim (a 'voluntary excess'), the cost of your insurance should go down – although not all insurers allow you to do this.

- **Avoid claiming** An increasing number of insurers offer discounts if you can show that you have a claim-free record. If you know that you have not claimed on your contents insurance in the last couple of years or so, it is worth asking whether a no-claims discount is available.

- **Avoid accidents** Cover against accidental damage pushes up the price of your insurance because there is a greater likelihood of your claiming.

Too much cover

Will had accumulated a lot of books, records and other personal possessions which were of little second-hand value but would cost a lot to replace as new. He did not think it was worth insuring them, but under most insurance policies he needed to include them in the total value of his belongings or risk being under-insured. After trying several insurers, he finally found one willing to let him exclude all the items that he would not replace. Not only did Will get the cover he wanted, he was able to avoid the risk of being under-insured because his insurer agreed to his own personal exclusions – and he has halved what he pays for his cover.

Buying your policy

When it comes to buying contents insurance you are spoilt for choice: there is no shortage of advertisements in the press, your bank or building society will usually have leaflets on display and you will also find entries both for direct insurers and insurance intermediaries in *Yellow Pages*. It is always worth getting several quotes but before you make contact, you will need to have the following information to hand:

- the total value of your possessions (or the number of bedrooms you have, if you want a bedroom-rated policy)
- the value of your high-risk items (see page 52)
- the kind of cover you want (e.g. accidental damage cover or contents cover away from the home)
- any special requirements – you want cover for your garden ornaments or pets, say
- the date you last claimed on any contents insurance.

How to pay

Once you have compared several quotes and have decided on a policy, ask what payment methods are available and check that there is no credit charge for paying by monthly instalments. You should also check that the price quoted includes insurance premium tax. When you have accepted a quote and decided how to pay, the policy documents will be sent to you. You should check these very carefully. If you are unclear about any documents the insurer sends you, ask for an explanation. (If you have been offered a discount because you have taken certain security measures, or it is a condition of the insurance that you do, you may be sent a form to complete confirming the measures you have taken *before* you get the final policy.)

Keeping your insurance up to date

Contents insurance policies that index-link the sum insured automatically increase the amount you are insured for in line with the consumer durables element of the Retail Prices Index (RPI), but this will not take into account things you have bought during the year or items you have got rid of. If you make a substantial purchase part of the way through the year – you buy a new sofa, for example – it is worth telling your insurer about it, especially if the item falls into the high-risk category (see page 52). You should also tell your insurer about anything which may (in the insurer's mind) affect the security of your belongings, such as:

- taking a lodger or letting your home (in whole or in part)
- having work done on your home – especially if you have scaffolding erected or your builder suffers from 'leave-the-front-door-wide-open' syndrome
- starting to work from home (you may need specialist business insurance, see Chapter 15)
- changing your job or employment status
- moving house
- your child taking his or her hi-fi and computer to university
- anyone whose belongings are insured under the policy being convicted of a criminal offence
- any break-in or attempted break-in – even if nothing was taken and/or you did not make a claim.

How to claim

If your belongings go missing, report the loss to the police *as soon as possible* and make a note of the crime number the police give you and the name and address of the police station where you reported the loss. Even if you think that the item was lost rather than stolen, if you do not report the loss to the police the insurer may reject your claim. If your purse or wallet and/or cheque book have disappeared, report this to your bank and all credit and shop card issuers so that they can cancel your cards.

Emergency measures

If your belongings are stolen following a break-in at your home, first concentrate on the damage to the building. Although the cost of repairing the damage is covered by your buildings insurance, it will be a condition of your contents policy that you take immediate steps to make your home secure in order to prevent further loss –

such as boarding up a broken window (see page 37 for advice on emergency repairs). You should also take immediate steps to prevent further damage if your home and possessions have been damaged by fire, flood or severe weather – putting plastic sheeting over a hole in your roof, for example.

Lost or stolen?

When Charles lost his Mont Blanc fountain pen at work, he did not think to report the loss to the police but he did tell the security guard and emailed his colleagues to ask them to look out for his pen. When he tried to claim, his insurer told him that because he had not reported the loss to the police, it would not pay for a replacement. However, when Charles wrote explaining what other actions he had taken to retrieve his pen, after a long silence he received a cheque – but no explanation for the delay.

Making the claim

Once you have reported the loss to the police and/or organised any emergency repairs, make a list of the stolen or damaged items and take photographs of any damage. Do not throw away anything that has been damaged since your insurer may ask to see it. Once you have established what you need to claim for, check your policy to make sure that you are covered then contact your insurer – using its helpline if one exists – for a claim form and advice on what to do next.

Warning

Do not repair or replace items until you have your insurer's written agreement to do so – some insurers will arrange for the repair or replacement directly with certain suppliers.

Fill in the claim form, giving details of what has been stolen or damaged and how this happened. Your claim is likely to be processed more quickly if you back up your claim with the original receipt for the item, a professional valuation (if appropriate) or other proof of ownership. You should also give estimates of the likely replacement and/or repair costs. If you have not yet obtained estimates, send the claim form in anyway but add a note explaining that the form does not represent your final claim.

Tip

When you make a claim after a burglary, make clear that the list of stolen items is complete 'so far as I can see at present'. If lots of things have been stolen, you may not notice that some things – jewellery you do not wear that often, for example – have gone missing until weeks after the break-in.

Checks on your claim

Provided that you have sent the necessary information in support of your claim, your insurer should agree to your replacing and/or repairing your lost or damaged belongings. However, if you have claimed to replace a damaged item, your insurer may send a claims inspector to confirm that the item cannot be repaired before agreeing to a replacement. If your claim is very complex, your insurer may appoint a loss adjuster – see page 40.

Some insurers replace or repair items using their own suppliers, rather than giving you the money to do this yourself. However, if the insurer cannot replace the item with the same model or a similar alternative – for example, if you are claiming for a piece of antique jewellery – you can insist that the company pays you the value of the item. Alternatively, you can agree to pay the difference for a better version of what you lost.

Agreeing to an upgrade

When Paul lost his Nikon camera, he expected his insurer to replace it with one that was as good as the original. After much discussion about what constituted an equivalent model – Nikon had stopped making the type that Paul lost – he finally decided to choose a camera that was better than his old one and make up the difference in price himself.

Getting problems sorted out

If your claim is not accepted in full, ask the insurer to explain why – and do not cash any cheques you are sent. Be cautious of accepting any offers of less than the amount you are claiming. If you are asked to complete a form agreeing to 'full and final settlement', do not sign if there is a possibility that you will have to claim more.

Common reasons why insurers reject or reduce a claim are:

- you are under-insured
- your policy does not cover you for what you are claiming for
- you are claiming for the full cost of replacement, but your policy only gives indemnity cover (see page 42)
- the insurer has made a deduction for wear and tear.

If your insurer will not pay your claim, or has offered you less than you claimed because you could not provide a valuation (see page 53), get new estimated valuations by describing the items to experts like antique shop proprietors and jewellers. If you cannot provide the original receipt and your insurer disputes whether you ever owned the item you are claiming for, try to find photographs depicting it – a snap of you sporting your new gold chain at your birthday party, for example – or take witness statements from people who have seen the things. If the disputed claim is very large, consider employing a loss assessor – see page 40.

If you and your insurer still cannot agree, and you think that your insurer is being unreasonable, you can complain – see Chapter 23.

Chapter 4

Appliance insurance

If you have an emergency fund or other short-term savings that you can dip into to pay for the repair or replacement of any of your domestic appliances or other electrical goods, it is unlikely that you need 'warranty' or 'breakdown' insurance. You definitely do not need it if a newly acquired appliance breaks down, since you should be covered by the manufacturer's one-year guarantee.

Appliance insurance could be useful if you do not want to worry about the cost of repairing or replacing your electrical goods. However, in financial terms this sort of insurance is not a good bet: the chances are that you will spend more on premiums than you will on repairs. If you are after peace of mind, the alternative to buying appliance insurance is to start building up your own emergency repair fund in an instant-access savings account.

Schemes to cover you against repair costs come under a variety of names including 'extended warranties', 'breakdown insurance' and 'maintenance contracts'. These used to be offered only by manufacturers and retailers but in recent years several insurance companies have got in on the act and are now selling stand-alone appliance insurance, either directly or through brokers, banks and building societies, other financial institutions and, more recently, the privatised utilities. You may find that you are offered special deals on this sort of insurance when you arrange a loan to buy an appliance, when you buy contents insurance (which does not cover you for repair bills), or in a mailshot with your electricity bill.

The most important question when considering this sort of insurance is: how likely is it that your washing machine, tumble drier, dishwasher, vacuum cleaner, microwave, television, video recorder, fridge-freezer (or whatever) will break down? Not that likely, according to regular surveys conducted by *Which?** magazine. These have revealed that even the most trouble-prone types of electrical appliances – washing machines and washer-driers – have become more reliable over the last five years. The other factor you should take into account is the cost of repairs. *Which?* surveys have also shown that the average amount that people spend on repairs in the first five years of the life of an appliance is far less than the price of an extended warranty – see the table below.

Appliance reliability and repair costs

Type of appliance	Percentage of breakdowns in first five years	Average repair bill	Average repair cost over five years	Cost of extended warranty
tumble drier	14%	£40	£12	£50–120
washing machine	50%	£50	£38	£130–220
washer-drier	50%	£60	£56	£160–260
dishwasher	30%	£50	£25	£85–170
cylinder vacuum cleaner	10%	£28	£10	£40–70
upright vacuum cleaner	20%	£19	£10	£40–70
microwave oven	12.5%	£40	£10	£40–120
television	33%	£44	£12	£55–200
video recorder	25%	£50	£21	£100–220
fridge-freezer	14%	£57	£17	£45–150

Even if you believe that your appliance will be one of the ones that breaks down, you can take comfort from the fact that unless you are extremely unlucky, it should still be cheaper to pay for repairs as needed rather than buy insurance – especially since appliance insurance does not cover the costs of *all* repair work – see 'What is not covered', page 65.

Insurance does not add up

When Gerald bought his microwave oven for £68.99, the sales assistant was very keen to sell him an extended warranty giving an extra four years' cover on top of the standard one-year guarantee from the manufacturer. But Gerald was adamant that he did not want the insurance. He had worked out that over four years the warranty would cost just one pound less than the microwave he had just bought.

What is covered

Appliance insurance policies aim to meet call-out charges and the costs of parts and labour (though some may not pay labour charges) if your appliances break down as a result of sudden and unforeseen mechanical or electrical defect. If you buy an insurance-backed extended warranty from a retailer or manufacturer, you will be covered only for the cost of similar repairs to one specific appliance.

Stand-alone appliance insurance offered by an insurer has the edge over a manufacturer's or retailer's extended warranty in that:

- you can insure against the costs of repair for several appliances under the same policy
- you can insure older appliances (although you may not be able to buy insurance for appliances which are older than eight to twelve years)
- you do not have to take out insurance until after the manufacturer's one-year guarantee has expired
- the insurer will replace the appliance or will make a contribution to the cost of replacing the appliance.

Buying an insurance-based warranty also means that you have access to a dispute-settling scheme if you have a problem with a claim – see Chapter 23.

If it would cost more to repair the appliance than it would to replace it, the insurer will not meet the cost of the repair. With a new-for-old policy, you should get the full amount of money required to replace the appliance with a new one of similar specification – the insurer may even arrange the purchase for you. However, new-for-old replacement may be available only for appliances up to a certain age – five years, say. With other policies, you may receive a *contribution* towards replacing the appliance with a new model. Many policies base the amount on the current value of the appliance less depreciation – so the older the appliance, the less you get (see the table opposite). Note that a policy will not pay towards the cost of a replacement if your appliance has given up the ghost because it is old and worn out.

The effect of depreciation on an appliance costing £500 to replace

Age of appliance in years	Percentage of original purchase price (depreciated value)	Maximum payable towards repair or replacement	Shortfall needed to replace appliance
up to 2	100%	£500	£0
over 2 and up to 3	90%	£450	£50
over 3 and up to 4	80%	£400	£100
over 4 and up to 5	70%	£350	£150
over 5 and up to 6	60%	£300	£200
over 6 and up to 7	50%	£250	£250
over 7 and up to 10	40%	£200	£300
over 10	0%	£0	£500

Washed out

When Eleanor's two-year-old washer-drier broke down, she assumed that the five-year extended warranty she had bought from the retailer would cover the costs of repairing or replacing the machine. But the insurer told her that the machine was 'beyond economical repair' and offered her only £240 towards a new washer-drier. Having paid a total of £565 for the washer-drier and warranty, Eleanor therefore had to find about £200 to make up the difference between the insurer's contribution and the cost of a new machine.

What is not covered

Appliance insurance will not cover all possible repair bills, nor will it cover the cost of an annual service to keep your machine in good working order. You may also find that a policy will not pay out if the appliance cost over a certain amount (e.g. £1,000) when new, was over a certain age when you first took out the policy, or when it reaches a certain age (although some policies have no age limit); or if repairs are needed in the first 30 days after taking out the policy.

It is also likely that the following will not be covered:

- accidental damage (e.g. your vacuum cleaner falling downstairs) – although some polices cover this
- cosmetic damage (e.g. damage to the surface or trim of the item)
- repairs needed because you failed to follow the manufacturer's operating or maintenance instructions (e.g. your dishwasher stops working because you let the filter get clogged)
- repairs needed due to misuse (e.g. you inadvertently block the washing machine filter with small change you forgot to remove from a trouser pocket)
- repairs you could have carried out yourself by following the problem-solving steps in the instructions
- repairs to breakdown caused by wear and tear (e.g. replacing the worn-out door seal on a washing machine)
- repairs needed because of fire, flood or attempted theft – although you would be able to claim under your contents policy (see page 43)
- repairs needed because of blocked pipes, damage to the external water supply or drainage hoses
- repairs needed because you let your fridge or freezer get over-iced
- repairs needed because your television or video was not tuned in correctly, or there was something wrong with the aerial
- frozen food spoilage (with some exceptions). You may already be covered if you have accidental damage or frozen food cover under your contents policy (see page 44)
- the replacement of 'consumables' such as vacuum cleaner belts, fridge light bulbs and hi-fi styluses; also batteries, fuses and plugs
- the call-out charge, if no fault is found
- costs incurred as a result of not being able to use the appliance (e.g. the expense of visiting the launderette)
- the cost of adjusting your appliance to cope with the date change from 1999 to 2000 (goods containing computer clocks)
- repairs covered by other insurance (e.g. your contents policy or a repairer's guarantee)
- repairs needed because your home was left unoccupied
- repairs if you let your home or share with tenants or lodgers (check with your insurer for their position on this)
- repairs carried out without the insurer's permission.

Choosing the right policy

When choosing a policy, it is important to remember that no appliance insurance policy will cover every possible repair cost. Before you sign up for a policy, you need to be very clear what the policy you are looking at will and will not cover you for. You should find out the following:

- Will the policy cover all your appliances or is there an age limit?
- If you want to cover only your essential appliances (e.g. your washing machine and tumble drier), can you do this?
- Will the policy pay all the costs associated with a repair – call-out charge, labour and parts – or will it pay only for parts?
- Will the policy pay out for all parts, including trims (if the look of the appliance is important to you) – or are some parts specifically excluded?
- If an appliance had to be replaced, would the amount you received towards the replacement cost be calculated on a new-for-old basis (see page 64) or would the amount be reduced by an allowance for depreciation?
- Will the insurer arrange and pay for repairs, or will you have to pay the repairer and claim the cost back?
- Can you pay the premium monthly, so that you do not lose out if you decide to cancel the policy?
- Is there a limit on what you can claim for each individual claim, or a maximum amount that can be paid out over the life of the policy?
- Will the insurer continue the cover you if you move house?

Buying your policy

When you buy your new appliance, it is very likely that commission-hungry sales staff will try to sell you an extended warranty – sometimes by offering the inducement of a discount if you buy the insurance on the spot. Despite what sales staff may tell you, there is no good reason to give into this sort of sales pressure. If you really want this kind of insurance, you may get a better deal elsewhere: a policy offered by an insurer for example, or the extended warranty

---

Cracking the code

In 1995, the British Retail Consortium launched a Code of Practice for the selling of extended warranties in response to pressure from both Consumers' Association and the Office of Fair Trading. It states that shops selling extended warranties should clearly display details of terms, conditions and prices, or make leaflets containing this information available to prospective customers. The code was devised to help people make informed choices about whether to buy an extended warranty and which type to choose. However, a recent undercover investigation by *Which?* magazine discovered that many stores fail to adhere to the code, and that dubious advice from sales staff is resulting in mis-selling of this type of insurance.

---

offered by the manufacturer – if details are not enclosed with the item you have bought, they will be sent to you after you have returned the guarantee registration card.

You should also bear in mind that you do not need to buy the extended warranty until the manufacturer's free one-year guarantee runs out – which means that you have time to compare the details and prices of other policies. Some department stores offer you a free two-year guarantee on new appliances, so you have even longer to make up your mind or to build up your own repair fund.

Blurred vision

When Donald bought a pair of binoculars, the salesperson tried to sell him an 'additional guarantee' costing £25, which would extend the manufacturer's free one-year guarantee to five years. Donald was not convinced and declined the offer. When he got home and opened the box, he realised he had made the right decision: the binoculars came with a free ten-year guarantee from the manufacturer.

Chapter 5

Car insurance

If you want to drive a car, motorcycle or any other motor vehicle on a public road, you must have a 'certificate of motor insurance' to prove that you are covered against any damage you do to other people or their property. That is the minimum required by law but it is likely that you will want insurance against your car being stolen or damaged as well.

What is covered

What your car insurance covers you against depends on the level of cover you choose to pay for. There are three main types:

Third party is the most basic cover and fulfils your legal obligations by covering you for your liability (and possibly your legal costs) for injuries to other people – including your passengers – and damage to other people's property. This type of car insurance, which is sometimes called 'Act only' because it fulfils your legal obligation, will also cover you for your legal liability for injuries to other people caused by your passengers (for example, if your friend does not look before opening the car door and knocks a cyclist over), and for injuries or damage caused by a caravan or trailer attached to your car.

Third party, fire and theft insures you for everything covered by a 'third party' policy and in addition pays to repair or replace your car if it is damaged or destroyed by fire or if it is stolen.

Comprehensive insures you against the same things as a policy for third party, fire and theft but also provides cover for accidental damage to your car, some cover for personal possessions left in the car – usually up to a limit of £100 – and medical expenses which you have to pay as a result of an accident involving your car.

Comprehensive policies also provide limited personal accident benefit which pays out a specified lump sum of around £5,000 if you (and sometimes another named person insured to drive under the policy) die or suffer certain specific injuries – typically loss of sight or loss of a limb – in a car accident. A comprehensive policy will generally cover you for damage to your windscreen and other windows and it may also provide a courtesy car if your own car is too badly damaged to drive, or while it is being repaired, after an accident.

Driving other cars

If you are going to drive a car that belongs to someone else, do not assume that you will be covered by your own insurance policy on the same basis as for driving your own car. Most policies, whether comprehensive or not, will cover you to drive a car that belongs to someone else provided you have the owner's permission – but the cover is limited to *third party liability* only, which means that you are *not* insured by your own policy for theft of the car or any damage that you do to it. However, if the owner of the car has comprehensive insurance on a policy which allows any driver (without exclusion), you *will* be fully covered. So if you are planning to drive someone else's car, do not rely on your own insurance to cover you for more than the legal minimum. If you are a young driver or you have a bad driving record, your insurer may exclude cover for driving another person's car from your policy so that you are only allowed to drive the car that you are insured to drive.

Driving abroad

All UK car insurers provide the minimum cover required by law in countries which have signed the Multilateral Guarantee Agreement (MGA). These countries include all the member states of the European Union (EU) plus Norway, Hungary, Iceland, Switzerland and the Czech and Slovak Republics. You are guaranteed the minimum level of cover provided by the country you are visiting or the UK statutory minimum, whichever is greater. This means that you do not have to take out extra insurance to meet the legal requirements for driving in these countries.

However, if you want to be covered for more than the legal minimum when driving abroad, check your car insurance policy: some insurers automatically extend the cover you get in the UK to trips abroad (although there may be a limit on the length of each trip) while other insurers will extend cover only at extra cost. So unless your car insurance policy specifically says that it provides the same level of cover as you get in the UK while you are driving abroad, you will need to read your policy carefully beforehand.

If you will be driving in a country which has not signed up to the MGA, you will need to ask your insurer for an international motor insurance card – called a green card – which proves that your insurance provides the minimum legal cover for the country you will be driving in. The green card does not itself provide any insurance cover. You can also get a green card for driving in countries which *have* signed up to the MGA and, since it is internationally recognised by the police and other officials, this may be worthwhile. However, your insurer is more likely to recommend that you take with you instead your certificate of motor insurance and policy booklet (which should give details of who to contact in the event of an accident).

If you plan to drive in Spain, you will need a 'bail bond' to prove that you can meet any claim for damages. If you cannot prove this, the police can detain you and impound your car after an accident. If a bail bond is already included in your policy (with appropriate Spanish translation), you should take your policy document with you. If your policy does not include a bail bond, you will have to ask – and possibly pay – for a separate bail bond from your insurer.

For hiring a car abroad, see page 123.

What might be covered

A comprehensive policy may cover you for certain extras but any claims you make may nevertheless be rejected or reduced if you fail to follow certain conditions or if there is a hefty 'excess' (the first part of the claim that you have to pay). For example:

- You may have to pay the first part of any claim for theft of the car if it was not kept in a locked garage.
- Claims for lost or stolen possessions may be refused if you did not keep your belongings out of sight in a locked car.
- Money and documents may be excluded altogether.

- There may be limits of around £500 on what you can claim for custom-fitted audio equipment, car telephones or other electrical accessories – although there may be no limit for such equipment fitted by the manufacturer as part of the standard specification for your car.
- It is very likely that you will have to pay the first £50 to £75 towards any claim for damage or loss, but this excess could be much higher if your car was being driven by a particularly young driver – under 24 or 21, for example – or by the holder of a foreign driving licence.
- You will have to pay the first £50 or so towards any claim for replacement glass – a smashed windscreen, for example – but it could be more if you do not use your insurer's preferred supplier(s).
- Personal accident benefit may not be paid for people over a certain age and it definitely will not be paid in the case of suicide or attempted suicide.
- Some policies will include insurance for legal expenses connected with your car, while others may ask you to pay extra for this.

What is not covered

No car insurance policy will cover you if you drive without a valid driving licence or if you do not keep your car in a roadworthy condition. You will also find that you will not be covered for:

- wear and tear on the car
- loss as a result of the car depreciating in value
- mechanical and electrical breakdown
- tyre damage caused by braking or by punctures
- theft of, or damage to, the car if you left it unattended with the keys in the ignition (e.g. while you went to pay for petrol)
- 'theft' of the car by deception (e.g. if you agreed to sell it to someone who managed to make off with the car before you had received payment for it).

If you buy a policy that insures you for third party, fire and theft, it should cover damage as a result of theft or attempted theft but theft itself may be excluded altogether if the car is not normally kept in a locked garage at night. Unless you choose comprehensive cover, you will not be covered for accidental damage to the car.

Choosing the right policy

For most people, comprehensive cover is the best choice. However, if you are young (under 25), you may find that comprehensive cover is prohibitively expensive – particularly if you drive a high-performance car. If this is the case, third party, fire and theft is the cheaper option. If you drive an old (but not classic) car, whether you choose comprehensive or third party, fire and theft depends on the value of your car: if the car is not worth much, paying to replace it with a similar car could well cost less than comprehensive insurance.

Cost is a significant factor in choosing a policy but the cheapest policy will not always be the best: you must ensure that it gives you the cover you need. Although most policies are pretty standard, there are subtle differences which can affect which insurer you choose.

If, for example, you depend on your car for ferrying your children to school and doing the shopping, or you cannot get to work on public transport, make sure that the policy you are buying will pay for a courtesy car while yours is off the road because of an accident or accidental damage. If you like to take your car abroad, a policy which does not charge you extra for doing this makes sense. If you do not want to take responsibility for getting repairs done after an accident or you do not want to have to pay upfront for repairs, make sure that the insurer operates a direct repair service. This may also include a free accident recovery service which takes an undriveable car to the nearest authorised repairer and puts you up in a hotel or drops you off at the nearest convenient source of public transport.

However, these extra services come into play only if you and the car have been involved in an accident: they will not be available just because you break down somewhere.

Special cases

If you drive a motorcycle or moped, you are legally obliged to have insurance in the same way as for cars and the choice of types of insurance and the cover are much the same except that there may be no personal accident cover, and discounts for not claiming (see page 78) tend to be lower.

If you own a caravan, you need to make sure that your car insurance covers you for towing – most policies do. Once the caravan is attached to the car, it counts as part of the car and so the third party liability covered under your car insurance automatically extends to the caravan. However, accidental damage to, or theft of, the caravan – whether it is attached or not – will not be covered. If you want this cover, you can either extend your contents policy (see Chapter 3) to cover your caravan and the things in it, or you can buy a specific caravan insurance through a broker.

If you own a classic, vintage, exotic, particularly expensive or 'high-risk' vehicle – a Lamborghini or Aston Martin, for example – or your annual mileage is low (in the jargon, you have a 'cherished' car), a standard car insurance policy might not be the best deal. It could be worth investigating the specialist policies on offer through a broker: contact the British Insurance and Investment Brokers' Association★ for a list of brokers in your area. Policies are also available to cover you against loss or theft of 'cherished' (i.e. personalised) number plates.

Calculating the cost

The type of policy you choose affects the cost of your car insurance because the higher the level of cover, the more you will pay. When working out the cost of your premium, insurers will also take the following factors into account:

- **Type of car** Insurers class cars using a group rating system of 20 groups which are based on the probability of the car being stolen, likely costs of repairs and parts, repair times, new car prices, the availability of the basic frame of the car, and performance in terms of the car's top speed and acceleration capabilities. The higher the rating, the more expensive the car is to insure.
- **Age of driver** Your age can have a dramatic effect on the price you pay. In general older drivers pay less – although the price may rise if you are over 70. The price will also take into account

the ages of all the drivers who are insured on the policy, not just the main driver.

- **Occupation** Your job may also affect how much you pay. People deemed to be in low-risk occupations, such as teachers and civil servants, generally pay less than people in what insurers view as high-risk occupations, such as actors, journalists and pub landlords. However, insurers are gradually realising that such blanket classifications do not give an accurate picture – a journalist who sits quietly at home tapping away on the keyboard is obviously less of a risk than a scoop-hungry paparazzo, for example – and are beginning to assess each risk on an individual basis.

- **Sex of driver** Generally young men pay higher premiums than young women because they are considered to be a higher risk. However, there tends to be little or no difference in the price paid by older men and older women.

- **Claims record** If you have a bad claims record or you have been convicted of motoring offences, you will pay more for your insurance – although if a motoring offence is more than a certain number of years old, your insurer may ignore it. If you have been convicted of drink-driving, you are likely to face a price increase of 100 per cent and you may find that you cannot buy comprehensive insurance at all. You must tell your insurer about any convictions.

- **Number of drivers** The more drivers who are insured on a policy, the more expensive it will usually be. The most expensive option is an 'any driver' policy under which anyone (with a valid driving licence) who has your permission to drive your car is insured to do so.

- **Where you live** The price you pay will also be affected by where you live. Insurance claims are more frequent in urban areas so motorists in cities usually pay more than motorists in rural areas. Insurers base this factor on your postcode.

- **Where you keep your car** You may pay less if you keep your car in a garage overnight rather than parked in a drive or on the street. The price may also be different if you usually keep your car somewhere different from your home address.

- **How you use your car** Most private car insurance policies give you cover for 'social, domestic and pleasure' use, which usually includes driving to and from your permanent place of work. If you intend to use your car for business-related travel (for example, to visit clients), your insurers will need to know. Your annual mileage will also affect the cost of your insurance.

- **Giving lifts** All insurers have agreed that if your passengers contribute towards your running costs your insurance will not be affected provided that you do not make a profit and that your car seats no more than eight people. This would cover examples such as a colleague contributing to the cost of petrol in exchange for a lift to work, or your sharing the school run with other parents.

Cutting the cost

Just as it is an offence to drive without proper insurance, so it is an offence to withhold information from an insurer in order to obtain motor insurance. So it is a false economy to try to cut the cost of car insurance by not telling the truth. However, there are several legitimate ways in which you can keep the cost to a minimum:

- **Do not claim** All insurers offer big discounts if you do not claim: for more details, see 'Discounts for not claiming', page 78.
- **Do not take the first quote you are offered** Although car insurance is pretty standard, prices are not.
- **Change to an insurer you have not used before** Many insurers offer start-up discounts to new customers.

Loyalty unrewarded

Kate owns a 16-year-old Triumph TR8 which she insures through a classic-car policy. When she received a renewal notice showing her premium had increased to £306, she decided to telephone other brokers for alternative quotes. By mistake, she phoned her original broker and was surprised to find that the quote she was given was less than the figure on her renewal notice. When she questioned this, she was told that quotes given to new customers were based on a different system from the one used for existing customers. Not impressed with this explanation, Kate carried on phoning around and eventually found a policy with another broker which was £172 cheaper than the figure on her renewal notice.

- **Volunteer to pay more towards any claim** If you agree to pay more than the 'compulsory excess' towards any claim (e.g. £250 rather than £100), you could save around 10 per cent a year on the cost of your policy.
- **Tell the insurer who you work for** Some insurers offer special schemes to people in certain low-risk occupations (although these are not always the best deal). If you work for a large company, you may find that your employer has negotiated a discount that you can take advantage of. You may also be offered a discount if you belong to a trades union, are a member of the Automobile Association (AA) or Royal Automobile Club (RAC) or other organisations such as the National Trust.
- **Tell the insurer about any security measures** Your insurance should cost less if you have fitted an immobiliser or car alarm, for example. You may also get a reduction if you have had your car registration number etched on to all your car windows, because this is a deterrent to thieves, who would have to replace all the windows as well as the number plate in order to hide the car's identity.
- **Take an advanced-driving course** If you are a newly qualified driver, some insurers will give you a discount if you take an advanced-driving course. These courses usually consist of around six lessons and cost around £80 – your insurer will be able to tell you which courses count towards a discount.
- **Check how you can pay** Some insurers offer a discount if you pay by credit card because this costs them less in administration.

Strike a bargain

When Edward changed his car, he was distinctly unimpressed that the large insurance company he used told him that his premiums would have to increase by about £200. However, when he told them he would look for another insurer, the company replied that it would be prepared to halve the increase. Edward accepted this but was left wondering what the 'right' price for insurance really is. He had no doubt that it was worth haggling.

- **Combine your insurance needs** If you are insuring more than one car and several drivers, you can save money by putting them all on one policy.
- **Haggle** Many insurers will reduce the price they quote if you show them you have found a cheaper quote elsewhere. Even if they will not reduce the price, they may offer extra cover at no extra cost.

Discounts for not claiming

If you make no claims on your car insurance, your insurance company will give you a discount when you renew the policy. Typically this 'no-claims discount' will be 30 per cent after one year, building up to a maximum of 60, 65 or 70 per cent after four to six years, depending on your insurer. If you change insurer, your new insurer will accept the same number of your claim-free years when setting your new no-claims discount.

Ex-company-car drivers

You do not have to have driven under your own policy to be entitled to a no-claims discount. If you have just switched from driving a company car to running your own car, you will find that most insurers will give you a no-claims discount if you can prove your claim-free record. To do this, you will need a letter from your employer, or the leasing company which ran your company car scheme, or their insurers, confirming that you have not made any claims.

If you claim on your car insurance, you lose the no-claims discount. However, most insurers will let you keep the discount if the claim is for replacing a shattered windscreen or other windows. Some insurers, but certainly not all, will let you keep your no-claims discount if you are involved in an accident which is not your fault, as long as they are able to reclaim all the costs relating to your claim from the person responsible or from his or her insurer. However, if your claim costs your insurer money, irrespective of who or what caused the claim to be made, you will lose up to two years' worth of no-claims discount.

> **Warning**
>
> A no-claims discount is a discount for not claiming. It is *not* a no-fault discount. You can still lose the discount if you claim as a result of an accident which was not your fault.

Protecting your no-claims discount

You can protect your no-claims discount in one of two ways: either by not claiming and paying for any repairs yourself, or by paying your insurer an extra premium.

Paying for repairs yourself

Paying for repairs yourself is worthwhile if they would cost less than the first part of any claim you have to pay, or they cost less than the no-claims discount you would lose. For example, if your no-claims discount saves you £600 a year and a repair would cost £300, you would be better off paying for the repair rather than claiming on your insurance. But when deciding whether or not to claim, you also need to take into account the no-claims discount you would lose in the future. The 'No-claims calculator', overleaf, shows you how to work out the effect on your no-claims discount of your making a claim. It is important to note that even if you decide not to claim, you must still tell your insurer that the accident happened and what form it took.

No-claims calculator

To decide whether to make a claim on your car insurance, you need to compare the estimated cost of the repair with the cost to you of making a claim on your policy. The calculator overleaf allows you to work out the cost of making a claim. The cost of making a claim includes the cost of any 'excess' that you have to pay towards any claim and the possible loss of your no-claims discount in the future.

No-claims calculator

	worked example
Step 1: Calculate the full cost of your premium This step gives you the figure you need in order to work out what your no-claims discount may be worth in the future	
At A, enter the current level of your no-claims discount — A %	60%
At B, enter the amount you currently pay for your car insurance — B £	£500
At C, enter the result of the following calculation, which gives the full cost of your premium without discount: $\dfrac{B \times 100}{100 - A}$ e.g. $\dfrac{500 \times 100}{100 - 60} = £1{,}250$ — C £	£1,250
Step 2: Calculate the discount you will lose in future Normally, you will lose two years' discount if you claim. The following calculation uses the full cost of your premium, your current no-claims discount and the reduced no-claims discount you will have in future years if you make a claim. You may need to ask your insurer for these figures.	
At D, enter the level of your no-claims discount on the first renewal after a claim — D %	40%
At E, enter the level of your no-claims discount on the second renewal after a claim — E %	50%
At F, enter the result of the following calculation, which shows the total amount of no-claims discount you will lose if you claim: $(A - D) + (A - E)$ e.g. $(60 - 40) + (60 - 50) = 30$ — F %	30%
Step 3: Calculate the total cost of making a claim To work out how much extra you will pay for your car insurance over the next two years if you lose your no-claims discount, multiply C by the percentage figure at F and enter the result at G — G £	£375
At H, enter the amount you have to pay towards any claim (the policy excess) — H £	£100
To find the cost of making a claim, add G to H and enter the result at I — I £	£475

You should make a claim if the figure at I – the total cost of making a claim – is less than the cost of the repair to your car. The calculator assumes that you make only one claim, followed by two claim-free years. The savings or costs will be altered if you have another accident during the two-year period. (It also does not take into account inflation of your premium.)

Worked example   Stephen pays £500 a year to insure his Audi 80 and has a full no-claims discount of 60 per cent. He has had a minor accident which would cost £425 to repair.

To work out whether or not to claim on his insurance for the cost of the repair, he calculates – at Step 1 – that the full cost of his insurance without the discount would be £1,250.

At Step 2, he works out how much no-claims discount he would lose if he made a claim. In the first year after claiming, his no-claims discount would fall from 60 per cent to 40 per cent; in the second year, it would be 50 per cent. So he would lose a total of 30 per cent of no-claims discount if he claimed for repairing his car.

Finally – at Step 3 – Stephen calculates the total cost of making a claim. The extra cost of his insurance would work out as £425 (30 per cent of £1,250) which, added to the £100 he has to pay towards any claim, gives a total cost of claiming of £475. He would save £50 by paying for the repair himself rather than claiming on his insurance.

Paying an extra premium

If you have built up the maximum no-claims discount (e.g. you have been claim-free for at least four years), most insurers will allow you to protect the discount by paying an extra premium that usually works out at around 15 per cent of the total premium you pay. This means that you can make a few claims without losing your no-claims discount. Some insurers allow two claims in three years while others allow two claims in five years and a few set no limits on the number of claims.

You have to weigh the extra cost of protecting your discount against the discount you would lose over the next two years if you made a claim. For example, if your premium was £500, it could cost you around £75 to protect your no-claims discount. However, if you were to make a claim and you had not paid extra to protect your no-claims discount (which would be about 60 per cent), you would pay £250 more for your car insurance in the first year after making a claim and £125 in the second year.

Buying your policy

You can buy car insurance either direct from an insurance company, or through a broker or other insurance intermediary listed in *Yellow*

Pages (look under Insurance agents, Insurance brokers and Insurance consultants). If you use an intermediary, rather than going direct yourself, you should be aware that although intermediaries sell policies from a range of insurance companies, they will not necessarily cover the entire market.

Give yourself plenty of time before the renewal date on your existing policy (or the purchase date of your car if you do not already have insurance) to get alternative quotes. Before you ring up for a quote, make sure that you have to hand all the information you need, including:

- the car's registration number
- the car's engine size
- the car's make and model
- details of any modifications made to the car
- the cost of replacing the car (although you will not necessarily be asked for this). If it is new, give the full on-the-road price even if you bought it at a discount; if the car is older, check local dealers or a specialist magazine such as *The Book* or *Parkers* (available from newsagents) for what it would cost to replace your car with the same model of a similar age and condition
- the type of cover you want (e.g. comprehensive)
- the names and ages of the people you want to be insured to drive the car
- the amount you are prepared to pay towards any claim (the 'excess')
- whether you will be using the car for business
- the date you last claimed on your car insurance, or the number of years you have been claim-free
- dates and details of any accidents you have been involved in as the driver of a car
- the number of years you – and any other drivers to be named on the policy – have had a full driving licence
- the dates and types of any motoring convictions (although parking offences are ignored).

Be prepared to volunteer information which may reduce the price you will pay, such as your age, the name of your employer, the fact that you have a car alarm, and so on. You should also tell the person giving you the quote about any health problems – such as epilepsy, or a disability for which you have had the car specially modified – that could affect the way in which the premium is calculated. If you want car insurance to cover you for less than 12 months, say this before the person gives you a price: there may be specially calculated rates for short periods.

How to pay

When you have decided which quote to accept, you will need to pay the premium, either in a lump sum or by completing a form agreeing to pay the premium in instalments. You can pay by any of the usual methods, such as cheque, credit or debit card, or direct debit.

Cover notes

While your payment is being processed, and before you receive your policy and the certificate of motor insurance, you should get a 'cover note' which is a temporary insurance document that typically covers you for a period of 30 days, although it could be longer. The cover note is evidence that you have the insurance you need to meet your legal obligations under the Road Traffic Act 1988 and can be used for all the purposes for which a certificate of motor insurance is required, such as registering the car or showing to the police, until you get the permanent certificate. This gives you time to send the insurers all the supporting documents they need to finalise your policy – for example, evidence for your no-claims discount. If necessary, a second cover note can be issued.

Warning

If you drive a car without having arranged a current cover note or certificate of motor insurance, you are breaking the law.

Once you receive the policy and the permanent certificate of motor insurance, check all the details very carefully to make sure that you have the cover you asked for and that there are no extra conditions or exclusions that might affect a claim. Do not keep your insurance details in the car: instead, keep a note of the policy number and the name of the insurer with your driving licence; alternatively, use the plastic-card version of the certificate which some insurers might send you.

Keeping your insurance up to date

You must keep your insurer informed about anything that could affect your car insurance. If you do not, you could face your insurer rejecting any claims you make, and you could even be guilty of breaking the law. You should tell your insurer if:

- you change your address
- you (or any named drivers) change the type of work you (or they) do or the basis on which you (or they) do it – e.g. if you become self-employed
- you change your car – even if your insurer classes the new car in exactly the same way as the previous one, you will need a new certificate of insurance with the new car's registration number on it (your insurer will probably tell you that you need a new policy)
- you (or any named drivers) have been convicted of a motoring offence
- the place where you keep the car has changed (e.g. your garage has become filled up with your student daughter's belongings and you are having to keep the car outside overnight)
- any new drivers have started to use the car – this is particularly important if the new drivers are under 25 or hold a foreign driving licence
- you – or the car – have been involved in an accident (however minor) even if you did not make a claim
- you have been prescribed drugs for a long-term illness or have become disabled in some way
- you have made modifications to your car
- you are taking the car abroad (if your policy does not cover foreign trips or your trip is longer than the maximum number of days given in your policy).

A date for your diary

Relying on your car insurance company to tell you when your policy is coming up for renewal could leave you driving without insurance, as Martin discovered. It was only after he had an accident and came to make a claim that he was told that his insurance had run out three weeks previously. Most insurers do remind motorists to renew their policy – after all, it is good for business – but they are not obliged to do so.

How to claim

If you want to make a claim, ask your insurer for a claim form (if it has not already sent you one) and/or – if you were involved in an accident - an accident report form.

Even if you do not intend to make a claim – for example, because you do not want to lose your no-claims discount – you have to tell your insurer about anything that happens to you and your car that results in something for which you could choose to claim. Send in the claim form or accident report form with the words 'for information only' written on it.

What to do after an accident

If you are involved in an accident, as well as having to tell your insurers about it (however minor it may seem) there are certain steps you have to follow to meet your legal obligations. You are legally required to stop after a road accident if someone else is injured; if any dog, horse, sheep, cow, pig, donkey, mule or goat not in your vehicle has been hurt; or if any vehicle or roadside property (apart from your own) has been damaged as a result of the accident. You are not legally required to stop if you injure a cat (although if the cat has an identification tag you may feel that you should let the owner know what has happened).

In any situation where you are legally obliged to stop, you must remain at the scene of the accident for a reasonable time, give your vehicle's registration number, your name and address and, if different, the name and address of the owner of the vehicle, to anyone else involved in the accident or whose property has been damaged. If you cannot do this, you must report the accident to the police as soon as possible.

If anyone else has been injured in the accident, you must show your certificate of motor insurance to those at the scene and report the accident to the police within 24 hours. If you cannot show your insurance certificate (or cover note) at the time of the accident – because you very sensibly do not keep it in the car, for example – the police will allow you up to five days after the accident to produce it.

The other driver

If another driver is involved in the accident, you should take a note of his or her name, address, phone number, insurer's name, policy number and the number of his or her certificate of motor insurance, the registration number and the make, model and colour of his or her vehicle. If the other driver does not own the vehicle, ask for details of the owner (at the least, his or her name and address). Although it may go against your natural inclinations, do not discuss what happened, apologise or admit liability – even if you think that the accident was your fault – since doing so could compromise your claim. If you think that the other driver has been drinking or has broken the law (he jumped a red light, for example) call the police to the scene.

Witnesses

If there are other people around, who were not involved in the accident but who have seen what happened and the circumstances leading up to the accident, get their names, addresses and phone numbers; and if there were other drivers who saw what happened, get the registration numbers of their vehicles. Witness statements can make a big difference to the outcome of an insurance claim, especially where you are convinced that the accident was not your fault.

Accident details

As well as getting the other driver's details and those of any witnesses, it is worth noting down:

* the date and time of the accident

- the state of the traffic at the time the accident happened – e.g. heavy or fast-moving
- weather conditions and visibility
- the condition of the road surface
- any signals given by the vehicles involved and whether the vehicles were showing any lights
- the state of other vehicles if there are any obvious signs of unroadworthiness – e.g. brake or indicator lights not working
- identity numbers of police (on the shoulders of their jackets)
- what was said and by whom.

Picture the scene

It is always worth making a sketch of the scene, especially if the accident has taken place somewhere that is not familiar to you. If you have a camera with you, it could also be worth taking a photo, but this is no substitute for a detailed diagram, which should include:

- **the road layout** Draw the immediate layout, including any junctions, and write on the road names. Show the position of any traffic signs or road markings, and any difficulties or obstructions such as a sharp bend or parked car.
- **vehicle positions** Show the positions of all relevant vehicles, including parked cars, both before and after the accident. Include details of the distances between the cars themselves, and from the cars to road junctions and the roadside.
- **additional details** Show the position and length of any skid marks, and write on your sketch approximate speeds and the direction of travel of all vehicles involved. If you have a camera, take photos of any damage. You should also show the positions of any witnesses.

Claiming after an accident

You will have to fill in your insurer's accident report form giving details of the accident (see page 85). Any other drivers involved will have to fill in their insurers' report forms too. The insurance companies will try to agree who was to blame for the accident. If it is very clear who was to blame – for example, another driver pulled

---

Adding £££ to injury

If you and/or any of your passengers are injured in a road accident, the hospital that treats you is entitled, under the Road Traffic Act 1988, to charge you £21.30 for every injured occupant of your vehicle who needs emergency treatment, even if the accident was not your fault. Under the Act, if accident victims need to stay in, or return to, the hospital, the hospital can claim up to £2,949 for in-patient treatment, and up to £295 for out-patient treatment. Hospitals have been entitled to reclaim the costs of treating victims of road accidents from the insurer of the person who caused the accident since the 1930s. This entitlement was brought into sharp relief towards the end of 1997 when the government announced plans to make full use of these long-standing powers.

---

out of a side road and drove straight into the side of your car, and you have the names and addresses of three witnesses who agree with your account – the insurer of the driver who was to blame will pay both claims. If the guilt or innocence of the drivers involved is less clear-cut, and the insurance companies are unable to agree who was to blame, each insurer pays the claim of its own driver.

Some insurance companies have 'knock-for-knock' agreements with each other, which means that they pay their own driver's claim and do not bother arguing between them about who is to blame for the accident. This saves the insurance companies time and money but may, if you cannot prove who was to blame, mean that you lose your no-claims discount even if you were not to blame for the accident and even if you did not make a claim yourself. However, if you *can* prove that the accident was not your fault, the insurer will probably let you keep your no-claims discount.

Claiming from the other driver

If you cannot persuade your insurer of your innocence, or you cannot claim on your own insurance for damage that another driver has caused (because you do not have comprehensive insurance), the alternative is to claim from the other driver. You will need to write to the driver explaining that you hold him or her responsible for the accident and that you intend to claim from him or her any costs resulting from the accident. At the same time, you should write to the other driver's insurer giving the number of his or her policy or certificate of motor insurance. You should also let your own insurer know that you intend to claim from the other driver.

The other driver then has the opportunity to settle your claim directly or to pass the matter on to his or her insurer. If the other driver's insurer agrees that its driver is wholly to blame for the accident, it will pay your claim as long as you have provided all the information required, such as evidence of the cost of repairs. The insurer will probably ask for two or three quotes, and may insist on your using a repairer of its choice (see 'Getting quotes for repairs', overleaf). If the other driver's insurer thinks that you are entirely or partly to blame, it may refuse your claim or may suggest a compromise. If you are not satisfied with the insurer's response and you still want to recover your losses, you will have to take legal action against the other driver. This will be your only choice if the other driver refuses to co-operate or if he or she has decided not to involve his or her insurer.

If you do decide to claim from the other driver, either through his or her insurer or by taking him or her to court, you can claim not only for the things your own insurance policy would have paid out for, had you claimed on it, but also your 'uninsured' losses, which are things like the cost of repairs if you do not have a comprehensive policy, the cost of alternative transport while your car is off the road, compensation for personal injury, loss of earnings, compensation for inconvenience, loss in value of your car and legal costs. If you win your court case, the other driver's insurer has to pay up – even if the other driver did not tell the company about the accident.

If you find that the other driver was not insured, you may still be able to recover some costs. See page 92.

Claiming for theft

If your policy covers you for theft (third party, fire and theft and comprehensive policies do) and someone breaks into your car and steals possessions from it, or steals the car itself, you should report this to the police as soon as possible after you discover what has happened, and then tell your insurer – even if the car is returned to you after a few hours. If your car is stolen, your insurance company will probably want to see the 'vehicle registration document' and the MOT certificate as well as receipts for items stolen from the car – including receipts for tyres – in support of your claim.

Getting quotes for repairs

If your car is damaged in an accident, or as the result of theft or vandalism, and you have decided to claim rather than paying for repairs yourself, your insurer will either ask you to use its direct repair service or an 'authorised dealer' of its choice, or will ask to see two or three quotes for the cost of repairs if no direct repair service is available or if you choose not to use it. If the estimated cost of repairs is more than a certain amount, the insurer will probably want to send its own engineer to inspect the damage and assess what needs to be done. If you get the repair done without first getting your insurer's approval, your claim may be rejected or scaled down.

The advantage of using your insurer's own direct repair service or one of its authorised dealers is that repairs can be started straight away and the insurer may pay the repairer directly. However, if you prefer to use the garage you usually go to – because it is more convenient or the mechanics know your car, for example – you will have to wait for the insurer's permission before getting work done.

Repair costs go through the roof

The roof of Louise's car was damaged when a lorry shed part of its load. She took her car to her garage which said that it could fix the dent for £364. Louise's insurer said that the garage could not start the repair until the damage had been inspected but if she wanted the repair done immediately, she could take it to one of the insurer's 'authorised' repairers. Louise took the car to the authorised repairer who recommended that the entire roof be replaced at a cost of £1,464. To her amazement, Louise's insurer recommended that she accept this quote. This left her in the unusual position of trying to persuade her insurer to pay out more than £1,000 less than they planned to. Eventually, the insurer agreed and Louise had her roof repaired perfectly by her usual garage for £364.

Write-offs

If the garage estimate for the cost of the repairs is more than around three-quarters of the value of the car, your insurer may decide that the car is a 'write-off'. This is because it is quite likely that when the garage starts the repairs it will find more damage, and because the repairs could end up costing more than it would cost to replace the car.

If your insurer decides to write off the car, it should pay you the full value of the car, according to its age and condition before the damage, and will sell the car for scrap. Your insurer has the right to decide whether or not to sell your wrecked car for scrap but if you are particularly keen to keep the wreckage and sell it yourself, you can ask your insurer to pay only the market value less the scrap value.

Valuing the car

If you write off a car which is less than 12 months old, most policies will pay to replace the car with a new one. If you write off a car which is older than 12 months, you are entitled to claim for the full market value of the car (what you would have paid to buy a similar

---

No better off

Geoff thought his troubles were over when the police recovered his stolen car – but the garage inspection arranged by his insurer found that not only did the steering column and locks need repairing, at a cost of £800, but that also the engine was so badly damaged that it would have to be replaced, adding a further £2,300 to the repair cost. His insurer was willing to pick up the £800 bill for the steering column and locks, but said that Geoff would have to pay 40 per cent of the cost of replacing the engine because the new engine would increase the value of his car, with the result that he would be better off than he was before the damage occurred.

Geoff didn't agree that he would be better off and – using information from a trade guide to used-car prices – argued that because the potential sale value of a used car is based on its age and general condition, a new engine would not increase its value. A few days later, the insurer backed down and agreed to pay the full cost of all the repairs.

---

car in a private sale) before the accident happened. This may not be the same as what you said it was worth when you took out your insurance, although insurers will use this figure as a guide. When calculating what to pay you, most insurers will consult trade guides to second-hand car prices (see page 82).

Insurers will also look at the market value of your car if they believe that any repair you have done at their expense has increased its value. If they think that you are in a better position than you were before the repair was carried out – called 'betterment' in the jargon – you may be asked to contribute to the cost of the repair. However, if you do not agree that the repair would make you better off than you were before the accident happened, you should challenge any request for a contribution to the repair cost.

Claiming against uninsured drivers

If you are the innocent victim of an accident caused by an uninsured driver, you may be able to claim from the Motor Insurers Bureau★ provided that you have not already claimed on your own insurance. You can claim for personal injury caused by an uninsured driver – whether or not the driver can be traced – and for damage to property where the guilty driver has been found but turns out to be uninsured.

Getting problems sorted out

If your insurer rejects your claim because you are not covered for what you are claiming for, there is not much you can do except change your insurance policy for the future. However, if you think that your insurer has rejected or reduced your claim unfairly, you should complain – see Chapter 23.

Chapter 6

Mechanical breakdown insurance

If you have just bought a new car, you do not need mechanical breakdown insurance – more commonly referred to as an 'extended' car warranty – because your car will be covered by the manufacturer's guarantee for the first year or so. If your manufacturer's guarantee is due to expire or you are buying a second-hand car, paying for mechanical breakdown insurance can offer peace of mind for a limited list of possible repairs. If you are offered this sort of insurance at no extra cost as part of the deal when you buy a second-hand car, you may as well take it.

Every new car comes with a basic guarantee or warranty – a statement by the manufacturer that it will not charge for fixing most of the things that go wrong with the car, provided that it is serviced properly and has not been misused. Most new-car warranties last between one and three years, depending on the type of car. New-car warranties vary in their detail but they all include an undertaking by the manufacturer to replace or repair, free of charge, most faults that can be traced to a manufacturing or assembly defect. Some also offer cover for other things such as roadside recovery or the loan of a vehicle if repairs take more than a few days. Very few warranties cover routine servicing costs or general 'wear and tear' and they may cover other repairs only if the car is serviced by a franchised dealer while the car is under warranty.

Once the new-car warranty expires, you can buy an 'extended warranty' or 'extended guarantee', which car makers and dealers typically use to mean mechanical breakdown insurance. Unlike a new-car warranty, which covers a broad range of defects, mechanical breakdown insurance is very specific about what is and is not covered. As with extended warranties for domestic appliances (see Chapter 4), if you buy this sort of insurance you risk spending more on insurance than you would paying for repairs as they become necessary. Also, like appliance insurance, you do not need to buy mechanical breakdown insurance from the car retailer: you can buy a stand-alone policy from an insurer.

What is covered

Mechanical breakdown insurance covers you against the unexpected failure of a specific list of components. This sort of insurance is not a maintenance contract, and it does not cover breakdowns which occur as a result of normal wear and tear on the car. Indeed, it is a condition of mechanical breakdown insurance that you keep your car in good condition by having it regularly serviced. It may also be mandatory that details of each service are recorded in the warranty handbook, that you keep the receipts relating to the services, and that the services are carried out by a dealer who is registered for VAT. If you cannot show that you have met the insurer's servicing requirements, any claims you make will be rejected.

Mechanical breakdown insurance covers the cost of parts and labour for factory-fitted components which need to be repaired or replaced as a result of sudden and unexpected mechanical, electrical or electronic failure. The components listed in the policy document may include some or all of the following:

- engine
- gear box
- cooling system
- fuel system
- clutch
- prop shaft
- differential and drive line
- electrics
- steering
- wheel bearings
- braking system – including anti-lock braking system (ABS)
- turbo unit
- suspension

- air conditioning
- gauges
- computers
- central locking
- screen elements.

Depending on the policy, cover may also include a contribution of about £50 a day towards hiring a car for a maximum of seven days if yours is off the road for more than 24 hours. However, you cannot claim for the cost of hiring a car if you are waiting for parts to arrive or for work on the vehicle to start or continue. You may find that you can claim something towards hotel costs and travel on public transport (in the UK) if your car breaks down as a result of something covered by the policy. Some policies also cover breakdown outside the UK, provided that the reason for the breakdown is covered by the policy. If the policy does include cover outside the UK, it is likely that there will be a limit on the number of days you and your car can spend abroad, and the amount paid out for repairs may be limited to the cost of having an equivalent repair carried out in the UK.

Roadside rescue

Some mechanical breakdown insurance policies include membership of a breakdown recovery service – e.g. the AA or RAC – as part of the package you are offered. This typically gives you access to roadside assistance if you break down for *any* reason (including things like running out of petrol, punctures and having a flat battery) and the recovery of your vehicle to a nearby garage or anywhere in the UK. Breakdown recovery service insurance can be purchased separately from mechanical breakdown insurance. It is worth considering if you want access to help if you get stranded, do not have the mechanical know-how to deal with a breakdown, or would feel vulnerable in such a situation. You can also buy breakdown recovery insurance to cover you for a specific number of days (e.g. 14 or 31) when you travel abroad. This can be useful if you do not like the idea of sorting out problems by yourself if your car breaks down overseas.

What is not covered

Mechanical breakdown insurance will not pay for routine servicing of your car, nor will it pay for repairs needed as a result of wear and tear on the car. You will also find that mechanical breakdown insurance will not pay out for:

- claims which exceed a certain limit (e.g. the purchase price of your car)
- claims which exceed the mileage limit given in the policy
- claims where you did not follow the claims procedure properly (e.g. you had work carried out without getting the insurer's permission)
- parts and labour costs which exceed the manufacturer's list price
- parts usually covered by normal servicing
- parts which are being recalled by the manufacturer (e.g. because they have design faults)
- replacement of glass, wheels and tyres, batteries, bulbs, water ingress, exhaust systems and catalytic converters, wiper blades, wheel balancing and alignment, and airbags
- replacement of spark plugs, plug leads, points, oils, filters and lubricants as a result of wear and tear
- replacement of body components such as strikers and hinges, or any component requiring adjustment or paintwork
- replacement of radio cassettes and CD players, or any component within the audio system
- repairs, replacements or alterations to a car which has been modified from the manufacturer's original specification
- repairs, replacements or alteration to electrical equipment, computer hardware or accessories unable to process the date change from the year 1999 to 2000 or beyond
- damage caused by you or other people (this should be covered by your car insurance, see Chapter 5)
- damage which, in the view of a qualified engineer, could have been avoided or which was caused by lack of maintenance or by misuse (e.g. damage to the clutch or gearbox)
- renewal of any brake components due to incorrect adjustment, misuse or wear and tear
- cleaning of fuel lines, filters, carburettors and pumps

- recharging of the air-conditioning system
- components which fail due to wear and tear caused by the vehicle's age or mileage.

You may also find that there is a 'betterment' clause in the policy which means that your claim will be reduced if, in the insurer's view, a repair has increased the value of the car with the result that you are better off than before the repair took place.

Being better off costs money

When Hugh needed to replace the engine of his second-hand car, he assumed that costs would not be a problem because he had taken out mechanical breakdown insurance when he bought the car. But when he had a factory-reconditioned (not new) engine fitted, his insurer claimed that the repair had increased the car's value and refused to pay the claim in full. By contrast, the mechanic who had fixed Hugh's car considered that the car was worth less because potential buyers might assume it had been mistreated. When Hugh went back to the insurer and put forward this argument, the insurer was unconvinced but did agree to meet him halfway by offering to pay a quarter as much again towards his claim.

Choosing the right policy

Whether you should buy mechanical breakdown insurance depends on how likely you think it is that one of the parts covered by the policy will suffer an unexpected mechanical breakdown, and whether you would be prepared to pay for the repair yourself if there was a breakdown of the sort covered by the policy. You should not buy mechanical breakdown insurance to cover your car for repairs it may need as a result of getting old: repairs due to wear and tear are not covered. (For information about the reliability of different models of car, see the reports in *Which?** magazine and *Which? Car*, published annually in June.) Likewise, do not buy mechanical breakdown insurance if what you really want is breakdown recovery insurance (see page 95) – although this may be included in some packages, it is cheaper to buy separately.

However, if you are worried about the reliability of your car and have decided that it is worth paying for insurance to cover specific faults, you need to ask certain questions before buying a policy:

- Which parts or repairs are specifically included and excluded?
- How does the claims procedure work – do you pay for the repair and then claim back the cost, or are repairs paid for directly?
- What happens if you move house or sell the car before the insurance expires?
- What are the conditions for routine servicing – does this have to be carried out at a franchised dealer and will you need to provide proof that it has been carried out?
- Is there a limit on what will be paid out for each claim, or a limit on the total amount of all claims?
- Are there limits on how much mileage you can build up?
- Is breakdown recovery included in the price?

An 'electrics' shock

When the central locking on Kath's car started to play up, she thought that the warranty she had bought would cover the cost of the repair because the booklet stated that 'electrics' were covered. So she booked the car into an approved garage (a condition of her policy), but on collecting the vehicle received a nasty shock in the form of a bill for nearly £150. The garage told her – quite correctly – that 'electrics' did not cover the central-locking wiring circuit.

Part 2

Insurance for you and your family

Chapter 7

Private medical insurance

If you are a fervent believer in waiting your turn for treatment under the National Health Service (NHS), private medical insurance (or private 'health' insurance as it is also known) is not for you. If you are among the growing number of people who want the option of 'going private', but you do not have access to private medical insurance as a perk from your or your partner's job, this sort of insurance can be worth considering. It is not cheap however, and there is no guarantee that the treatment you need will be covered.

Private medical insurance buys you the option of going private if you do not want to wait for treatment under the NHS, would like to be able to choose when and by whom you are treated, and are attracted by the idea of a hospital stay in a well-furnished private room. The insurance lasts for a year at a time but, provided you pay your premiums, most insurers will automatically renew the policy each year. If and when you need treatment, the policy pays out – provided your illness is covered. The alternative to buying private medical insurance is to meet the bills for private treatment from your income or savings, although there are drawbacks to doing this if you do not already have a substantial lump sum. The table overleaf gives a rough guide to the cost of private medical treatment (including hospital accommodation) for a range of operations. As you can see, medical treatment does not come cheap and you need to consider what you would do if you had to have a series of operations.

All-in costs of some common private treatments

Treatment	Cost	Treatment	Cost
appendectomy	£2,000–£7,200	hysterectomy	£3,000–£4,000
cataract operation	£2,000–£2,800	knee replacement	£5,200–£8,200
heart operation	£3,280–£8,250	slipped disc repair	£3,015–£8,250
hernia operation	£1,200–£2,000	tonsillectomy	£665–£1,635
hip replacement	£5,200–£7,200		

What is covered

Private medical insurance is designed to pay the bills for private treatment of 'acute' conditions – which means short-term and curable disorders. In general, policies do not cover the treatment of long-term illnesses which cannot be cured such as asthma, diabetes and multiple sclerosis, conditions commonly referred to as 'chronic'. Although there may be limits on the amounts you can claim for in each category, policies will usually pay out for:

- consultants' fees for private consultations
- physicians' fees
- operating expenses including surgeons', anaesthetists' and operating theatre fees
- accommodation and nursing charges – often the biggest part of the bill
- X-rays, dressings and medication while you are an in-patient
- radiotherapy, chemotherapy, physiotherapy and other types of specialist treatment
- home nursing charges, if this is recommended by the consultant and follows in-patient treatment
- out-patient and day-care treatment, if this is linked to treatment you have received as an in-patient.

What might be covered

The most expensive policies may also include cover for:

- cash benefits if you stay in hospital as an NHS patient
- out-patient care that is not linked to an in-patient stay
- emergency treatment while travelling abroad (although the USA and Canada may be excluded and you will not be covered if you go abroad specifically to get treatment)

- dental treatment
- some of the costs of giving birth in a private hospital, or complications resulting from pregnancy and childbirth
- glasses or contact lens prescriptions
- sight tests
- critical illness benefit.

Acute becomes chronic

When Neil was admitted to hospital for a serious eye operation, his insurer confirmed that the costs of treatment would be covered by his policy. However, various complications arose which left Neil in a coma. Because of this the insurer recategorised Neil's state as a 'chronic' condition and told Neil's family that the policy would no longer pay for treatment because chronic conditions were not covered.

What is not covered

Because private medical insurance covers the unforeseen, you cannot take out a policy to get treatment for a condition that has developed recently. And it will not cover all your health needs. The following are almost certain to be excluded:

- emergency treatment – you will almost certainly be treated by the NHS
- existing or previous health problems (but see 'Pre-existing conditions', overleaf)
- incurable or chronic conditions (including the terminal stages of cancer)
- long-term illnesses (e.g. diabetes, asthma, multiple sclerosis) – although initial treatment and relief of acute phases might be covered
- AIDS-related illnesses – although you may be covered for the initial diagnosis and a limited stay in hospital
- treatment on a kidney machine (renal dialysis)
- routine check-ups from GPs, dentists or opticians
- preventative medicine such as vaccination or cancer screening
- 'palliative' treatment designed to relieve rather than cure (see case history overleaf)

- long-term hospital or nursing care
- complementary medicine – although some policies pay for osteopaths and chiropractors if your GP refers you
- normal pregnancy and childbirth
- abortion
- vasectomy and sterilisation
- some out-patient costs (e.g. glasses, hearing aids and prescriptions)
- the services of your GP (e.g. the fee for filling in your claim form)
- self-inflicted injuries or suicide attempts
- treatment related to drug or alcohol abuse
- cosmetic surgery
- psychiatric treatment
- dental problems.

An unhealthy get-out clause

Mavis chose her private medical insurance policy specifically because it covered pre-existing medical conditions (see below) – she had already been treated for lymphoedema (swelling in her limbs due to impairment of her lymphatic system) and wanted to be sure that her policy would cover treatment for her condition in the future. However, when she eventually submitted a claim for manual lymph drainage treatment, which had been recommended by her consultant, her insurer refused to pay the claim on the grounds that the procedure constituted 'palliative treatment'. This was defined in the policy as 'any medical condition [sic] the primary purpose and intention of which is to offer temporary relief of symptoms rather than to cure the medical condition causing the symptoms' – in other words, because – in the insurer's view – the treatment only made Mavis *feel* better, she was not covered.

Pre-existing conditions

Private medical insurance policies always have some sort of clause covering claims for pre-existing conditions. Some will pay out for the treatment of existing (or foreseeable) conditions only if the insurer agrees to cover them when you take out the policy. In this case the insurer assesses the risk of paying out on the basis of a medical questionnaire and posssibly medical examination. You may find that cover is adjusted or premiums loaded accordingly and sometimes that you are refused cover altogether. Some will cover existing conditions on a 'moratorium basis', meaning that any illness or condition that has occurred in the five years before taking out the policy will not be covered for a specified period – usually two years – after the policy is taken out.

Check-ups not covered

When Caroline was looking around for private medical insurance, she knew that for the first two years her policy would not cover the costs of treating a malignant cyst similar to one that was removed from her breast four years earlier. However, she was worried to find that some insurers would cover her after two years only if she had no precautionary check-ups relating to her earlier condition during those two years – even if the check-up found nothing wrong.

Out of pocket on arrival of the bill

When Leila got back around £500 less than she had claimed for after her kidney operation at a private hospital in London, she was surprised – not least because her policy provided cover at the top of the London scale. The explanation given for the shortfall was that she had overshot the individual limits for surgeons' and anaesthetists' fees, as well as surpassing the limit for consultations and other treatments, because of the many pathology tests her condition had required.

Choosing the right policy

With private medical insurance, the more you pay, the more you get in terms of cover and choice. However, your choice of policy may be restricted because of your age: some insurers will sell you a policy up to the age of 74 while others will turn you down if you are 59 or over.

Once you have bought your policy, most insurers offer 'guaranteed renewability' which means that they will undertake not to

---

Medical insurance for pets

There is no NHS for cats and dogs – not to mention horses, rabbits, hamsters, birds and snakes – so pet owners have to meet the full cost of vets' bills unless they take out insurance. However, just like private medical insurance for humans, pet insurance will not cover all forms of treatment or all pets (you may not be able to buy cover for ten-year-old cats and dogs, for example, because they are older). Even where treatment is covered, there are limits on what will be paid out. Where pet policies differ from the human kind is that they provide cover against the damage your pet might do to another person or their belongings – although you might be able to extend the 'liability' cover you get with your contents insurance (see Chapter 3). For more details on pet policies, see Chapter 17.

---

cancel your policy at renewal or penalise you as a result of the number of claims which you make. However, there is no guarantee that changes won't be made to the scheme overall, nor that your premiums will not go up.

Although not necessarily advertised as such, there are broadly three sorts of policies: top-of-the-range, standard and budget.

Top-of-the range policies give the most cover and impose the fewest limits on how much you can claim. Cover typically includes extras such as complementary medicine (e.g. osteopathy and chiropractic) and home nursing. Some add in the costs of private consultations with a GP, plus dentists' and opticians' charges. Cover may even extend to treatment abroad. There is usually no limit on the amount you can claim for in-patient treatment (within the terms of the policy), though there may be individual limits for bills relating to out-patient treatment.

Standard policies cost less but impose limits on what you can claim in a number of ways. For example, they may:

- restrict the overall amount you can claim in any one year
- allow you only a certain number of days' treatment each year
- place cash limits on specific items
- limit your choice of hospital.

If you go over any limits, you have to meet the difference between the cost of treatment and the amount the policy will provide.

Budget policies are about one third cheaper than standard policies and consequently pay out for fewer things. To keep costs down, as well as applying similar limits to standard policies (see above), budget policies tend to restrict cover by:

- paying out only if the waiting time for NHS treatment is longer than six weeks – although these policies are becoming rarer
- excluding the cost of the initial consultation and diagnosis
- covering a limited range of illnesses only
- paying for treatment only if you use an NHS pay-bed (private treatment in an NHS hospital) rather than a private hospital.

Aftercare an afterthought

Colin was in his 80s when he suffered a stroke. Although he was treated by the NHS, in accordance with the terms of his private medical insurance he was paid a daily cash allowance for a maximum of 35 days' treatment. Before he could return to the home in which he lived alone, he subsequently required extensive nursing – including five weeks in a private nursing home – but did not receive any further financial assistance. Even though this aftercare was essential to his recovery, his insurance policy did not cover it.

Hospital bands

The biggest chunk of the bill for private treatment is often accommodation and nursing charges – but all the costs associated with private medical treatment can vary considerably across the country and between different types of hospital (and even between different types of room in the same hospital). For all types of plan, insurers often divide hospitals into three or four bands according to the amount they charge. The premium you pay is affected by the band you choose. However, paying more does not necessarily mean that you will get better treatment since the higher cost may simply buy you a more luxurious room. If you opt for a budget policy, your choice of hospital could be limited to just one band.

If you are offered a choice of different bands of hospital, which band you choose depends on how much you are prepared to pay to get the surroundings and facilities that you want, and which band your preferred hospital is in (if there is one situated particularly conveniently for your home, for example). Once you have chosen your band, you have to stick with it – otherwise you may find yourself having to top up what the policy pays out towards your bills.

What it costs

How much you will have to pay for private medical insurance depends largely on where you live, your age, your state of health and the number of people covered by the policy. A yearly premium can cost anything from £120 for someone in their twenties taking out the cheapest policy, to well over £5,000 for a top-of-the-range plan for a couple in their sixties. The premium is likely to increase every year as the cost of private medical treatment rises (which tends to be at a faster rate than inflation), in addition to automatic increases at certain as you get older (although some insurers claim not to make age-related increases).

Increasing costs

The annual cost of Ralph's policy has risen by more than £1,000 in the last four years: when he first took out the policy, it cost him £296 a year; now the yearly premium has risen to £1,385. Ralph and his wife have made a number of claims totalling more than £8,000 but their insurers discount this as a reason for the increase, saying it is due to the fact that medical costs have risen and Ralph is four years older. If he wanted to cut the cost of his premium, Ralph could switch to another insurer but if he did this, he would not be covered for some of the illnesses that he has already claimed for under his current policy since they would be regarded as pre-existing conditions (see page 104).

Cutting the cost

If you get private medical insurance through an employer's scheme, it should cost you less than buying your own policy. If your employer pays the premium, you pay tax at your highest rate on whatever the premium costs your employer.

If you cannot get insurance through your employer, the main way of keeping the cost of private medical insurance down is to limit what you are covered for. However, you may also be able to cut the cost if the insurer offers you a discount for doing any of the following:

- not putting in a claim
- agreeing to an 'excess', meaning that you pay the first part of any claim yourself
- paying by direct debit
- being a first-time buyer of the insurer's private medical insurance.

If you are buying insurance for more than one person – either as a couple or for your family – you can save money if you buy a joint policy. However, if there is a wide age gap between you and your partner, it may be cheaper to buy separate policies since the age of the older partner is what sets the premium rate.

Children under 18 can normally be included relatively cheaply and you may also be able to cover offspring older than 18 provided that they are in full-time education and still dependent on you. New-born babies may be covered for free in their first year, provided that you let your insurer know that you want them covered as soon after they are born as possible. Some policies do not limit the number of children that can be covered.

Since tax relief on private medical insurance premiums was scrapped in the July 1997 Budget, people aged over 60 can no longer save money on premiums because of their age.

Cheaper alternatives

If you are happy for your insurance cover to be limited to surgical treatment only, you could consider **Major Medical Expenses** (MME) insurance, which pays out a tax-free cash sum if you undergo surgery – though it is sometimes limited to certain operations. MME costs significantly less than full private medical insurance and has the advantage that you can spend the money as you choose (on child-care costs while you are in hospital or a recuperative holiday, for example); although some insurers halve the payout if you are treated under the NHS. The main disadvantage is that there is no guarantee that the payout will be enough to pay for private treatment.

This is certainly also true of a **hospital cash plan**, which pays a small tax-free cash sum for each day you are treated as an in-patient or day-patient, either privately or on the NHS. This type of insurance may be combined with a range of other cash benefits: cash payments if you need dental treatment or chiropody, for example, or if you become pregnant. However, because the payouts are small and because they may not be paid until you have had the policy for at least six months, the benefits you are likely to get from a hospital cash plan will be too low to make it worth considering.

Buying your policy

In the past few years the number of insurers selling private medical insurance has increased dramatically, as has the range of plans on offer. Private health insurance is often advertised in the press and leaflets extolling its virtues regularly fall out of magazines.

What to ask

When choosing a policy, it is important to remember that no private medical insurance policy covers the cost of every possible type of private treatment. Before you sign up for a policy, you need to be very clear about what you are buying and equally what the policy will not cover you for. You should find out the answers to these questions:

- Does the policy cover you for all the illnesses and/or types of treatment that you think you might need?
- If you have a pre-existing condition, after what length of time will the policy cover you?
- Are you happy with the choice of hospitals?
- Will you have to wait for a certain period of time before the policy pays out for treatment?
- Is there an overall limit on the amount the policy will pay out?
- Are there individual limits on certain types of treatment?
- Are you limited to a certain number of days' treatment per year?
- Will the policy meet the costs of treatment directly, or will you have to pay initially before claiming the money back?
- Will you have to pay anything towards your claim?

- What discounts are available?
- Can your partner and/or children get cover?
- If you want to be able to stay overnight while your child is in hospital, does the policy cover the costs?

What is required

Some insurers require you to have a medical examination or fill in a detailed questionnaire about your medical history before they will agree to insure you. However, most do not. Instead, you are likely to be insured on a moratorium basis (see page 105) and asked to sign a declaration like the one below:

> I understand that the Policy excludes the costs of any investigation and/or treatment of any medical condition for which I or any of my insured dependants underwent treatment, sought medical advice, were aware existed or were aware of the symptoms thereof existing within the five-year period prior to the Policy inception date. I also understand that following two years' continuous cover, I and my insured dependants will be eligible for any benefit for any such pre-existing medical condition, provided the condition is not chronic or long-term and that a two-year period has expired without consulting a medical practitioner for treatment, medication or advice for the medical condition.

How to claim

As soon as you know that you are likely to claim, and before you commit yourself to paying for treatment, check that your policy covers you (or ask your insurer) and get a claim form from the insurer. It may be a condition of your policy that you have to get your insurer's consent to treatment before it begins but even if not, it makes sense to get written confirmation that your treatment will be covered. If possible, it is helpful to send your insurer an estimate of the costs of treatment together with an estimate of possible hospital charges. If your insurer runs a telephone helpline, use it to get advice on how to claim.

Check which bills will be met directly by the insurer, and which you will have to pay for and claim back. If possible, get hold of a claim form before the initial medical consultation takes place so that the consultant can sign the form on your first visit. Keep a detailed record of all visits, letters and telephone calls to both your insurer and your doctor.

After treatment, send your claim form in promptly since some insurers refuse to meet claims received six (sometimes three) months after the date treatment *started*.

Getting problems sorted out

If you are dissatisfied with the level of service you have received from your insurer, or it has paid less than you claimed for and you cannot understand why, contact your insurer. Policy booklets usually tell you who to contact. If you get nowhere with your insurer's complaints procedure, you can take your complaint further – see Chapter 23.

Chapter 8

Dental insurance

You cannot take out stand-alone dental insurance if you are treated under the NHS. If you pay for private dental treatment, whether or not it is worth your buying dental insurance depends on the state of your teeth and the fees your dentist charges. If you are still able to say 'no fillings, Mum' after every check-up, it is unlikely that your dental charges will be high enough to warrant buying insurance.

If you have private medical insurance (see Chapter 7) – either as a perk from your job or because you pay for it yourself – you might already be covered, although there are limits on what these policies will pay out for dental costs. An increasing number of employers are offering dental insurance as part of a job package: if you are eligible to join an employer's scheme, it will almost certainly be cheaper than paying for dental insurance yourself.

What dental treatment costs

NHS fees are set by the government and are the same across the country. Under the NHS you pay 80 per cent of your dental costs, up to a maximum of £330 per course of treatment. The other 20 per cent, or anything over £330, is paid by the state.

With private dental treatment, there are no standard charges or maximum expenditure limits. Costs are nearly always higher than NHS fees, and will vary according to where you live. Prices are highest in London and the south-east.

Costs of dental treatment

Type of treatment	NHS cost	Private cost
two small X-rays	£3	£12–16
small filling	£4.64	£18–42
gold crown	£36.08	up to £345
full set of plastic dentures	£88.88	£225–385

Free dental treatment

You should be eligible for free dental treatment on the NHS if you are:

- pregnant or have a child under the age of one
- under the age of 18
- under the age of 19 and in full-time education
- on Family Credit or income-based Jobseeker's Allowance
- receiving income support on top of a state pension.

Choosing the right policy

If you choose to pay for private treatment, you may want to consider an insurance plan to avoid being hit with any unexpectedly large bills and to help you spread the cost of payments across the year. One attraction of a private plan is that it may cover you for more expensive cosmetic treatments – such as white fillings in back teeth – which may not be available under the NHS. What is covered by the insurance plan depends on what sort of scheme it is. There are three main types:

- **Capitation schemes** These are budget plans for private dental treatment which you take out through a specific dentist. Once registered as a private patient, you are given an initial dental-health check. The dentist then makes an assessment of how much you should pay based on the amount of future treatment you are likely to need and the level of cover you want. You are then charged a regular agreed amount, usually monthly. According to the terms of the plan, you agree to see your dentist on a regular basis for *preventative* treatment. Capitation schemes therefore encourage you to look after your teeth.

- **Dental insurance schemes** These are straightforward insurance policies which repay the costs of private treatment. You can either pay for a stand-alone scheme or you can buy dental cover as part of a private medical insurance policy (see Chapter 7). You must have a check-up before the policy starts and may be refused cover if your oral health is not satisfactory (because there is a greater risk of the insurer having to pay out for expensive treatment).
- **Health-care cash plans** Usually, these cover the costs of dental treatment as part of an overall package of health-care benefits such as maternity benefit and opticians' fees. You will be unlikely to be able to buy this sort of insurance to cover just dental costs. Premiums are calculated on a flat-rate basis and do not depend on the state of your oral health. You pay a regular amount on a monthly basis and the insurance pays out a proportion of any dental bills (both private and NHS) you incur – usually 50 to 75 per cent, subject to an upper limit of, say, £100 a year. You can claim on the policy any number of times until you reach the maximum annual limit on claims: the amount paid depends on the level of cover. However, there is usually a waiting period of around six months after taking out the policy before you can make a claim.

What is covered

Both capitation schemes and dental insurance plans cover you against the costs of regular treatment from a private dentist after an initial consultation. Health-care cash plans pay part of the costs of treatment from either an NHS or private dentist after you have had the policy for a certain period of time.

What is not covered

Capitation schemes are, in effect, mouth-maintenance contracts which encourage preventative treatment – so if you choose this form of insurance you may not be covered for expensive treatment like root-canal work, or the plan may meet only part of the cost. In addition, because you cannot take out a plan until after you have had an initial check, you may need to pay for treatment to bring your dental health up to scratch before you can take out the policy.

The extent of cover from a dental insurance scheme varies from policy to policy, but generally it is very unlikely that any plan will meet the full cost of expensive treatment or major procedures such as laboratory work for crowns and bridges. You may not be covered for the first £5 to £25 of any claim, and there may also be an upper limit on what the insurer will pay out in any one year – which means that you will have to meet these extra costs yourself if you exceed the limit.

Health-care cash plans will usually not cover you for the cost of any treatment you have in the first six months of taking out the plan. Even after this waiting period, your dental costs will not be met in full. There will also be a limit on what the plan will pay out in a year, which means that you will not be covered for costs that exceed the limit.

Calculating the cost

The cost of a capitation scheme depends on how much treatment your dentist thinks you are likely to need. The monthly payment can range from £5 for someone with a healthy mouth to around £25 for someone who needs extensive dental work. Dental insurance schemes cost around £10 a month, while dental cover bought as part of a health-care cash plan can cost from £5 to £10 per month. If you want your whole family covered, the costs per person may be reduced.

Dental insurance will not necessarily meet your dental bills in full, and you should check the details of what is and is not covered very carefully before you buy. If you visit your dentist regularly and generally look after your teeth, paying as you go could well be cheaper than paying £100 a year for insurance.

Chapter 9

Travel insurance

If you buy a package holiday from a tour operator or through a travel agent, it will be a condition of the booking that you have adequate travel insurance. If you are making your own arrangements to travel abroad, whether or not you buy travel insurance is up to you – but it makes sense if you do not want to find yourself out of pocket as a result of serious holiday mishaps. If you are staying in the UK, it is unlikely that you need travel insurance (but see page 123).

What travel insurance covers

The main reason for buying travel insurance is to cover yourself against the costs of emergency medical treatment abroad and the potentially very expensive bill if you are legally required to pay damages to someone whose property you have damaged or whom you have injured while on your travels (your 'personal liability'). Travel insurance can also cover you against the costs of having to cancel or cut short your holiday due to circumstances beyond your control and against theft, loss or damage or delayed arrival of your belongings – including your passport, other travel documents and cash. It also covers costs resulting from a whole host of other travel-related mishaps such as any legal costs incurred in getting compensation from someone because you have become ill or have been seriously injured or killed, lump sum payments following such injury or death, and delayed or missed departure.

Most standard travel policies include the following sections:

- medical expenses
- personal liability

- cancellation and curtailment
- money and personal belongings
- personal accident
- legal expenses
- delayed or missed departure.

Note that standard policies do not cover you for certain activity holidays such as skiing (see 'Insurance for skiing holidays' page 131, and Chapter 17).

Most policies will extend the cover for some elements of the policy at no extra cost if you cannot get home before the date the policy is due to expire because of the death, serious injury or illness of you or your travelling companions. You should also benefit from extended cover if you cannot get home because public transport let you down.

Don't duplicate

Because travel insurance is a lot of different types of insurance rolled into one, you may find that you already have insurance for some of the things it aims to cover. If you have top-of-the range private medical insurance (see Chapter 7), for example, you may already be paying for cover for emergency medical expenses anywhere in the world. It may be possible to extend the 'personal liability' section of a contents policy (see Chapter 3) to cover you against the cost of being sued for damages while abroad. If you have an 'all-risks' extension to your contents insurance, this can cover both baggage and belongings – including cash – that you take out of the home, however far you choose to take them (although there may be a limit on the number of days you can take them abroad). If you are travelling in the UK, making sure that your belongings and cash are covered by an all-risks extension to your contents policy may be all the 'travel' insurance you need – unless you want cover against the costs of cancelling your holiday. Nearly all travel policies do not include travel in the UK, although a handful do.

What travel insurance does not cover

Travel insurance does not cover you when driving abroad because this cover is provided by your car or motorbike insurance (see Chapter 5). No policy will meet claims made as a result of war (which includes general hostilities, civil war, rebellion, revolution, insurrection or military or usurped power), so if you were caught in the cross-fire of a military coup, for example, any claim for injuries would be rejected. You will typically find that the policy will not pay out for any claims as a result of:

- HIV, HIV-related illnesses and AIDS
- being detained or having belongings confiscated or destroyed by Customs or any other government officials
- damage suffered by you or your belongings where caused by radioactive contamination from nuclear fuel, waste or installation
- loss owing to exchange rates moving against you
- hiring a moped (although medical bills may be covered)
- travel in the UK.

As well as the general exclusions, each section of a travel insurance document – or policy within a policy – has its own terms and conditions which are discussed in more detail below.

Medical expenses

Insurance for medical expenses covers you against the cost of treatment while you are on holiday abroad. Unless you already have private medical insurance which covers you worldwide, you should aim for minimum cover in a travel insurance policy of £1 million, although you will find that some insurers provide unlimited cover.

What is covered

You will be able to claim for bills for a stay in hospital, out-patient treatment, emergency dental treatment and consultations with a doctor, as well as the cost of prescriptions. You may also be able to claim a small daily allowance (of anything between £10 and £20, for example) to cover incidental expenses – such as phone calls – while you are in hospital.

Because of the expense of treatment in some countries and the poor medical conditions in others, many insurance companies would rather you were treated in the UK so will pay to bring you back, by air ambulance if necessary. Many policies will also cover the costs of a close relative or friend staying behind with you, or travelling out, in order to look after you.

If you die abroad, the policy should cover burial or cremation costs in 'a foreign field' (including transporting your ashes home) or the cost of getting your body back to the UK – although there will be a limit of around £1,500.

Form E111 and what it gives you

Form E111 (available from post offices) entitles you to free, or reduced-cost, treatment in member states of the European Union, plus Iceland, Liechtenstein and Norway. Should you need treatment while in one of these countries, you present your completed E111 together with proof of UK residency. Depending on the agreement that the UK has with the country in which you fall ill, you may still need to pay for treatment (keeping all receipts for any drugs or treatment that you receive) and then claim a refund either abroad or when you get back home.

The E111 can be useful – some insurers will not make you pay the first part of a medical expenses claim if you use an E111 to cover your medical costs – but it is no substitute for the medical expenses part of travel insurance if you want cover for other possible costs such as emergency repatriation or the costs of a relative or friend staying behind to look after you.

What is not covered

Typically, the first £35 of any claim under the medical expenses section will not be paid unless you used an E111 (see box above) to meet your medical bill. Claims under this part of the policy are not generally paid if:

- you travelled against your doctor's advice

- you received treatment for an illness or on-going condition (e.g. asthma or diabetes) which you already had when you took out the policy but did not tell the insurer about
- you attempted to commit suicide
- you were treated for a self-inflicted injury
- you were injured as a result of deliberately putting yourself at risk – although if you were trying to save someone's life, your claim would be paid
- you needed treatment because you were taking drugs – but not prescribed drugs (unless they were prescribed for the treatment of drug addiction)
- you were under the influence of alcohol (e.g. you fell down the stairs and sprained your ankle after one too many gin and tonics)
- you were injured as a result of participating in a 'hazardous activity' (which the policy should define); see also the sections on insurance for skiing and other hazardous activities, pages 131–3
- treatment was non-urgent or was not related to the reason for your being admitted to hospital
- you had treatment in the UK
- your treatment could have waited until you got home.

Depending on the policy, treatment relating to pregnancy or childbirth might also be excluded, although conditions vary. If,

Money well spent

If Alison and Richard had not taken out travel insurance for their holiday in Florida, they would have faced a bill for $250,000. The policy they bought excluded pregnancy-related claims from women over 32 weeks pregnant. However, Alison was fully covered because she was only 25 weeks pregnant and she was not travelling against the advice of her doctor. While on holiday, Alison went into premature labour and had to be airlifted to a hospital in Orlando where she gave birth to her son Alexander. The $250,000 bill resulted from Alexander having to stay in hospital for over three months because he was so weak. Alison's insurer also paid for her accommodation in the USA while her son was in hospital.

when you took out the policy, you told the insurer that you were pregnant, or you did not know you were pregnant, or you were in the early stages of pregnancy (usually defined as the first 28 weeks), you may be covered. However, some policies will include all treatment relating to pregnancy while others will not cover you at all. Insurers also vary in their attitude to age and mental illness so it is worth checking whether there is an age limit or if mental disorders – including stress and anxiety – are covered.

Personal liability

This part of the policy is to cover you if you are legally liable to pay compensation because you have injured someone or damaged their property. If you cannot extend the personal liability cover under your contents insurance, you should aim for minimum cover from your travel insurance of £1 million, or £2 million if you are travelling in the USA.

What is covered

This section of the policy should cover you for costs that you are legally required to pay because you have done something that results in:

• someone unrelated to you being injured or becoming ill
• damage to someone else's property
• damage to your holiday accommodation (e.g. your hotel room or rented apartment) unless it belongs to you or a member of your family.

What is not covered

The personal liability part of your travel insurance policy will not pay out if the claim:

• is a result of your driving a car or motorbike – which should be covered by your car or motorbike insurance
• was caused by your piloting a boat or plane – you would need other insurance to cover this

- is from a member of your family
- is for damage to a property owned by you or a member of your family
- could be paid by other insurance you may have (e.g. your contents insurance)
- is for damage which you caused on purpose or which was caused by your being careless
- is related to any paid work you have done
- is as a result of damage done by your pet.

Hiring a car abroad

When you hire a car, the rental agreement should include cover if you have an accident and damage property or injure other people. However, it is worth paying for collision damage waiver so that if you have an accident, you do not have to pay for the whole cost of repairing damage to the rental car – although you may need to pay the first £100 or so of any repair costs. It is also important to have personal accident cover. This should be available as an extra from the car hire company but it will be cheaper to make sure that you are covered for driving a hire car by your travel insurance.

Cancellation and curtailment

'Cancellation' cover ensures that you are not out of pocket as a result of having to cancel your holiday after paying for it (but before you set off). (This can be a useful insurance for pre-booked holidays in the UK as well as abroad.) Cover for 'curtailment' ensures that you get part of the cost of the holiday back if you have to cut your holiday short, and should also cover any travel costs you incur. To get the most benefit from this sort of cover, you should make sure that you are covered for the full non-refundable pre-paid costs of your holiday, which you would otherwise risk losing if you have bought a package holiday, or a non-exchangeable air ticket to visit your sister in Australia, or if you have paid up-front for a villa in the Dordogne, for example. You do not need this kind of cover if your ticket is fully flexible and/or refundable, or if you are paying for your holiday as you go and there is nothing to cancel.

If you do want this sort of cover, it is very important to buy the insurance as near to the time that you book the holiday as possible. If booking with friends, it is worth booking on the same form so that it is very clear who your travelling companions are. This is because certain cover extends to a problem encountered by your travelling companion(s) that affects you too (see below).

What is covered

Most travel insurance will pay out under this part of the policy if circumstances *beyond your control* force you to cancel or cut your journey short because:

- you, your travelling companion(s), or the person you are going to visit becomes seriously ill or dies
- a close member of your family or a close business associate (the policy should define what these mean) falls seriously ill or dies
- you (or your travelling companions) are called to do jury service in the UK
- you (or your travelling companions) are called as a witness in the UK – although you may not be covered if you are called as a technical witness
- you are made redundant – although there may be limits on the amount of time you have to have been employed by your employer before being made redundant
- the police have asked you (or your travelling companions) not to go away, or to come home, because of a burglary, serious fire, storm or flood damage at home or at work.

'Curtailment' also covers you for a member of your party being recommended to return home on medical grounds.

What is not covered

The first £35 or so of any valid claim under the cancellation and curtailment section of the policy will not be covered. In general, all the things for which you cannot claim under the medical expenses section of the policy will also be listed in this section. You will also find that your claims will not be paid if you cancel or cut short your holiday for one of the following reasons:

- you fail to get a passport
- you are refused entry because you did not get the necessary visa
- your car breaks down or is stolen
- you no longer fancy going
- there is a crisis at work
- you missed your flight, train or boat out of the UK (unless as a result of severe weather conditions – a freak snow storm cutting off road access, for example)
- you are not enjoying yourself or the weather is bad
- there is a riot (or other civil commotion)
- a pre-existing illness or condition that you did not tell your insurer about when you took out the policy
- a close relative has a recurrence of, or dies from, an illness which you knew about before you were due to go on holiday but did not tell the insurer about when you took out the policy
- a close relative, or the person you were planning to stay with, is injured or dies as a result of taking part in a 'hazardous' activity.

Depending on the policy, you may or may not be able to claim for cancelling or cutting short your holiday to look after a close relative who suffers from mental illness.

Cancellation cover curtailed

Last year, Barry booked a holiday for him and his wife and one of his two daughters and her friend. He was not happy at being told that he had to buy the travel insurance offered by the tour operator but, since the price seemed reasonable, he went ahead. Unfortunately, his other daughter developed stress problems and she needed medical treatment to help her through the crisis. The doctor agreed that the full support of her family would aid her recovery so Barry cancelled the holiday. He sent off the necessary claim form but was astonished to find that his claim was rejected on the grounds that the policy did not cover anxiety, stress or depression – although policies he had bought independently in the past did have this sort of cover.

Money and personal belongings

Policies typically cover you for a total of £1,000 to £1,500 for the belongings that you take with you and around £300 for cash (see opposite for what this covers). Although it may be a boring task, the only way to find out if this is enough is to make a list of everything you will be taking with you, including suitcase, clothes, shoes, books, personal stereo/CD player, pre-recorded tapes and CDs, camera, camcorder, radio, jewellery, watch and so on. If you are way over the total limit, or anything you are taking exceeds the single-item limit (typically £300, although it can be as little as £150), you would be better off getting an all-risks extension to your contents policy.

The main advantage of extending your contents policy is that you do not pay twice for the same cover: remember that if you are covered twice for the same risk, you can make only one claim which the two insurers will share. The other advantages are that the limits on the contents policy are likely to be higher, that valuable items (such as a camera or camcorder) can be fully covered and that your claim is likely to be paid on a new-for-old basis (where you get the cost of replacing the item as new) rather than on an indemnity basis (where an amount is deducted for wear and tear) which is what travel insurance typically offers. Most insurers will give you a discount of around 25 per cent on your travel

---

Share and share alike

Linette had her camera stolen while she was on holiday in Zanzibar. When she got home, she claimed on her contents insurance. Because the cover was 'new for old' she claimed £500 – the full replacement value of the camera. She also told her contents insurer that she had claimed on her travel insurance, as she was required to do. Her travel insurer paid her £200 because its policy gave her only second-hand replacement cover, and her contents insurer made up the difference. If she had not duplicated this insurance, she would have been paid the full amount by the contents insurer and would have saved herself the bother of claiming on two policies.

---

insurance if you exclude money and personal belongings from their policy and use an all-risks extension to your contents insurance instead.

What is covered

This section of travel insurance covers you against loss, theft or damage of the things you take with you, including money and your passport. Cash, cheques, air and other travel tickets, petrol coupons and vouchers all usually count as money. Traveller's cheques and credit cards may also be included in the definition of money but if the cheque or card issuer has an emergency replacement service, you will be expected to use that. Your passport may also be covered under this part of the policy, but you will usually be able to claim only for the cost of replacing it (a limit of £100 is common) and not for the extra costs – such as travel or any extra nights' stay in a hotel – involved in getting it replaced.

Delayed baggage

Within the 'Money and personal belongings' section of your policy, you will usually find details of an allowance which is paid if your baggage is delayed. This pays out for the replacement of essential items – washing things and underwear, for example – while you wait for your luggage to catch up with you. Most policies which offer this sort of cover will pay out if your baggage is delayed by more than 12 hours, although some make you wait for 24 hours. There is usually a limit of around £100. If your baggage fails to turn up, any allowance you were paid to replace essential items is deducted from your overall claim for loss of baggage.

This sort of cover is unnecessary if you will have your baggage with you at all times – if you are driving to your holiday destination or you pack essential items in your hand baggage, for example. It is also unnecessary if the carrier that caused the baggage delay has some arrangement to cover out-of-pocket expenses while you wait for your baggage to arrive.

What is not covered

What the 'Money and personal belongings' part of your travel insurance will not cover you for is:

- the first part of any claim (the excess); there will be separate 'excesses' for belongings and for money
- the full cost of replacing items as new, since most claims will be reduced by a deduction for wear and tear (although some policies give new-for-old cover if an item is less than two years old)
- the full amount of replacing expensive items if they go over the 'single-article limit' specified in the policy
- loss or theft not reported to the local police within 24 hours of your making the discovery
- loss or theft because you did not take 'reasonable care' of your belongings (e.g. you went for a quick dip and left your camcorder on your beach mat with nobody looking after it)
- damage to very fragile or breakable objects
- confiscation of your belongings by Customs or other officials or authorities
- loss or theft of glasses, contact lenses, hearing aids or dentures.

Depending on the policy, you may or may not be covered against loss or theft of valuables or cash which you left in your car – even if left out of sight and locked in the boot. There may also be a condition that you carry valuables in your hand baggage if you are travelling by air.

Personal accident

Personal accident cover pays out a lump sum – £10,000, for example – which is supposed to compensate you (or your heirs) if you are disabled (or die) as a result of an accident. If you already have life insurance which pays out on your death and/or permanent health insurance which pays out if you are injured, personal accident cover is of limited value.

What is covered

The situations in which the lump sum will be paid out are very specific. The cause of the accident must be violent and not of your own making – you will be covered if you are knocked down by a hit-and-run driver, for example – and your death or the injuries you sustain must be as a direct result of the accident. Provided those conditions are met, the lump sum will be paid if the accident causes:

- your death
- total and permanent loss of sight in one or both of your eyes
- total and permanent loss of the use of one or both of your hands or feet (which includes your hands and/or feet being cut off)
- you to be so disabled that you cannot work – policies vary on whether this means that you cannot do the job you usually do or you cannot do *any* sort of paid employment.

What is not covered

The lump sum will not be paid out if the accident was caused by you or if you died or were injured as a result of:

- piloting a plane
- suicide or deliberate self-injury – including drug, alcohol or solvent abuse
- putting yourself at unnecessary risk – unless you were attempting to save someone's life
- taking part in a hazardous activity.

Policies may also reduce the amount of the lump sum paid for children under 16 or older people over a certain age – 76, for example.

Free travel insurance with your credit card?

A lot of credit card issuers offer free travel accident insurance if you buy a package holiday and use their card to pay for it. This travel accident insurance pays out a lump sum – usually a maximum of between £50,000 and £100,000 – if you die or if you are seriously disabled while travelling. It is of limited value to most people and no substitute for proper travel insurance – although proper travel insurance is offered free with some gold cards. You may also find that you get free comprehensive travel insurance if you belong to a frequent-travellers' loyalty scheme and have reached a certain membership level. However, do not make a decision not to buy your own travel insurance until you have made sure that the free insurance on offer gives you the cover you need.

Legal expenses

Most policies will have some sort of provision for covering the legal costs of pursuing claims for compensation and/or damages if you are killed, injured or become ill when on holiday. The insurer will probably want to be convinced that you have a winnable case and may wish to take control of any legal proceedings by appointing the lawyers and so on. It is in the insurer's interests to include this sort of cover because any legal costs your insurer incurs in fighting your case will be included in the compensation and paid direct to the insurer, which can deduct its costs before passing the remainder to you. Free advice for legal problems related to your travel cover under the policy may also be available under this part of the policy. Legal expenses for action unrelated to the policy or legal action against your travel company or insurer will not be covered. (But see Chapter 16 on Legal expenses.)

Delayed departure

This covers you for expenses – such as food and accommodation – that you may incur because your plane, boat, train or whatever is late leaving. Most policies will pay out a small allowance, and only after you have been delayed for 12 hours, followed by an even lower amount for subsequent 12-hour periods of delay. Some policies will pay back your holiday cost if you decide to cancel after having been delayed for more than 12 hours.

Missed departure

This pays your extra expenses if you miss your plane, boat, train or whatever and have to make other arrangements to get to your holiday destination which cost you extra. If you have a fully flexible ticket, you do not need this kind of cover because it will not cost extra to change your ticket and travel later. However, if you have a non-refundable ticket or you are travelling on a chartered flight and would have to pay more to buy a new ticket to get you to your holiday destination, this kind of cover can be worth having. Some policies also offer cover for missed departure of *internal* flights in the country (or continent) you are visiting, which is useful if your trip involves this sort of travel.

The circumstances in which you can claim are carefully defined. The policy should pay out if you missed your flight (or whatever) because public transport let you down as a result of bad weather, mechanical breakdown or industrial action (unless advance warning was given). It is less common to be covered because your own mode of transport breaks down or because you are involved in an accident. You definitely will not be covered because you did not leave enough time to get to the station, port or airport.

No cover for internal flights

Paul and his wife have been on holiday to Africa several times over the past few years. While there, they have sometimes taken extra flights to get them to and from different countries within the continent – South Africa and Zimbabwe, for example. Paul had always assumed that if they missed their flight because public transport had let them down on the way to the airport, he would be able to claim the cost of new tickets under the 'missed departure' section of his travel policy. It was only after chatting with a friend that he checked with the insurance company to see whether his assumption was correct. He discovered that, in common with a lot of policies, his policy covered only his flights to and from the UK and not internal flights he took while away.

Insurance for skiing holidays

If you are going skiing, you need to buy special insurance – and pay more – to cover you against the greater likelihood and cost of your claim, and also for particular expenses related to a skiing trip. As well as the kind of cover you get with a standard travel insurance policy, you should also be covered for:

- mountain rescue if you have an accident and are too badly hurt to get off the mountain under your own steam
- the cost of refunding 'pre-paid expenses' (such as your ski pass, ski and boot hire and lessons) if you have to cancel your holiday or injury prevents you from skiing

- loss or theft of your ski pass
- loss, theft or damage of *hired* ski equipment – if your policy covers this, you do not need to buy the insurance offered by the hire shop
- extra expenses you incur as a result of being held up by an avalanche on the way to the resort
- the cost of having to hire skis and boots while you wait for your own to turn up
- the cost of being transported to another resort if there is not enough snow at yours
- piste closure – although this usually means all lifts being closed for more than 24 hours, which is very unlikely.

If you take your own skis and boots, they should be included under the 'Money and personal belongings' part of the policy but the cover may not be enough, and there may be unreasonable exclusions such as covering you for theft or loss only if your skis are safely locked away in a ski locker or locked to a ski rack on top of the car. You should avoid any policy that has these types of exclusion because you would not be covered if your skis were stolen when propped up outside a mountain restaurant while you had lunch, for example. It is also worth checking whether the cost of hiring skis would be covered if yours were lost, damaged or stolen.

Insurers also vary in their attitude to other ways of hurtling down the slopes and you are more likely to be covered for the following activities if you are accompanied by a trained instructor or guide. However, if you fancy trying any of the following, check your policy carefully to make sure you are covered for:

- snowboarding
- racing
- mono-skiing
- tobogganing
- skiing off-piste
- heli-skiing.

Insurance for other hazardous activities

If you are off on any other kind of activity holiday, or you are planning to take part in some of the activities on offer at your destination, you need to make sure that your travel insurance will cover you. Not all policies list what they consider to be hazardous or not hazardous so it is always worth checking before you buy. Hazardous activities may include:

- rugby
- football (if playing in an organised team, not a friendly knock-about on the beach)
- mountaineering with ropes or guides
- water-ski jumping
- aquaplaning
- paragliding
- sub-aqua diving
- scuba diving below a certain depth
- pot-holing
- hang-gliding
- motorcycling
- motor racing
- professional sports
- parachuting
- ballooning
- flying or gliding.

Choosing the right policy

The right travel insurance policy is the one which does not duplicate insurance you already have and covers you for what you need to be covered for. However, because most travel insurance is sold as a package, it may be difficult to avoid duplicating insurance you already have – although if the insurance you already have gives better cover than the travel policy, it means that you do not need to worry so much about low limits that the travel policy may impose. The main choice you have to make is between a pay-as-you-go policy and an annual policy.

Pay-as-you-go policies cover you for one specific trip so are the best choice if you do not go abroad very often – less than once or twice a year, for example.

Annual policies cover all your foreign travel for a whole year and some include winter sports cover – typically for up to 17 to 21 days. An annual policy is a good choice if you travel a lot and you like to know you are covered for spur-of-the-moment weekends away, for example. Not only do you get the convenience of not having to arrange insurance each time you go away, but an annual policy should work out cheaper than buying insurance for each separate trip.

If you are buying insurance for more than one person – you and your family, for example – a joint policy should be cheaper than buying separate policies for each individual. Before buying a joint *annual* policy, however, ask whether you and/or any of the other people named on the policy will be covered when travelling alone. It may be that the first-named person *only* is covered for individual travel. This will not be a problem if you tend always to travel together, but if you do not, you would be better off buying separate policies unless only one of you ever goes off alone on foreign trips (in which case this person should be the first name on the policy).

If you are a skier intending to buy an annual policy, make sure that it covers you for winter sports (to save buying separate ski insurance) and check the detail of the cover. There will be a limit on the number of days you will be covered and the policy may or may not cover you for the kind of skiing you do: for example, if you are keen off-piste skiers with snowboarding children, this will be particularly important (see 'Insurance for skiing holidays', page 131).

Once you have chosen the type of policy, you need to make sure that it covers you for the country or countries that you are planning to visit. A worldwide policy is exactly what it says. However, what counts as Europe can vary from insurer to insurer. One policy, for example, defines 'Europe' as 'all countries to the west of the Ural mountains (but excluding the United Kingdom), Mediterranean Islands, Morocco, Algeria, Tunisia, Turkey, Canary Islands, Madeira and the Azores'. It is worth checking this definition because if your chosen destination falls into 'Europe' it will be cheaper than buying a worldwide policy.

If you have decided to buy an annual policy, you should also check if there is a limit on how long an individual trip can be and whether there are any additional conditions such as not having had treatment for a health condition for two years or not being covered if you do paid manual work while abroad.

Getting the right cover

The kind of cover you need depends on the insurance you already have, the value of the possessions you will be taking with you, your state of health (and that of your travelling companions and immediate family), what you have already paid for the holiday, and the kind of holiday you are going on.

Although there is no guarantee that you will be able to negotiate for a discount on your travel insurance policy because you have cover elsewhere, you are likely to find that insurers can be more flexible about tailoring a policy to meet your requirements than an intermediary selling an off-the-peg policy. However, most sellers of insurance should be willing to exclude cover for money and personal belongings if you have an all-risks extension to your contents insurance. If you do not already have this cover, it is worth finding out how much extra your contents insurance would cost so that you are in a position to compare prices. It is definitely worth extending your contents insurance if you are taking expensive equipment such as a camera or camcorder or skis with you, since a travel policy is unlikely to give you sufficient cover.

Sellers of insurance are supposed to tell you about the things that will cause them to reject a claim (the policy exclusions) before you buy. When you buy travel insurance you will not necessarily have to fill in an application form, so it is worth volunteering information about your state of health, such as being pregnant, having a long-term health condition such as diabetes or asthma, or being on the waiting list for medical treatment of some kind, and about any sporting activities you propose to indulge in. The same applies for your travelling companions because it will affect whether claims for medical expenses or for cancellation or curtailment will be paid or rejected. Cover for cancellation and curtailment will become worthless if you knew that you might have to cancel or come home early to look after a member of your immediate family either because he or she has been seriously ill or because he or she takes part in a dangerous activity – if your daughter is a keen hang-glider, for example.

Warning

Do not book and pay for a holiday if you *know* that there is a chance that you will have to cancel or come home early, unless you are prepared to pay for the consequences: your insurance will not cover you.

If you have not paid up-front for your holiday (and have not bought non-exchangeable or non-refundable travel tickets), you do not need to worry about cover for cancellation and curtailment. You do, however, need to make sure that you are getting cover for the length of time that you will be away, for the country or countries you are going to and for all the people who need to be covered. It is also worth checking that the cover will be extended if you cannot get home before the insurance expires.

Curtailed cover for curtailment

When Tom and Liz booked a week's holiday in Turkey, they naturally took out travel insurance. Shortly before the holiday, one of Liz's relatives fell ill. She seemed to make a swift recovery once she had started medication, so they went on the trip. But while they were away, the illness recurred, causing Tom and Liz to cut short their trip and return home early. However, they could not use their return flight tickets because they had booked on a charter flight which could not be changed, and had to buy tickets on a scheduled flight. When they tried to claim for the unused tickets, they were turned down: their policy excluded the recurrence of a pre-existing condition. Their insurer told them that because they knew their relative was on medication, they should have bought scheduled-flight tickets, which could have been changed.

Buying your policy

You do not have to buy travel insurance from the travel agent or tour operator who arranged your trip. A good reason for looking elsewhere used to be that the rate of insurance premium tax you pay was 17.5 per cent if you bought from a travel agent but 4 per cent if you bought direct from an insurance company or from an insurance intermediary (which includes insurance brokers, banks and building societies). From 1 August 1998, *all* travel insurance will attract tax at 17.5 per cent. However, another good reason for avoiding the insurance policy offered by your travel agent is that it may be harder to find out exactly what the policy does and does not cover.

The Association of British Insurers★ (ABI) has a Code of Practice which says that anyone selling insurance from an ABI member should give you an explanation of what is and is not covered by the insurance policy being sold, should point out the main exclusions, ask you about anything relevant (whether you are pregnant, or take part in dangerous sports, for example), and should give you a specimen copy of the full policy wording if you ask for one. This is fine in theory but surveys by *Which?* magazine over the years have consistently found that theory does not always translate into good practice – in the worst cases, the policy had to be bought before its wording was made available.

If you do not get the answers you need to be happy that you are getting the cover you require, do not buy the policy. If you are sat-

---

Tied to a travel agent

Some travel agents offer discounted holidays to customers only if they buy the travel agent's in-house insurance (although this is an improvement on the situation ten years ago where they could refuse to sell you any holiday unless you bought their insurance). Unless the cost of the compulsory insurance is included in the discounted price of the holiday or made very clear at the outset, you could find that the cost of the insurance pushes up the price of the holiday by around 40 per cent. More importantly, you may find that the compulsory insurance does not give you the kind of cover you need. As we go to press, the Department of Trade and Industry is planning to ban travel agents from giving holiday discounts only to people who buy their over-priced travel insurance. This decision follows an investigation by the Monopolies and Mergers Commission.

isfied that the policy will give you what you want at a reasonable price, check that the insurance premium tax is included in the price and make it clear when you want the policy to start and end. You will have to pay for the insurance in full in advance either by cheque or by debit or credit card. Even with an annual policy, you will not be able to pay monthly premiums.

As soon as you are given or sent the policy, check that the cover is what you expected and contact the insurer if there is anything that you are not clear about. If the cover is not what you expected, cancel the policy and look for another insurer.

How to claim

The insurance industry is paranoid about fraudulent travel insurance claims and may regard with the deepest suspicion any claim which does not have the necessary proof to back it up. It is therefore particularly important to take a copy of your policy – and any helpline card – with you when you go on holiday so that you can check what you have to do when faced with a holiday mishap. If you fail to take the action outlined in the policy guidelines, your claim will be rejected.

Waiting until you get home to see how to claim is not a good idea since it may then be too late to do what is required. It *is* a good idea to read through the 'How to claim' part of your policy before you set off so that you do not throw away receipts and other back-up material that might be needed. Guidance on the kind of back-up material you will need to provide – which depends on which part of the policy you are claiming under – is given below, but check your own policy for details of exactly what you will be expected to supply in support of any claim. You should also claim as soon as possible after getting home. If your claim is for less than the excess given in the policy, there is no point claiming.

Medical expenses
Most policies will have an emergency phone number to call if you have to be admitted to hospital because of a serious illness or accident and it may be a condition of meeting your claim that you use the emergency number. This is worth doing anyway since they should be able to give advice on what to do and can even arrange for

payment to be made directly to the hospital. If you are treated for a minor illness or accident which does not involve a stay in hospital, you will have to pay the bill yourself and keep all receipts to back up your claim when you get home.

Personal liability

You will need to provide full details of what happened to make you legally liable to pay damages, together with any supporting evidence that will prove that you are entitled to claim under this part of the policy.

Cancellation and curtailment

If you need to cancel your trip for medical reasons – if you or a close member of your family becomes ill, for example – you should get hold of a medical certificate from your general practitioner (or the GP of the person whose illness is causing you to cancel) *before* you cancel your trip. Your insurer may also require a cancellation invoice from your travel agent.

If you are curtailing your trip (cutting it short), in order to ensure your claim will be met you should contact your insurer before you pay for any travel expenses involved in getting home, and you should keep all receipts. If you are coming home early on medical grounds, you will also need a medical certificate from the local doctor which gives the reason why it is necessary for you (or your travelling companion) to return home.

If you are cancelling or cutting short your holiday because someone has died, it is likely that your insurer will ask to see a copy of their death certificate.

Money and personal belongings

If you lose belongings or suspect that they have been stolen, you must report the loss to the local police within 24 hours of discovering the loss and get hold of written evidence from the police that you did this. Your insurer may also require you to report any loss to your holiday representative or the management of your hotel or apartment (if applicable), and may also ask for proof of ownership in the form of receipts for the items lost.

If your money is lost or stolen, you should take the same action but you may also be required to produce evidence that you had the cash, in the form of receipts for currency exchange, cash-dispenser withdrawal slips or – if these were in the wallet that went missing – confirmation from your bank that you bought currency or with-drew sterling from your account. If your passport is lost, stolen or destroyed, you will need a letter from the Consulate where you reported the loss, together with receipts for the cost of replacing your passport.

For damaged belongings, you will need the original receipt plus an estimate for repairing the damaged item.

Delayed baggage

If your baggage goes missing – either temporarily on your way to your destination or permanently on your way there or back – you should keep your tickets and the baggage tags (which may be stuck onto the tickets by the carrier and stand as their 'receipts' for your baggage), and obtain a 'property irregularity report' from the carrier (airline, railway or shipping line) responsible for your baggage. If you are claiming for the replacement of essential items because your baggage went missing, you will also need to provide receipts for the things you bought.

Personal accident

You will need to get a medical certificate giving details of your injury – or in the case of death, a death certificate will have to be provided. Evidence of how the accident happened (a police report and witness statements) may also be required.

Delayed departure

You will need to get a letter from the airline, shipping line or railway confirming the reason for the delay and giving details of the sched-uled departure time and the time you actually got underway.

Missed departure

You will need proof that you were prevented from catching your flight (or whatever) for a reason beyond your control that is covered by the policy – the train or coach taking you to the airport broke down, for example.

Dog days

During a fortnight's holiday in Portugal, John went for a walk and was bitten by an alsatian dog. He went straight to a medical clinic as the wound needed stitches. He also received a tetanus jab and a prescription for antibiotics. He later went to the local police to report the incident and to register a complaint against the dog's owner. The medical bill was almost 47,000 escudos, which John paid using his credit card. When he got back to the UK, he submitted a claim under his travel insurance enclosing copies of his medical and pharmacy bills, the police record of the incident and his insurance certificate. Within one month, the insurer sent a cheque that met John's claim in full.

An unreported loss

While Michael was having a look around Milan on the last day of his Italian motoring holiday, someone tried to force the lock of his car. The car had not been broken into but the door lock needed replacing. He asked directions to the police station but realised that he did not have time to report the incident if he was to catch the train on which he and his car were travelling. The next Motorail was not for two days and his ticket was not transferable so, rather than incurring the extra expense – which would have been considerably more than a new lock – Michael continued his journey home and explained the circumstances to his insurer on his claim form. The insurer refused to pay up because Michael's policy stated that attempted thefts must be reported to the police – although it did later offer to pay something towards his claim.

Getting problems sorted out

Provided you are not claiming for something you are not covered for, and you have followed the policy guidelines for claiming to the letter and have sent off all the written evidence required to back up your claim, the insurer should pay up. If your claim is rejected and the grounds for rejecting your claim are unreasonable – for example the insurer introduces an exclusion or condition you did not know about – you should complain (see Chapter 23).

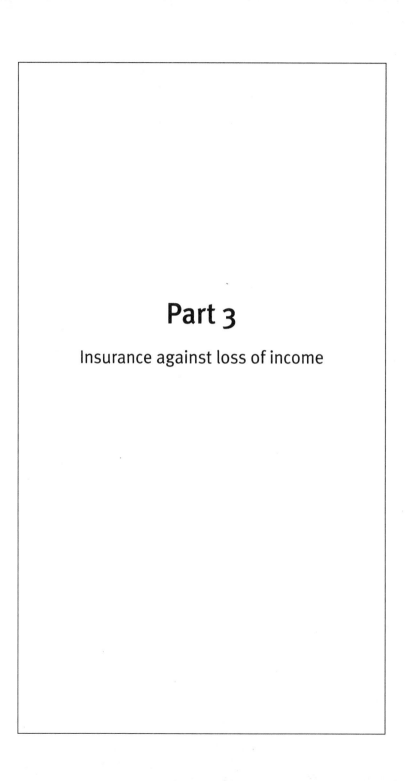

Part 3

Insurance against loss of income

Chapter 10

Life insurance

If anyone would suffer financially if you died, either because of the income that would be lost or because of the extra money that would be needed to pay for the free services you provide – childcare, for example – you need life insurance. If no one is financially dependent on you, life insurance is unnecessary.

The main reason for buying life insurance is to provide financial protection for your dependants in the event of your death. It may be that you already have some life insurance through your job, or that some is linked to your mortgage in the form of a mortgage protection policy (see page 155) or as part of an endowment mortgage (see Chapter 20). In this case, whether you need to buy more life insurance depends on how much replacement income your dependants would need, and whether they would need a lump sum to pay for large additional expenses as a result of your death – such as having to replace a company car or pay an inheritance tax bill. For more details of how to work out your life insurance needs, see 'How much cover?' on page 147.

Insure or invest?

If your prime motivation for buying life insurance is to protect the people who are financially dependent on you, the cheapest and simplest way is to buy protection-only or 'term' insurance which is the type of life insurance described in this chapter.

Term insurance pays out only if you die within a specific period of time (the term) – usually between 5 and 25 years, although it can be longer. If you survive to the end of the term, you get nothing back (in the same way that you get nothing back if you do not claim on your buildings, contents or car insurance). You can also buy investment-type life insurance. This is basically an investment with life insurance tacked on for tax reasons. The apparent attraction of this type of insurance is that you get something back whether or not you die – although you should expect this with *any* sort of investment. You should also bear in mind that you do not get back the part of your premium which was used to pay for life cover, nor do you get back any commission paid to the person who sold you the insurance (which is invariably higher in cash terms than the commission paid when you buy term insurance). The main disadvantage of investment-type life insurance is that it is a very expensive way of buying protection for your dependants. For example, a man and woman aged 40 who want £100,000 of cover would pay around £50 a month for straight term insurance, while the monthly payment for investment-type life insurance would be around £250.

Tip

If you want life insurance and you have money to invest, it is usually better to take out term insurance and put your spare cash into other investments. For more on investment-type life insurance, see Chapters 20 and 21.

What is covered

In terms of what it covers, life insurance is the most straightforward of all the types of insurance you can buy. Provided that you are still paying your premiums at the time of your death, life insurance will pay out. How much depends on the amount your life is insured for (see 'How much cover?', opposite) and the type of policy (see 'Choosing the right policy', opposite).

What is not covered

Life insurance may not pay out if you did not tell the truth (i.e. disclose all material facts) on your application form. The policy may also state that no payment will be made if you commit suicide within a specified period (typically one year) after taking out the policy.

Choosing the right policy

There are two types of term insurance policy. You can choose one that pays out a lump sum or the sort that pays out a guaranteed regular income.

Lump-sum policies pay out a cash sum when you die. They are useful if your dependants will need a substantial amount of cash in the first few months after your death. They are also flexible because the sum can be spent or invested as they wish. The policy will pay out the full amount of the lump sum you have insured for regardless of whether you die at the beginning or end of the term.

Family income benefit policies pay out a series of regular lump sums on your death which can be used as income for as many years as the policy has to run. For example, if you die after six years of a fifteen-year policy, it will pay out for nine years (fifteen minus six). These policies tend to be cheaper than lump-sum policies because the amount the insurer has to pay out decreases with every year of the term that you survive. They are useful if your dependants do not have much experience of investing a large lump sum (e.g. young children) and so would prefer a regular income. They are also a good way of providing cover for a specific period – say until your children are no longer dependent on you.

Tip

Both lump-sum and family income benefit policies offer certain advantages, and there is nothing to stop you buying a combination of the two types to fund the different financial requirements your dependants may have.

How much cover?

There is no easy way of working out the right amount of life insurance you need. You may come across set formulae – such as a lump sum of five or ten times your before-tax income – for working out how much cover you need. These may make doing the sums simple but they do not take account of your personal circumstances, so you could end up insuring for too much or too little. The best way is to estimate what your dependants will need and for how long. The Calculator on pages 150–1 shows you how to work out the amount you need to insure for, assuming that your main aim is the provision of income for your dependants and that you would want them to maintain the same standard of living as they enjoy now. If you are married or live with a partner, you should each work through the Calculator separately. Before you can fill in the Calculator, you need to make a list of:

- lump sums that will be needed on or after your death
- lump sums that your dependants will receive on your death
- income that would be lost on your death
- extra expenses that your dependants will have to meet after your death
- income gained after your death
- outgoings that will be saved by your death.

Examples of what the list might include are explained in more detail below.

Lump sums needed on or after your death

Unless you have already set money aside to pay for your funeral(s) or have taken out some kind of funeral plan (see page 149), you will need to make an allowance for funeral costs. An average funeral costs £1,100 but what you pay depends on where you live, whether you choose burial or cremation and how simple or elaborate you want the funeral – and wake – to be. As well as funeral costs, you should add to the list lump sums needed to pay any of the following:

- debts (including your mortgage if you don't already have a mortgage protection policy – see page 155 – or an endowment mortgage – see Chapter 20)
- possible inheritance tax bills
- gifts of money you have made in your will to people other than your dependants
- the cost of replacing large items, such as a company car which would no longer be available after your death.

You should also consider making an allowance for about two months' worth of lost income, that your dependants may spend while they sort out their longer-term finances and wait for the life insurance policy to pay out.

If you have savings or investments that your dependants would be happy to use in order to meet these immediate expenses, you do not need to enter an amount in the Calculator. However, if these expenses would wipe out your emergency fund, for example, or you would need to borrow money to meet them, you should add an amount to either replenish your savings or pay off any loans. Note that you should make sure that any savings that would be used on your death are readily accessible in a joint account.

Paying for your funeral in advance

A handful of insurers offer life insurance specially packaged to cover funeral costs. They are usually linked to a whole-of-life investment-type life insurance policy (see Chapters 20 and 21) and are designed to pay out enough to cover the insurer's estimate of future funeral costs. Be warned: there is no guarantee that this estimate will provide enough to pay for your funeral, nor that the underlying investment will perform sufficiently well to pay out an adequate amount – especially if you were to die in the first few years after taking out the policy. Including an estimate of your funeral costs in the amount you are insured for with your term insurance is a cheaper and more flexible option. Funeral insurance is different from pre-paid funeral plans, where you pay in advance directly to a funeral company – the regulation of these schemes (or lack of it) is currently being scrutinised by the Office of Fair Trading.

Lump sums your dependants will receive on your death

The lump sums that your dependants might receive on your death could include:

- payouts from any existing life insurance policies

- life insurance – often called 'death-in-service benefits' – from your employer
- a refund of your contributions if you have a personal pension plan
- a modest lump sum that a widow would receive from the state, provided that her spouse's National Insurance payments were up to date
- capital raised from the sale of assets – if your dependants wanted to move to a smaller home, for example, or sell shares and unit trusts
- other lump-sum savings that could be used.

Life insurance calculator

Step 1: Will you need a lump sum?		worked example	
		David	Sharon
Lump sums needed on or after your death	A	£3,400	£3,400
Lump sums your dependants will receive on your death	B	£70,000	£44,880
At C, subtract B from A and enter the result	C	–£66,600	–£41,480
If C is a plus figure, this is the lump sum you will need. If C is a minus figure, you do not need a lump sum.			
Step 2: Will you need to replace income?			
Yearly income that would be lost on your death	D	£15,996	£9,720
Extra yearly expenses	E	£6,000	£6,000
Yearly income gained after your death	F	£6,480	–
Yearly outgoings saved by your death	G	£7,500	£7,296
Add D to E, then subtract F and G and enter the result at H	H	£8,016	£8,424
If H is a plus figure, this is the amount of income that needs to be replaced. If H is a minus figure, you do not need to replace income. If both C and H are minus figures, you do not need life insurance.			

Income that would be lost on your death

In this part of the Calculator you should include both regular monthly income (multiplied by 12 to give a yearly amount) and any irregular income that your dependants would no longer receive after your death, such as:

- your pay after all deductions
- your pension (both state and other), if it will not provide for dependants
- state benefits
- any maintenance payments you receive
- monthly income from savings and investments
- annual bonuses from your job

Step 3: Decide which type of insurance you need

If you need to replace income (the figure at H is a plus figure), you can choose a family income benefit policy (see page 147) to provide the required amount – in which case the figure at H is the amount you need to insure for – and lump-sum insurance to provide the amount of lump sum needed at figure C (if this is a plus figure).

Alternatively, you can buy lump-sum insurance which could be invested to provide the income that would need to be replaced. To work out the size of the lump sum you need to insure for, go to Step 4.

Step 4: What size of lump sum?

To work out what size of lump sum will be necessary to provide the income you need, you will have to take an informed view about future investment returns and decide for how long you want the lump sum to be used to pay out an income.

		David	Sharon
At I, divide the figure at H by 1,000 and enter the result	I	8	8.4
At J, enter the appropriate lump sum from the table on page 153.	J	£16,800	£16,800
At K, multiply I by J and enter the result	K	£134,400	£141,120
If C is a plus figure, add it to K If C is a minus figure, subtract it from K Enter the result at L	L	£67,800	£99,640

The figure at L is the total lump-sum insurance you need.

- income from investments which would be used to pay for expenses on your death and which would not need to be replaced.

If you are a couple with children or you care for another relative, you should also enter lost income if the surviving partner would give up work to look after any dependants. If you keep your personal finances strictly separate from your partner's, the amount of income lost will be the amount that the dead partner used to contribute to the running of the household.

Extra expenses your dependants will have to meet on your death

You should include here any extra expenses that would be incurred after your death, such as:

- paying for services currently provided for free (e.g. cleaning and child care)
- running a car – if your dependants would need to replace a company car
- replacing other perks from your job.

Income gained after your death

Include here any widow's or widower's pension that your partner would receive or dependants' pension if you have children and any income that would be gained if your surviving partner increased his or her earnings.

Outgoings saved by your death

The type of outgoings you should include here are:

- all or part of your mortgage payments – if the mortgage will be paid off on your death
- the amount by which your living expenses will be reduced – i.e. food bills, travelling expenses and so on – but bear in mind that the cost of heating and lighting your home is unlikely to fall dramatically
- personal expenditure (e.g. spending on clothes and leisure activities)
- payments into a personal pension
- life insurance premiums.

The table below shows the lump sum you would need (to the nearest £100) to provide £1,000 of income each year, assuming investment returns of 3, 5 and 7 per cent after tax plus an allowance for the income to be increased by 3 per cent each year as some protection against rising prices. You should choose the rate of growth which best reflects your assumptions about future investment returns. If you are not confident about doing this, you could use an independent financial adviser.

Lump sum needed to provide each £1,000 of income			
	assuming the income goes up by 3% each year and the annual rate of return on the invested lump sum is:		
Period for which income is to be paid (years)	3%	5%	7%
5	£5,000	£4,800	£4,650
10	£10,000	£9,200	£8,500
15	£15,000	£13,200	£11,650
20	£20,000	£16,800	£14,300
25	£25,000	£20,000	£16,450

Worked example David and Sharon recently had a daughter, Phoebe. They have no life insurance. David is a lecturer and Sharon a psychiatric nurse who works three days a week. Both of them are entitled to lump-sum death-in-service benefits from their employers which should more than take care of the lump sums they would need in the event of death to pay for funeral costs and cover outgoings for a couple of months – see Step 1.

The longer term is a different matter. If David died, Sharon would work full-time but the increase in her income would not be sufficient to make up for the loss of David's income as well as meeting childcare costs. Although the mortgage would be paid off and other living expenses would fall slightly, when David and Sharon did their sums they discovered that if either of them died, the other would be worse off by around £8,000 – see Step 2.

David and Sharon had the option of taking out a family income benefit policy (see page 147) to cover this loss of income for a fixed period – say, until their daughter leaves home. Or, they could insure to get a lump sum which could then be invested – see Step 3.

Eventually, they decided that they would prefer a lump sum to pay an income for 20 years. They did not want to over-estimate the return they would get on their investment, so assumed that the lump sum would grow by 5 per cent. They also allowed for an increase to the income of 3 per cent a year. After calculating the lump sum needed to produce the income they required, they deducted the cost of payouts likely to be made (see Step 1) to arrive at figures of £67,800 for David and £99,640 for Sharon – see Step 4.

Allowing for future increases

Both lump-sum and family income benefit policies can pay out a 'level' (i.e. fixed) amount: the amount you are insured for stays the same over the term of the policy which means that its real value is likely to go down because of inflation. Alternatively, if you want to guard against inflation eating away at the amount you are insured for, you can choose an 'escalating' policy where both the amount you are insured for and your premiums increase each year – either by a fixed percentage, or in line with the Retail Prices Index (RPI). Escalating policies cost more than policies which pay a level benefit, but they are a good way of making sure that the value of your cover is maintained – a particularly important factor if you are insuring for more than ten years, say.

Increasable term insurance

For an extra premium, you can also buy the option to increase the amount you are insured for: either at set intervals, such as on each anniversary of taking out the insurance, or when a particular event occurs – marriage or the birth of a child, for example. As you would expect, if you choose to increase the amount you are insured for your premiums will become more expensive. The advantage of buying this sort of add-on to a basic policy is that the premiums are worked out on the basis of your health at the time when you first took out the original policy, even if your current health is not so good.

Term extension

As well as – or instead of – being able to increase the amount you are insured for, it may be possible to extend the term of the policy (i.e.

increase the length of time it runs for). This should be cheaper than taking out a new policy at the end of the term: premiums increase as you get older.

Decreasable term insurance

It is also possible to buy 'decreasing benefit' policies where the amount you are insured for goes *down* each year. This type of policy is useful if the amount you are insuring for will also decrease – the amount of an outstanding loan, for example. These policies are not advisable if the amount you need to insure will remain the same or go up during the life of the policy.

Mortgage protection policies

If you have a repayment mortgage, you may already have a decreasing benefit policy in the form of a mortgage protection policy. This kind of term insurance is designed to pay off your mortgage if you die before the mortgage comes to an end. If you have an endowment mortgage, life insurance is already included as part of the package, see Chapter 20.

If you have dependants, this type of insurance is usually well worth having. However, if you have no dependants and there is no one you want to leave your home to in your will, there is no need for this sort of cover because your mortgage should be paid off after your death using the proceeds from the sale of your house.

Mortgage protection policies are not the same as mortgage *payment* protection policies (see Chapter 13) – insurance against not being able to pay your mortgage because you stop earning as a result of illness or redundancy.

Keeping your options open

While increasable insurance (see opposite) lets you increase the amount you are insured for during the policy term, renewable insurance allows you to take out another policy regardless of your state of health at the time. Premiums will be based on your age at the time you renew but there will be no increase if your health deteriorates. Although you may pay more for this option, it could be worth considering if you are worried about future health problems which would make life insurance expensive (or even unobtainable). However, the option of renewing your policy may not be available if you want the renewed policy to end after your 65th birthday.

Flexible whole-of-life policies

One form of investment-type life insurance that could be worth considering is the maximum protection option of a flexible 'whole-of-life' unit-linked policy which, as the name suggests, gives you cover for the whole of your life – provided you keep paying the premiums. By choosing the maximum protection option, you are guaranteed life cover for the rest of your life, whatever your state of health. With term insurance – unless you pay extra for a renewable policy – you may not be able to renew your insurance if your health deteriorates.

However, unlike term insurance, your premiums may have to go up (usually after ten years) unless you are prepared to reduce the amount of life cover. This is because these policies are unit-linked, so the premiums you pay go into an investment fund which is divided up into units which are cashed in to pay for the life insurance. The value of your policy depends on how the price of these units moves, which in turn depends on the underlying value of the investments in the fund. For more on unit-linked life insurance see Chapter 20. One of the main uses of this type of life insurance is as a way of providing a lump sum to pay an inheritance tax bill.

Waiver of premiums

Usually, if you stop paying the premiums on any sort of term insurance policy, cover stops too. 'Waiver of premiums' – for which you may have to pay extra – ensures that cover continues, even if you can't afford the premiums because you have stopped earning as a result of illness or disability. This is a useful extra safeguard, although normally it comes into effect only after you have been disabled for three to six months.

Convertible insurance

This sort of term insurance could be viewed as a deferred selling method employed by insurance companies in the hope that you will buy investment-type life insurance at a later date. The way it works is that on specified dates (agreed at the outset), you have the option to convert your protection-only policy into an investment-type insurance policy based on your health at the time you took out the original term insurance. This option is of limited use and it ties you to the products of one insurer from which you may not get the best deal. However, if you are older and/or your health isn't what it was – and you are considering switching from a term insurance policy to a flexible whole-of-life policy (see opposite) – there is no harm in comparing the price of what your current insurer offers with what is on offer elsewhere but bear in mind that premiums may have to go up in the future.

Calculating the cost

What you pay for term insurance is set when you take out the policy and depends on a number of factors. Naturally, the larger the sum you want to be insured for and the longer the length of time you want the policy to cover you for, the more expensive your premiums will be: lump-sum policies also tend to be more expensive than family income benefit policies. The other main factors which influence the cost of your premium are your age, sex and state of health.

Your age
The older you are when you take out a term insurance policy, the more it will cost for a given level of benefit. For a 20-year policy, a man of 29 might pay one-and-a-half times as much as a 19-year-old male; at 49, the cost is almost two-and-a-half times that for a man aged 39.

Your sex
Term insurance policies are cheaper for women because women have a longer life expectancy than men. Typically, the cost for a woman is the same as for a man four years younger.

Your health
Premiums for life insurance are calculated on the assumption that you are in good health. If you have a medical condition, or a family history of one, your life insurance will cost more.

Genetic testing

At the end of 1997, the Association of British Insurers (ABI) responded to concerns about advances in the field of genetic testing and screening by issuing a mandatory Code of Practice outlining how insurance companies should use and handle genetic test information when considering applications for life (and other health-related) insurance. Its main points are:

- Insurers will not insist on applicants undergoing genetic tests.
- Applicants will not be asked to take a test, but existing test results should be given to the insurer if relevant, unless it has been stated that information about genetic tests is not required.
- Where someone has undertaken a genetic test voluntarily, the test results will affect the insurance only if they show a clearly increased risk of illness or death.
- Insurance companies will seek expert medical advice when assessing the impact of genetic test results on insurance.
- Insurers may take account of a test result only when the reliability of the test method and the test's relevance have been established.
- Insurers will not ask about existing genetic test results in applications for life insurance up to £100,000 which are directly linked to a new mortgage for the purchase of a house to be occupied by the applicant (for example, a mortgage-protection policy).
- People applying for insurance will not be required to give the result of a genetic test undertaken by another person – such as a blood relative – and one person's test result may not affect another's application.
- If someone has an application for insurance turned down, or if there is a premium increase, the insurer will explain to that person's doctor the reason for the rejection or increase.
- Insurers will not 'cherry pick' by offering a lower premium to someone on the basis of the results of genetic tests that a person may have undertaken.

Smoking

If you smoke, you are likely to pay more for life insurance because smoking is bad for your health. Premiums will typically be a third higher for a smoker than they will for a non-smoker. Some insurers treat smokers of cigars and pipes the same as non-smokers.

HIV and AIDS

In the 1980s, insurers responded to the scare over the perceived AIDS risk by increasing their premiums significantly – particularly for single men. However, premiums are now falling because there have been far fewer AIDS-related deaths than anticipated. In addition, since 1994 the Association of British Insurers* (ABI) has recommended that its members ask only for information about *positive* HIV/AIDS tests on life insurance application forms (and application forms for other forms of health-related insurance). This means that you will *not* be refused insurance if you have had a test and the result was negative. This should ensure that people are not discouraged from taking tests, which have been important in controlling the spread of AIDS.

Your occupation

If you have a high-risk occupation – such as deep-sea diving or working on an oil rig – you are likely to have to pay more than someone who works mostly in an office.

Your leisure pursuits

The cost of your life insurance may also be affected by the type of leisure activities you indulge in: for example, hang-gliding enthusiasts and some scuba divers can expect to pay more.

Cutting the cost

The main factors which affect the cost of life insurance are your age and state of health (see page 157), so if you want to take out insurance in the immediate future there is not much you can do to change these components. However, there are a limited number of ways in which you can cut the cost of life insurance:

- **Take advantage of competition in the market** One of the advantages of buying term insurance is that once you have decided how much cover and which optional extras you want, the deciding factor is the price. The advent of direct insurers has increased competition in the field, which in turn has made the premiums the cheapest they have been for years.
- **Go for term extension** If the insurer offers you the option to extend the term of the policy while it is still running, this should be cheaper than taking out a new policy at the end of the term because premiums increase as you get older.
- **Limit the term** If the premiums you would have to pay for the amount of life insurance you need are likely to overstretch your budget, consider buying a renewable policy (see page 155), or a policy which lets you extend the term in future without giving fresh evidence of your state of health. You can save money now by paying for a policy with a shorter term than you may need, but which incorporates the option of increasing the term in future when money may be less tight.
- **Don't switch** If you have serious health problems, it is likely to be cheaper to stick with the insurer you currently have.
- **Take out a joint policy** It can be cheaper to take out a joint-life policy rather than two single policies if you and your partner need to be insured for roughly the same amount and this will be sufficient if you both die. You can arrange for a joint-life policy to pay out either initially on your death – a 'first life' arrangement – or after both of you have died: a 'last survivor' policy. For the purposes of protecting dependants, a first-life policy is usually the most suitable.
- **Link your life insurance to your pension** If you are eligible to pay into a personal pension plan, you can use part of your contributions to provide term insurance for your dependants. The advantage of doing this is that you currently get tax relief at your highest rate on the premiums you pay (within certain limits). The disadvantage of pension-linked term insurance is that the amount you pay for life insurance reduces the amount you can pay into your pension. For more on personal pensions, see Chapter 18.
- **Don't give in** If you have decided that term insurance offers adequate cover to protect your dependants, and you want a free choice in how you invest any spare cash you may have, don't give in to pressure to buy investment-type life insurance (see page 145).

Writing life insurance in trust

When you die, the proceeds from a life insurance policy will normally be paid into your estate free of tax. However, there could be inheritance tax to pay if your total assets exceed £223,000 (in the 1998–9 tax year). There may also be a delay because the insurer cannot hand over the money until legal matters concerning your estate have been resolved – i.e. probate has been granted. To avoid the possibility of having to pay inheritance tax on what the insurance policy pays out, and to make sure that your dependants get the money as quickly as possible, you can arrange for the policy to be 'written in trust' for the benefit of the person(s) you specify.

Most insurers give you the option of writing a policy in trust at no extra charge and have standard forms to cover common situations. Solicitors can also help with trust-writing (if your affairs are more complicated or if your insurer does not provide a trust-writing service) but they will charge a fee.

Using life insurance to pay inheritance tax

If you are married and are planning to leave everything to your spouse, he or she will not face an inheritance tax bill when you die because gifts to a husband or wife are exempt from this. However, if you are not married or your estate would pass to your children or other relatives on your death, there may be an inheritance tax bill depending on what you are worth and how your finances are arranged.

The cheapest way of using life insurance to cover any possible tax bill is to include the amount in your life cover calculations and to have the policy written in trust for your beneficiaries so that the proceeds from the policy don't count as part of your estate when you die. However, the disadvantage of using term insurance to cover a possible inheritance tax bill is that once the policy comes to an end, so does the insurance against the tax bill.

If you would want the cover to continue until your death, consider whole-of life insurance (see page 156) to cover the future tax liability. For more details on using life insurance to pay inheritance tax bills, see *The Which? Guide to Giving and Inheriting*.

An alternative to writing a policy in trust is to buy a policy on a 'life-of-another' basis. Your husband, wife or partner takes out life insurance based on your life. If you die within the policy term, the policy pays out to him or her as owner of the policy. Note that you cannot take out a life-of-another policy on just anybody's life: you must stand to lose financially if the person on who's life you took out the policy were to die – in the jargon, you must have an 'insurable interest' in the other person. You are assumed to have an unlimited insurable interest in your own life and that of your spouse. When it comes to other people, your insurable interest is limited to the amount you would lose if they died.

Buying your policy

You can buy term insurance direct from an insurance company or through a broker. Because term insurance has no investment element and getting the cheapest policy for the cover you require should be a high priority, you do not necessarily need financial advice. However, if you do not feel comfortable about calculating the amount you need to insure for, or you would like advice on what assumptions to make about future investment returns and so on, it would be worth approaching an independent financial adviser. You should also use an independent financial adviser if you are considering a flexible whole-of-life unit-linked policy (see page 156), because this type of policy has an investment element.

However you choose to buy your term insurance, you will need to know certain things before purchasing a policy:

- the amount you want to insure for
- whether you want lump-sum insurance or a family income benefit policy (page 147)
- how long you want the policy to last
- whether you want the policy to be written in trust (see page 161).

What is required

When you apply for life insurance, you will need to give details of your medical history so that the insurer can assess how likely it is that you will die during the term of the policy, and by extension the probability that it will have to pay out.

If you have had health problems in the past, or if you want to insure for a particularly large amount (what is considered a large amount varies from insurer to insurer), your insurer is likely to ask you to provide a medical report from your GP – and/or you may be asked to attend a medical examination by a doctor chosen by the insurer.

Your rights

If you are refused life insurance, or you are made to pay higher-than-normal premiums on medical grounds, your name may be recorded on the 'Impaired Lives Register'. Under the Data Protection Act, you are allowed to see the entry made in your name. If your own doctor has prepared a report on you for the life insurance company, you have the right to see this. But if you go to a doctor nominated by the insurance company, it is up to the company whether you can see the report or not.

How to claim

If you have to claim on a life insurance policy, send the policy to the insurance company with the death certificate. You will usually have to send the original certificate, not a photocopy – so keep copies and use recorded delivery if you are worried about the document going astray. If the policy was written in trust (see page 161) to the person making the claim, the insurer ought to pay out reasonably quickly. If this is not the case, the insurer will not pay out until probate has been granted. However, if the wait for probate is longer than two months, the insurer should add interest – calculated from the date of death to the eventual date of payment – to the amount insured.

Chapter 11

Permanent health insurance

If you have dependants, your first priority should be making sure that they would be able to manage financially if you died. However, if you are self-employed, buying permanent health insurance comes a close second to life insurance if you could not work because of ill health or an accident and this left you with not enough to live on. If you are an employee, whether it is worth a look depends on what your employer would provide in the way of sick pay and/or retirement benefits if you were too ill to carry on working. If you do not do paid work but your family would have to pay to replace the services you supply if you fell ill, permanent health insurance could be worth considering. If you are already retired, permanent health insurance is not for you.

Income when you are ill

If your income was cut off because you had to give up work – either temporarily or permanently – as a result of illness or long-term disability, what would you do? If you are an employee, there are four possible sources of replacement income: your employer, the state, your pension (if you pay into one), and your other resources. If you are self-employed, the last three are the only possible ways to replace your earnings.

Help from your employer
If you earn enough to pay National Insurance, and you are off work for at least four consecutive days, your employer must usually pay you statutory sick pay (set at £57.70 per week in the 1998-9 tax year)

for the first 28 weeks that you are off work through illness or injury. However, your employer may run a sick-pay scheme which is more generous than the minimum required by law: you may receive full pay for the first six months and then reduced pay after that, for example. Alternatively, your employer might offer you membership of a group permanent health insurance scheme as a part of your package of salary and perks. These work like the permanent health insurance schemes described in this chapter except that the income you get from a group scheme is taxable – although the value of the perk itself is not taxed.

Help to fight cancer

After two major operations for cancer, Jean was off work for a total of five months. When she eventually returned to work, it was part-time for a year while she was still spending a few days each month receiving treatment in hospital. However, the monthly treatment was followed by more major surgery and a further three months off work. Throughout this time, even when Jean worked part-time, her employer topped up her statutory sick pay so that she was still receiving full pay.

Help from the state

If you do not qualify for statutory sick pay – if you are self-employed, for example – you may be entitled to incapacity benefit. In the first 28 weeks of illness you would be entitled to the tax-free short-term incapacity benefit of £48.80 per week (in the 1998-9 tax year) if your doctor certifies that you are unable to carry out your normal job. From week 29 onwards, you will be eligible for incapacity benefit only if the strict medical test which you must undergo assesses that you are incapable of doing *any* job. If it is found that you could do some work – even though not your normal job – incapacity benefit will cease. If you are assessed as unfit for work of any sort, you will get a higher rate of short-term incapacity benefit of £57.70 per week but this is taxable – so depending on what other income you have, you could end up receiving less than you did up to week 29. After a year, you move to long-term incapacity benefit, worth £64.70 per week in the 1998-9 tax year. However, if you are terminally ill or you are very seriously disabled, the long-term rate will be paid from week 29 onwards.

If you live with a husband, wife or other long-term partner, you have children, or you are over 60, you may also be eligible for extra benefits.

If you do not qualify for incapacity benefit, there may be other benefits you can claim depending on your personal circumstances. For more information, contact your local Benefits Agency.

Your pension

If you are unlikely to be able to return to work at all and you belong to a pension scheme, you may qualify for early retirement on grounds of ill health. If you are a member of an employer's final salary scheme, you may qualify for a 'disability pension', whereby you get a bigger pension than you would from normal early retirement. It is often calculated by assuming that you have built up the number of years' service that you would have at normal retirement age but based on your current salary. Whether this would be an option depends on the rules of the scheme and on whether you would meet Inland Revenue guidelines which say that you must be unable to follow your normal occupation because of physical or mental deterioration.

If you have a personal pension or belong to an employer's money purchase scheme, retiring early will not give you the advantages of a disability pension from an employer's final salary scheme, where a minimum amount is guaranteed. The Inland Revenue allows you to take benefits from a personal pension or money purchase scheme early on health grounds but the benefits you get will depend

---

Pension pays out for Peter

When Peter had only five years to go before retirement, he was diagnosed as having a brain tumour and was able to retire early on the grounds of ill health. This meant that his employer's pension scheme paid him the same proportion of his salary at the time he retired early that it would have paid at normal retirement age.

---

entirely on the amount of the fund you have built up, i.e. what you have paid in plus investment growth. If the fund is small it may be better to leave the money invested and to make other arrangements to replace your income.

Your other resources

If you could not rely on your employer, or you do not think that you could live on the help that the state would provide, and/or you do not have a suitable pension, you need to consider how you would cope using your own resources, and the extent to which you could rely on a partner's income. This involves making a list of:

- how much you spend
- what you spend it on
- what you could cut down on if you were ill
- what you would save if you were ill (e.g. travel expenses)
- which extra expenses you would have to meet (e.g. extra heating bills because you would be at home all day)

Sums for the self-employed

David and Janice live and work in a small Surrey village. David gave up the security of a good job in the Civil Service to become self-employed. When he left his job, he also left behind a good sick-pay scheme. Fortunately, David has never had a long illness but if he did, he and his family would find life very hard indeed. David and Janice reckon that they need around £350 a week to cover basics such as rates, mortgage, food, heating and so on for themselves and their son Christopher. If David were to become ill and could claim incapacity benefit, the family would still have around £300 to find.

Janice works part-time as a freelance journalist and although her income fluctuates, it is enough to mean that David would not qualify for an increased amount of incapacity benefit for both Janice and Christopher. They would not be able to claim any other benefits because their savings are too high. To make ends meet, they would have to eat into their savings and if David were ill for a year or more they would be really struggling. Since they could not manage on state benefits and Janice's income alone, they decided that they need to buy permanent health insurance.

- the income that you would get from your employer (if applicable) and the state
- how much money you would get from other sources
- how long any savings you would be prepared to use would last (having worked out how much income you need for essentials).

Are these enough?

If you would have to take a sharp cut in your standard of living and you are not prepared to do this, or your sums show that you would be able to maintain your current, or reduced, standard of living for only a limited time (less than six months or a year, say) before feeling the pinch, you need to arrange your own protection against loss of income through illness. The main way of making sure that you would have enough to live on is by taking out permanent health insurance.

Insuring your income

Permanent health insurance – sometimes called 'long-term disability' or 'income protection' insurance – aims to replace part of your regular income if you are unable to work because of illness or disability. Since 6 April 1996, the income paid out from a permanent heath insurance policy has been tax-free. It is called 'permanent' health insurance because once you have taken out this sort of insurance, and provided you carry on paying the premiums, the insurer cannot refuse to renew your policy (which typically happens every five years), even if your health has deteriorated and even if you have already claimed on the policy.

In the past, 'permanent' also meant that the premium you paid when you took out the policy was guaranteed to stay the same throughout the life of the policy (assuming the level of cover did not change). These days, premiums are usually reviewed every five years or so; but the permanent nature of the insurance means that any increases have to apply to *all* policyholders, not just to selected individuals – i.e. the insurer cannot weight what you pay because you have made a claim.

What is covered

Permanent health insurance pays out when you become ill or suffer an accident and as a result are left unable to work. How 'unable to work' is defined varies from policy to policy and can be any of the following:

- an inability to do your own job
- an inability to do your own job or a similar job for which you are qualified
- an inability to do any kind of paid work.

A policy which pays out if you cannot do your own job is obviously better than one which insists that you have to be unfit to do any job. Normally, schemes continue paying either until you get better or until you reach retirement age (whichever comes first), although newer 'budget' schemes may limit payment to a maximum of five years (see page 174).

Some policies also pay a 'partial' or 'rehabilitation' benefit for a limited period if you are able to return to your original job but in a reduced capacity: part-time for example. If you take a different and lower-paid job, either with your existing employer or with a different employer, some policies will pay 'proportionate' benefit which usually carries on being paid until retirement. In both cases, the insurer supplements earned income to make up the amount you are insured for.

What is not covered

Most policies will not pay out until you have been off work (without pay) for at least four weeks, although some policies have a longer 'deferred period' (or 'deferment period') for what insurers regard as people in high-risk occupations. If you become ill and recover during the deferred period, no payment will be made. You can find policies that pay out from day one (called 'immediate payment' polices) but they cost more than policies where payment is put off for longer. No policy will pay out while your employer continues to pay your full salary.

As well as not paying out until after you have been ill and off work for a certain number of weeks, there is also likely to be a 'waiting period' after you signed up to the policy. For example, a policy may not pay out for any illness which occurs within three weeks of the insurance being issued.

To make sure that no one is better off by staying away from work, all insurers put a limit on the income they will pay out if you claim. The most common rule is that the income paid out by the policy, plus income from any other insurance that pays out if you are ill or injured, plus any statutory sick pay and state benefits, must not come to more than three quarters of your before-tax earnings over the previous 12 months. If you are self-employed or you are an employee whose income fluctuates – if you earn a proportion of your income as bonuses, for example – your annual earnings will usually be taken to be an average of three years' worth of taxable earnings. Some insurers set lower limits (two thirds rather than three quarters, for example) for earnings over £45,000. For very high earnings, the fraction that will be paid out goes down further.

No payment will be made if you are unable to work as a result of:

- health conditions disclosed on the application form and which have been specifically excluded from the policy
- pre-existing medical conditions or other health defects or partic-ipation in dangerous sports which you *did not* tell the insurer about when you took out the policy
- intentional self-inflicted injury
- alcohol or drug abuse
- pregnancy or childbirth – usually until three months after the birth
- air travel – apart from ordinary passenger flights
- HIV- and AIDS-related illnesses
- war, riot or other civil disturbance.

There is also a limit on what the policy will pay out if you live per-manently outside the UK or Western Europe.

Choosing the right policy

If you are considering buying permanent health insurance because you are worried about the financial consequences of being too ill to work, you need to make sure that the insurance will not add to your worries by not paying out when you need it to, or by not paying out enough. Apart from checking that the definition of 'unable to work' is as generous as possible (see 'What is covered', page 169) and that you would not have to pay premiums while you are claiming (under what is called a 'premium waiver'), you should pay particular attention to the amount you are insured for and the income you get during illness.

Because it may be a long time before you need to make a claim, and because when you do the payment may have to go on for a long time, you need to allow for increases both in the amount you are insured for (to reflect the fact that your earnings are likely to rise in the future) and in the income that will be paid out in the event of a claim. Most insurers offer index-linking either as part of their standard policy or as an optional extra which you arrange at the time you take out the policy. Depending on the insurer, you may be able to choose for the cover (and/or the replacement income paid when you claim) to rise by a fixed percentage each year, in line either with the Retail Prices Index or with National Average Earnings. Note that if you do not arrange for increases when you take out the policy, you will not be able to have the replacement income increased once it is being paid out.

How much cover?

The most that the insurer will pay out is usually 75 per cent (three quarters) of your before-tax earnings (less if you are a high earner and/or you would be eligible for incapacity benefit and sick pay from your employer), so do not insure for more than that because you would be wasting your money. For example, if 75 per cent of your before-tax earnings, less any benefit and sick pay, is £15,000 and you insure for £20,000, the monthly replacement income you get will still be based only on the figure of £15,000.

You may also waste money if you automatically insure for the maximum allowed by the insurer, since you might only need the insurance to pay enough to cover essentials – if you would be able to rely on all or part of your spouse's earnings, for example, or you would be prepared to dip into your savings for non-essentials. For a rough check, use the 'Quick calculator', overleaf. Note that the calculator assumes that you would want the insurance to start paying out after you stop receiving sick pay and/or state benefits.

Quick calculator

Add up the monthly expenses you would want the replacement income to cover, and enter the figure at A.	A
Multiply your annual before-tax earnings by the insurer's maximum permitted percentage (e.g. 75%) and divide by 12. Enter this figure at B.	B
If A and B are about equal, you would not be over-insured. If A is substantially less than B, it could be worth insuring for less than the insurer's maximum. If B is substantially less than A, you need to consider how you will make up the shortfall between what the insurance will pay and what you spend.	

Cover for unpaid work

The amount you can claim on permanent health insurance is linked to your earnings from work, which means that there is no point taking out a policy if you are out of work. The exception to this is the unpaid role of housewife or househusband. If you are responsible for running the home, you can take out a policy which pays out when you are ill. Your earnings are assumed to be around £10,000 which is an estimate of the cost of replacing your unpaid services.

What it costs

As with all insurance, how much you pay for permanent health insurance depends on how much you are insured for, whether you choose optional extras such as increases in cover and payouts (see 'Choosing the right policy' on page 170), and whether you are prepared not to claim – by choosing a long deferred period, for example. The cost also depends on how likely it is that the insurer will have to pay out: the greater the risk of your claiming, the more the insurance will cost. To assess the risk, the insurer takes into account a broad range of factors including:

- **your job** This is a key factor in determining what you will pay, since some jobs carry bigger risks to health than others. Insurers generally split jobs into four occupational groups ranging from low-risk to high-risk. Jobs in the lowest-risk group include office jobs, such as accountants and lawyers, and attract the lowest premiums. The highest-risk group includes manual workers such as bricklayers and firefighters. If, in the view of the insurer, you are in a particularly high-risk occupation – such as motorbike courier or musician – you may be able to get a policy only on special terms and sometimes not at all. A few insurers have a fifth low-risk group for people in certain professions but dentists and teachers are often excluded from this group since they have a relatively high claims record.

Each insurer uses its own claims experience to determine which occupations it puts in which group, and their lists are not identical. If you find that you are in a particularly high-risk occupation, it will be worth approaching several different insurers to compare prices.

- **your sex** Women typically have to pay around half as much again as men for the same cover. This is because women tend to make more claims and for longer periods.
- **your age** Permanent health insurance is more expensive the older you are because older people tend to have more health problems.
- **your health** It will come as no surprise to learn that this sort of insurance will cost more if you and/or your close relatives have a history of medical problems. However, once you have taken the policy out, the insurer cannot refuse to renew the policy, nor can your premiums be increased on the basis of your *own* claims record – but they can go up for other reasons provided that all policyholders would face an increase.
- **your leisure activities** If you indulge in what insurers term 'hazardous' sports such as rock-climbing, flying light aircraft or pot-holing, for example, your insurance will cost more.
- **your habits** Smokers are generally charged more for permanent health insurance, as are heavy drinkers. You will be expected to own up to how much you smoke and/or drink on the application form.

Cutting the cost

Permanent health insurance can be expensive: often £500 to £1,000 a year but rising to several thousand pounds for an older person in a very high-risk occupation. However, there are ways in which you can cut the cost.

- **Wait before you claim** Most policies have a compulsory deferred period of at least four weeks before they will start paying out, although if you are in a particularly high-risk job (according to the insurer), the deferred period may be longer. However, it will save money if you actively choose a longer deferred period than the standard one the insurer will insist on. If your employer's sick pay scheme means that you would continue to be paid your full salary for the first six months of any illness, it makes sense to choose to wait 26 weeks before being able to claim. Not only will the premium be lower, but nor will you be wasting money, because even if the policy has a shorter deferred period, it will not pay out until your employer stops paying you.

    If you are self-employed and draw a regular income from your business, your personal deferred period could coincide with the number of weeks that you would be able to keep paying yourself. If you have savings that you would be prepared to use to tide you over when ill, the deferred period should correspond to the length of time after which your savings will run out (plus any time when you would be receiving pay from an employer or from your business).
- **Limit the cover** If you could get by on less than the proportion of your earnings that the insurer would pay out in a claim, choose a lower level of cover (see the 'Quick calculator' on page 172). This is worth doing if you would want only to cover your essential spending, or you regularly save a significant chunk of your monthly income and would be prepared to spend the money you usually save, while you are ill.
- **Consider a budget policy** Some insurers are starting to offer budget policies which either put a maximum on what will be paid out or limit the amount of time for which the policy will pay you a replacement income. The first option could be a reasonable choice if the maximum the insurer will pay out would meet your needs. The second option, whereby you would stop receiving a replacement income after two to five years, is worth considering only if you would be prepared to make alternative arrangements for replacing income after the time limit ends. Traditional polices are justifiably more expensive because they

would carry on paying you until retirement age. If you need this kind of safety net, do not buy a budget policy.

Waiting saves money

David has worked out that he needs to buy cover to replace £18,000 a year (£350 a week). He has also decided that although he is self-employed, he will not opt for the standard four-week deferred period but will save on premiums by choosing a deferred period of 26 weeks (six months). As he says, 'It's a question of balancing the extra premiums against the probability of being ill for a long period and if I wait 26 weeks before the policy starts to pay out, the premiums are halved. Janice and I have come to the conclusion that if the worst happens, we would be prepared to manage on Janice's income and dig into our savings for a while rather than pay out extra in premiums.'

Buying your policy

You can buy permanent health insurance direct from an insurance company or through a broker or other intermediary. You will need to know:

- how much you need to insure for
- what your before-tax earnings are, or the average of three years' worth of earnings if your income fluctuates from year to year
- what you would get from the state and/or your employer
- how long you are prepared to wait before receiving a replacement income (e.g. if you are an employee, you need to know how long you would carry on getting sick pay)
- whether you want to provide for increases both in the cover and in the payments, and how you want them to increase
- whether there is a waiver of premium option so that you do not have to pay premiums while the policy is paying out.

You will also need to give the name and address of your doctor (and that of your previous doctor if you have recently changed). If you are under 45, it is unlikely that you will have to go for a medical examination unless your answers to the medical questionnaire suggest that you need to, or you are insuring for a particularly large amount (this varies from insurer to insurer). You may also need to provide evidence of your age (a birth certificate for example, or the personal details from your passport) and/or proof of your marital status (if you are a married woman).

Insurance or investment?

Permanent health insurance policies can either be straight insurance – like contents or car insurance where you pay premiums for the cover you require – or they can be linked to an investment. With an investment-linked policy, your monthly payments are invested and the premiums for the permanent health insurance are paid for by cashing in part of the investment fund. You take the risk that the investment fund will not do as well as is necessary to pay your premiums. If the investment fund does not do as well as it needs to, either your premiums will go up or your policy will come to an end earlier than you might have intended. If your main purpose in buying permanent health insurance is to protect yourself against loss of income when ill, buy straight insurance and invest any spare cash separately.

How to pay

If your application is accepted, you normally pay premiums either annually or monthly. However, if you choose to pay monthly, it may cost more, so check that the monthly premium is not more than one twelfth of the annual premium. You should also be prepared to pay a policy fee or administration charge however you choose to pay the premiums.

Keeping your insurance up to date

Once the insurer takes you on, you *must* be offered the chance to renew your policy each year except when:

- you have changed your job to one which is considered to be an *unacceptable* risk. Most occupations are viewed as acceptable but

changing jobs can mean a higher premium to pay if the new job is in a higher-risk category
- you have moved to live permanently (for more than one year) outside Europe.

If you let the policy lapse – by failing to renew, for example – the insurer may ask for evidence that your health has not deteriorated before agreeing to carry on insuring you as before. The insurer cannot ask for this information if you carry on paying the premiums without a break.

How to claim

Your policy document will usually contain information about the point at which you should tell your insurer that you are ill and likely to claim – bearing in mind that you get no payment during the deferred period. However, if you are still ill when this deferred period ends, the policy should pay out once you have completed the claim form to the insurer's satisfaction and once the insurer has checked things out with your doctor (if it thinks this is necessary).

As well as giving medical details and the dates when you were first ill and went to the doctor, you will also have to give details of your earnings before you fell ill, together with details of other income you are getting *while* ill, such as sick pay from your employer, incapacity benefit from the state and any income from other similar insurance. The amount the insurer will pay out will be reduced if these other sources of income plus the amount you are covered for go over the insurer's maximum limit on payouts – usually 75 per cent of your pre-tax earnings less other forms of sick pay or benefits. Note that if you are eligible to claim incapacity benefit, the insurer will assume that you have claimed it, even if you have not, and your payment will be reduced accordingly.

While you are claiming

Once the deferred period is over, you will usually be paid monthly in arrears (so you will have to wait another month after the deferred period is over before you get any money). While you are receiving payments under the insurance, you will usually have to provide

Accident and sickness insurance

The fact that personal *accident* insurance is often offered free as an inducement to buy other financial products should alert you to the fact that the probability of your suffering the particular injuries covered by this sort of policy is very low. Some policies will pay out a modest lump sum if you die from bodily injuries as a result of a violent accident; some will pay out a lump sum if you die or are injured in an accident – if you lose a limb or you lose your sight, for example; others combine personal accident with sickness insurance (you cannot buy sickness insurance on its own). These accident and sickness policies pay out a lump sum if you suffer one of the injuries listed in the policy but may also pay a set amount for a limited period (usually a maximum of two years) if you cannot work because of illness or accident. However, unlike permanent health insurance, insurers can refuse to renew your policy if your health has deteriorated and they can put up the premiums you pay if you have had a lot of claims.

The possible attraction of these policies is that they are cheaper than permanent health insurance. However, because the conditions and exclusions that apply to accident and sickness insurance can be stringent and restrictive, you take the risk that you pay for a policy which will never pay out – even if you become ill. If you want to protect your dependants from financial hardship in the event of your death, you should buy life insurance (see Chapter 10) which will pay out whatever the cause of your death. If you want to protect yourself and your dependants from loss of your income as a result of illness or injury, permanent health insurance is a better bet because it gives much wider cover and – unless you stop paying the premiums, or take up a particularly dangerous job – you can keep a permanent health insurance policy going until you retire.

monthly medical certificates from your doctor. The insurer may also check with your GP on the reasons for your continuing disablement and ask for an estimate of when your GP thinks you will return to work. If the insurer is not happy with the GP's evidence, it may ask for a report by an independent doctor, which will be arranged and paid for by the insurer. Where it is very unlikely that you will return to work, the insurer may accept medical certificates at quarterly intervals and eventually annually. Unless you buy a budget policy, payment will carry on if necessary until you reach retirement age.

Going back to work

When you are able to return to your job and start receiving pay again, the policy stops paying out and you start paying premiums again (if the policy waived payment of premiums while you were claiming). Some policies will make partial payments if you will be earning less when you go back to work than you did before your illness, provided that the reason for the reduction in pay is related to your state of health. If, for medical reasons, you return to your old job on a part-time basis, you may receive partial 'rehabilitation' payments (if your insurance covers these), typically for up to 12 months. If for medical reasons you go back to a lower-paid job – either full-time or part-time – and your policy covers you, you will receive 'proportionate' payments until retirement if necessary (unless you buy a budget policy which puts a time limit on payments).

Chapter 12

Critical illness insurance

If you have dependants to protect, your first priority should be making sure that you have adequate life insurance (see Chapter 10). Whether you have dependants or not, if you would be in serious financial difficulty if you could not earn because of *any* sort of ill health or injury, you should consider buying permanent health insurance (Chapter 11). If you already have your life and earnings covered, it is unlikely that you need critical illness insurance. However, if you are single and do not need life insurance because there is no one who is financially dependent on you, this sort of insurance *might* be worth considering.

Critical illness insurance – previously called 'dread disease insurance' – is designed to pay out a tax-free lump sum (not income) if you are diagnosed as having one of a defined list of life-threatening conditions. Because it is designed to cover the costs of living with the illness, most policies require you to survive at least four weeks (called the 'deferred period') after diagnosis for a claim to be valid. If the policy pays out, you can use the money in any way you choose: for example, you could pay off the mortgage, cover living expenses for a time, pay for private medical treatment, adapt your home or take a holiday.

Nearly two thirds of the population suffer a critical illness at some time in their lives. In the past, they would often have died, but advances in medical science mean that more people with a critical illness are likely to survive for a significant time. For example, 40 per cent of cancer sufferers survive for five years or longer, and nearly half of the 130,000 people a year who suffer their first heart attack will survive for 13 years or more. This could mean having to manage on a reduced income if you had to give up work or change job. You might also need to buy special equipment or modify your home to cater for reduced mobility.

It is easy to see that the lump sum that critical insurance might pay out could be very useful at such a difficult time. However, although the flexibility of having a lump sum may seem attractive, critical illness insurance should not be regarded as a substitute for permanent health insurance if you would be in serious financial difficulty if you could not work due to ill health. The reason for this is that permanent health insurance covers more illnesses and can provide a monthly income for as long as you cannot work (up to retirement age if necessary), which is particularly important for self-employed people who cannot rely on the cushion of sick pay from an employer. Although permanent health insurance will pay out only after you have convinced the insurer that you are unable to

Permanent health insurance and critical illness insurance compared

You need to replace income because:	Permanent health insurance	Critical illness insurance
you are off work sick	covered	not covered unless reason for absence is covered by the policy
you have an accident that seriously maims you	covered	covered by some policies
you are diagnosed with a life-threatening disease	covered if you cannot work as a result	covered if you survive beyond the deferred period
you cannot work because of a chronic (but not life-threatening) illness	covered	not covered unless the illness is specifically included in the policy
you cannot work because of disability	covered	not covered unless the disability is total and permanent (and meets the definition given in the policy) or is as a result of one of the conditions covered by the policy

Note: Both types of insurance normally have a deferred period of at least four weeks.

work, it will cover both critical and non-critical illnesses such as stress and back pain if they prevent you from earning.

Despite the fact that permanent health insurance should be a higher priority and more suitable than critical illness insurance for most people, sales of critical illness insurance have risen sharply in the last ten years while sales of permanent health insurance have remained fairly static. One reason for the difference in sales could be that, on the face of it, critical illness insurance is cheaper and simpler than permanent health insurance. However, it is worth bearing in mind that you may pay less because you get less in terms of what is covered – see the table. You should also be aware that because the payment from a critical illness policy is a lump sum, once it is spent, you do not get any more. With a permanent health insurance policy the replacement income carries on being paid as long as it needs to be paid; there is also no limit on the number of claims you can make – provided you are still paying the premiums and provided that the claims are valid.

What is covered

Critical illness insurance policies vary greatly in the range and definition of illnesses they cover. Some specify more than 30; others fewer than 10. However, it is debatable whether cover for some of the 'extra' illnesses is of much value, given their rarity. In an attempt to make critical illness policies easier to compare, the Independent Financial Advisers' Association★ has drawn up standard definitions of the medical conditions that are most likely to give rise to claims. These are:

- heart attack
- coronary bypass surgery
- stroke
- cancer
- kidney failure
- major organ transplants.

Between them these conditions account for about 90 per cent of all claims, with cancer, heart attack and stroke accounting for the vast majority of those claims. Most policies also cover multiple sclerosis which accounts for about 5 per cent of claims.

Total and permanent disability

If you are diagnosed with one of the illnesses covered by the policy and you survive beyond the deferred period (see page 180), the policy will pay out. In addition to the list of specified illnesses, most policies will also insure you against 'total and permanent disability'. This should mean that you can make a claim if you are unable to work because of permanent disability following any serious illness or injury, even if the illness or injury is not specifically named in the policy. The best policies will pay out for total and permanent disability if you are unable to do your own job; however, only a handful of insurers define total and permanent disability so generously. Most policies will pay out if you are unable to do a 'similar' or suitable job (taking your experience, education and training into account). The most restrictive policies will pay out only if you are unable to do *any* job, irrespective of your training and experience.

Most insurers will assess a claim for total and permanent disability in relation to your ability (or lack of it) to do work (however that is defined in the policy). However, some insurers apply a more stringent test by using a system based on 'activities of daily living' to decide whether a claim is valid. If this sort of assessment is used, the insurance will pay out only if you are unable to perform at least three out of five 'activities of daily living', which cover things like moving from one room to another, continence, dressing, going to the lavatory and eating. If you want the insurance to pay out because you are too ill to work, insurers that use the 'activities of daily living' type of assessment are best avoided.

If you are not working when you claim, most insurers will base their assessment of your claim on activities of daily living even if they normally use an occupation-based assessment.

Warning

Over two thirds of claims made for total and permanent disability are rejected because of differences in interpretation of what is meant by 'total and permanent disability'.

Loss of limbs

You may also find that the policy will pay out if you lose a limb – but you should check the definition of what constitutes losing a limb very carefully since it can differ significantly between insurers. The most generous policies will pay out if one or more of your limbs is severed above the wrist or ankle. Less generous are those that pay out only if two limbs are severed above the wrist or ankle or if one limb is severed above the knee or elbow and a second limb above the wrist or ankle. However, many insurers will pay out for loss of limbs only if two limbs are severed above the elbow or knee.

Children

Some policies include cover for children as standard if you ask for them to be covered, but any claim is usually limited to a lump sum which is much lower than the total level of cover.

What is not covered

Most policies will not pay out if the claim is as a result of:

- self-inflicted injury
- alcohol or drug abuse
- flying – apart from normal passenger flights
- war, foreign invasion and other hostilities
- HIV- and AIDS-related illnesses.

Very few policies will pay out as soon as you are diagnosed with any of the listed illnesses and most will pay out only after a 'deferred period' of four weeks. If you die between diagnosis and the end of the deferred period, the policy will not pay out.

Cover for total and permanent disability and against loss of limbs may not be covered if you have a particularly high-risk occupation in the view of the insurer, or if you participate in a hazardous activity.

Choosing the right policy

If you are convinced that you want critical illness insurance rather than permanent health insurance, you can either buy critical illness insurance as a policy on its own – a stand-alone policy – or you can

---

Warning

You are likely to be refused cover if there is any evidence – from your own health records or those of your family members, or from genetic testing – that you might be susceptible to any of the conditions covered. However, if you think the reasons for refusing cover are unreasonable, ask the insurer to justify its decision. Insurers should not refuse cover unless they have specific grounds for doing so. (See 'Insurance, disability and health problems' on page 16 and 'Genetic testing' on page 158.)

---

buy this sort of insurance in combination with, or as an add-on to, another form of insurance.

Stand-alone policies cover you for a specific amount and term (25 years, for example) or sometimes for life. If you are buying critical illness insurance on top of life insurance, a stand-alone policy is your best option.

Combined life and critical illness policies With this type, a claim is paid either when you are diagnosed as having a critical illness or when you die, whichever happens first. The main disadvantage of these combined policies is that the lump sum is paid out on an either/or basis, so if you make a claim for critical illness you will be left with no life cover. If, for example, you suffer a stroke, make a claim, then die three years later, the lump sum may have been used up by the time you die, leaving nothing for your dependants. If you make a claim for a critical illness, you will also be left in a position where, given the deterioration in your health, it will either be virtually impossible or very expensive to buy more life cover. So if you want both life cover and critical illness cover, buy separate policies, otherwise you risk a critical illness claim nullifying your life cover. You should also avoid this sort of policy if you do not actually need life insurance (see the 'Life insurance calculator' on pages 150–1 for how to work out your life insurance needs).

Add-on critical illness insurance A limited number of insurers offer critical illness as an add-on to a permanent health insurance policy, which might possibly be worth considering if you want both an income and a lump sum (although this is likely to be smaller than the lump sum you would get with a stand-alone critical illness policy).

More commonly, you may be offered critical illness cover as an add-on to a newly arranged life insurance policy linked to your mortgage. Add-on cover is cheaper than a stand-alone policy because (in this case) it is designed to pay off only your mortgage, either on your being diagnosed with a critical illness or on your death (whichever comes first). If paying off your mortgage would be your only financial worry if you were ill or injured, compare the cost of a permanent health insurance policy (or possibly mortgage payment protection insurance: see Chapter 13), which would cover the cost of your mortgage repayments. However, if you would need to replace other income, you should consider either a stand-alone critical illness policy – so that you can insure for a lump sum that would be big enough both to pay off the mortgage and leave enough to provide you with an income – or you should take out permanent health insurance and separate life insurance (if necessary) instead.

As well as deciding which type of policy to buy (if you are convinced that you really want critical illness insurance rather than permanent health insurance) you should think about the range of illnesses covered. Some insurers give you the option of 'standard' cover or (for a higher price) 'extended' cover which includes more illnesses. However, a longer list of serious illnesses may not actually add much value. For example, some companies cover Alzheimer's disease only up to the age of 60 or 65, while others cover diabetes if you become insulin-dependent only after the age of 45. In fact, fewer than 3 per cent of people with Alzheimer's are under the age of 65 and the vast majority of cases of insulin-dependent diabetes occur before the age of 40. Before you worry about how many illnesses are covered, ensure that a policy gives comprehensive cover against the most common illnesses (listed under 'What is covered' on page 182) and that it has a generous definition of 'total and permanent disability' (see page 183). If they are serious enough, rarer medical conditions should be covered by 'total and permanent disability'.

What it costs

The bigger the lump sum you want the policy to pay out, and the longer the term you are covered for, and the longer the list of illnesses covered, the more your policy will cost. However, as with most health-related insurance, the cost is also affected by:

- **your age** The cost of critical illness insurance rises as you get older and becomes particularly expensive after the age of 40. For example, a mortgage-related policy with a 25-year term could cost around £13 a month for a 29-year-old man but £40 a month for a 39-year-old man. A 49-year-old man would pay £70 for the same cover.
- **your sex** In general, critical illness insurance is cheaper for women than for men because statistics suggest that they are less likely to suffer from one of the illnesses typically covered. The price for a woman and man aged under 30 is about the same, but at 39 a man can pay almost half as much again as a woman.
- **your medical history** If you have a poor health record, or if there is a history of serious illness in your family, you are likely to pay more.
- **your job and leisure activities** If your job involves manual work or if you take part in hazardous activities, this could push up the price or – more likely – reduce the cover in terms of which illnesses and conditions would be covered.

Your premium may also cost more if you choose 'waiver of premium' cover where the insurer will pay your premiums if you are left without income because you are off work ill – but not critically ill. This usually costs an extra couple of pounds a month, although some policies include it as standard.

Buying your policy

Do not buy critical illness insurance without first reviewing your other insurance needs and do not think of critical illness cover as a replacement for life insurance. If you are worried about the consequences of not being able to cope financially because you are seriously ill, you should also ask yourself how you would cope if you were unable to work because of *any* illness or injury. The main thing to focus on is the seriousness of the financial consequences of being too ill to earn and not the seriousness of the illness itself. If you decide to buy, you should check:

- whether the cover is for life or for a fixed term
- if the core illnesses (listed on page 182) are covered
- that the definition of 'total and permanent disability' is offered on an 'own occupation basis' – i.e. that the policy will pay out if you are unable to do your own job as a result of a disabling illness or injury
- whether the premiums are guaranteed for the term of the policy or whether they will be reviewed every five or ten years or so
- if there is 'guaranteed insurability' which means that you can increase your cover in future without giving new medical evidence
- if there is an 'indexation option' so that you can make sure that your cover – and premiums – can be automatically increased either by a fixed percentage or in line with inflation
- how long the deferred period is – i.e. how long you would have to wait after being diagnosed with a critical illness before being able to make a claim.

When you apply for critical illness cover, you will have to give details of your own medical history and that of your immediate family. The insurer may get a report from your doctor and you may be asked to have a medical examination. If there is a history of a serious illness in your family, premiums are likely to be much higher or you may be refused cover. Make sure that you give all the information requested: if you do not, the insurer can reject your claim.

Keeping your insurance up to date

Many policies allow you to increase the amount you are insured for (your 'sum assured') with no further medical evidence required, if you move house, get married or have children, for example. You may also be able to index-link your premiums and sum assured so that they rise with inflation.

Whether or not you choose built-in increases to keep pace with inflation, your premiums are likely to go up when they are reviewed by the insurer, usually every five or ten years. Most policies invest your premiums in a special fund: if the fund does not achieve the growth rate assumed by the insurer, or if the total value of all claims paid out to all policyholders is higher than anticipated, your premiums will have to go up. If, in these circumstances, you choose not to pay a higher premium (assuming that the insurer allows this), the amount of cover will have to fall. A few insurers offer stand-alone policies that have premiums guaranteed not to go up throughout the term of your cover.

How to claim

If you have to make a claim, always follow the guidelines in your policy. There is normally a time limit for claiming (often three or six months after diagnosis) and a deferred period typically of four weeks beyond which you have to survive before you can make a claim. The deferred period is usually longer for claims relating to total and permanent disability. The insurer will ask for detailed medical evidence before it pays a claim. This evidence will normally be supplied by the doctor treating you, but the insurer may choose to get a second opinion from another doctor.

Help for a holiday

Four months after buying her critical illness insurance, Helen was diagnosed with cancer, so she made a claim. She received a lump sum of £6,000. Almost six months later, following treatment and two operations, Helen was declared free of cancer. She had set aside the money to cover loss of earnings but when she was given the all-clear, she used some of the lump sum to pay for a holiday.

Getting problems sorted out

Around one fifth of all critical illness claims are rejected, as are two thirds of claims made for total and permanent disability. Some are fraudulent, some are for things which this sort of insurance clearly does not cover: a broken leg, for example. However, many rejected claims reflect a misunderstanding of, or disagreement about, what the policy does or does not cover and so when it will and will not pay out. If you feel that your claim has been unfairly rejected, you should complain – see Chapter 23.

Chapter 13

Loan payment protection insurance

Whether or not you need loan payment protection insurance – also called 'accident-sickness-unemployment' (ASU) insurance, or a 'payment protection plan' (PPP) – depends on what arrangements you have already made to protect your income in case of illness or unemployment. If you already have permanent health insurance, for example (see Chapter 11), or your employer runs a decent sick-pay scheme, you should be covered against inability to make any loan repayments (including mortgage repayments) due to illness or injury. If you become unemployed, you may have savings that could be used to meet your monthly outgoings. However, if you do not already have insurance and you would not be able to fall back on savings, buying loan payment protection insurance could be a wise precaution – although if you are past retirement age, already unemployed or know that you are about to be made redundant, you are unlikely to find a policy that will pay out. You might also find loan payment protection insurance to be a waste of money if you are self-employed, if you work fewer than 16 hours a week or on short-term temporary contracts, or if you already suffer poor health.

If you have a mortgage, one of the biggest problems if you lose your job or are ill for a prolonged period is having to carry on making your monthly repayments on a substantially reduced income. You may also worry about how you will make repayments on other loans such as personal loans and credit cards. Although you may be entitled to limited help from the state for your mortgage (see page 191), the state will not pay the interest on any other debts you have. For this reason, lenders will encourage you to take out insurance when you arrange a loan. However, this sort of insurance can almost double the cost of the loan and in some cases the promised protection will not be available when it is needed.

What will the state provide?

You will get no help from the state if you have more than £8,000 in savings or if you are entitled to claim Jobseeker's Allowance because you have paid enough National Insurance. However, if you are unemployed and your savings and income (or the joint savings and income of you and your partner) are low enough to qualify you for Income Support, you should also qualify for limited help with the interest payments on a mortgage of up to £100,000.

If you qualify for Income Support and you took out your mortgage before 1 October 1995, you must wait for two months before any payment is made, after which point you will receive half the monthly interest on the mortgage for the next four months. After this period, you should receive the full amount of monthly interest. If you took out your mortgage on or after 1 October 1995, and you qualify for Income Support, you must wait for nine months before receiving all the interest on a mortgage of up to £100,000. Note that payment from the state is for the interest part of your mortgage repayments only: you will receive nothing towards any capital repayments (which you start to make after the first few years of a repayment mortgage) or towards any insurance linked to your mortgage.

The insurance option

In theory, loan payment protection insurance will help to meet the repayments on your mortgage, a personal loan or a certain percentage of your outstanding credit card balance. However, you cannot buy a single policy to cover all your debts – instead, you will have to pay for an individual policy for each loan.

You will be able to buy insurance that will pay out if you are made redundant and/or you cannot work because of illness or injury, provided that:

- you have not yet reached retirement age
- you work at least 16 hours a week
- you have been in employment for at least six months, or sometimes one year

- you do not already suffer ill health – although redundancy should be covered if unrelated to your health problems.

If you do not meet the criteria above, loan payment protection insurance will not pay out. You should also be wary of this sort of insurance if you are employed on short-term contracts: most policies will pay out only if your contract comes to an end early and unexpectedly, and then only if the contract was due to run for a minimum of six months – although sometimes the minimum amount of time can be as much as a year. So if you work on short-term contracts which generally last for less than six months, you are unlikely to find a policy worth paying premiums for. However, if you work on a short-term contract basis for a single employer who has consistently renewed your contract for at least two years, you may find that an insurer will treat you as though you are in permanent work, with the result that the policy should pay out if you are made unemployed.

If you are self-employed or a company director and you are considering taking out this sort of insurance against the risk of periods of unemployment, tread very carefully. Some insurers will pay out only if you have permanently ceased trading – if you have been declared bankrupt, for example – or if the company of which you

---

Unforeseen disaster

When Ian bought his new car, he paid 50 per cent of the total up front and signed an 18-month finance agreement to pay off the rest. He also bought insurance to cover his repayments in case he fell ill or lost his job. Four months later, the company he worked for went into receivership and Ian was made redundant. He claimed on the insurance but the insurer refused to pay up, arguing that as a director and minority shareholder of the company, Ian must have known about the impending receivership (which he hadn't). When the company was declared a viable proposition by the company's bank the insurer reinstated its refusal to pay out, and claimed it had proof that the company was in trouble even before Ian took out his insurance.

---

are a director has failed. It is very unlikely that loan payment protection insurance will pay out if you have stopped trading temporarily or if you are faced with a shortage of work.

What is covered

If you are eligible for loan payment protection insurance, the amount that the policy will pay out depends on whether you have bought insurance against redundancy only, or if you have also bought cover against illness and accident. The amount of the payout also depends on the type of loan for which you have bought the insurance:

Mortgage payment protection policies usually cover the whole of your monthly mortgage payment, up to a maximum of around £750 to £2,000 per month. You can usually pay for an extra allowance to include your house insurance payments and other regular outgoings. Typically, the insurance will stop paying your mortgage if you return to work or after nine or twelve months – whichever comes first.

Warning

Do not confuse mortgage payment protection insurance with mortgage protection insurance (see page 155) – the latter is life insurance designed to pay off the whole loan if you die before your mortgage comes to an end.

Insurance for personal loans will usually cover your monthly repayments, including the insurance premium, for a set period if you are unemployed or until the loan is paid off in case of accident or illness. Some policies will pay the full amount of the loan if you die while still paying it off.

Insurance for credit cards and store cards will pay a fixed amount – typically 10 per cent – of your outstanding balance each month, for a set period of anything between 6 and 36 months, but most often a year.

Mortgage indemnity insurance

If you borrow more than a certain percentage of the value of your property (usually 75 to 80 per cent), your mortgage lender may insist that you pay for mortgage indemnity insurance. This covers the lender – not you – against the risk of your defaulting on the loan, and the sale of your repossessed property realising less than the amount needed to pay off the mortgage. Not all lenders insist on this type of insurance, and it is better to avoid those who do because mortgage indemnity insurance is expensive: it can add around £1,000 to the cost of a £50,000 mortgage, for example. In addition, if the lender claims on the insurance the insurer can try to recoup from you the amount of money paid to the lender by the insurer – through the courts if necessary.

What is not covered

Loan payment protection insurance is rife with restrictions and cover may be more limited than you think. Regardless of the length of the loan, most policies pay out for only 12 months or less. The amount paid out – both each month and in total – may also be limited depending on the type of loan you are insuring (see page 193).

Most policies impose two waiting periods before paying out. The first occurs after you have taken out your policy and often lasts for one month, but can sometimes be as long as three months. If you lose your job or become ill during this period, most insurers will not pay anything. After claiming, you are likely to encounter another delay – usually one month, sometimes two – before repayments will be made on your behalf by the insurer.

Most policies that cover unemployment will not pay out if:

- you knew you were going to be made redundant when you took out your policy; if your company has experienced recent job losses, your claim could be rejected on the grounds that you knew your position was potentially under threat
- you were sacked for negligence or misconduct
- you have taken voluntary redundancy or early retirement

- you are frequently unemployed; after you have made one claim for unemployment, you will usually be expected to have worked for at least six months continuously before being entitled to claim again
- you take up temporary work – although some (but not many) policies will start paying out again after the temporary work has come to an end
- you are self-employed and do not meet the insurer's definition of 'unemployment' (e.g. because your company has not officially been declared bankrupt)
- you usually work on short-term contracts of less than six months
- you have been claiming on the policy for more than a year (typically – although the length of time may be less).

If the policy covers sickness and accident as well as unemployment, it is likely that any waiting period before the policy will pay out will be shorter than for unemployment-related claims. However, policies covering sickness and accident will be unlikely to pay out for claims relating to:

- existing medical conditions
- stress-related conditions, psychiatric illness or nervous disorders
- back ache and related conditions
- the HIV-virus and AIDS-related illnesses
- pregnancy, childbirth, miscarriage, abortion or related complications
- alcohol and drug abuse.

Calculating the cost

As you would expect, cover against unemployment only is cheaper than cover against unemployment, accident and sickness. The cost also depends on the type of loan you are insuring:

Mortgage payment protection policies cost from less than £3 to over £7 for every £100 of your monthly repayments. So if your usual monthly mortgage repayment is £500 for example, insurance will cost between £15 and £35 per month. The cost of the insurance will rise if your monthly repayments go up and fall if your monthly repayments go down. Some lenders offer free (although limited) cover as an incentive to new borrowers.

Personal loan insurance can push up the cost of borrowing quite considerably: on a three-year loan of £3,000, for example, you might pay, on average, an extra £16 per month.

Credit and store card insurance costs around 70 pence for each £100 outstanding on your credit-card balance – so the cost goes up and down each month according to the amount you owe.

Warning

Buying payment protection insurance can cost more than the monthly premium if it affects your eligibility to means-tested state benefits. If the policy pays the lender directly, your entitlement to benefits will not be affected – nor will they be affected by any payments from a mortgage payment protection policy. However, if the insurance for a personal loan or credit/store card pays you rather than your lender, the money will count as income which will be taken into account when calculating how much state benefit you may receive. As we go to press, the government has announced its intention to change the rules so that in future payments from this sort of insurance will *not* affect state benefits.

Choosing the right policy

This sort of insurance is expensive, and a complete waste of money if you are unable to claim because it transpires that you are not covered. Since most policies will not pay out until one or two months have elapsed (see page 194), you will in any case need to work out how you would cope during this period. You also need to think about how you would cope after a year, when most policies stop paying out. To help decide whether it is worth your buying loan payment protection insurance, consider:

- how much you pay out each month for the loan you are considering insuring
- what income would be available to you if you were sick or lost your job

- what you would be prepared to cut down on to make money available to pay your debts
- whether you are eligible for sick pay from your employer, or entitled to a redundancy payment (e.g. one that could pay off a credit card debt, or be used to pay the mortgage for a time)
- whether you would be able to take early retirement on being made redundant, and therefore receive an income from your pension
- your present job security – note that if there has already been a round of redundancies at your workplace, it is unlikely that a policy will cover you
- the length of time it might take you to find another job, and whether you could do temporary work while looking for a permanent job
- whether or not you would take any other steps to reorganise your mortgage if the worst happened; for example, paying only interest for a time or extending the term of your mortgage – most lenders are prepared to be flexible and would rather come up with a temporary solution than go to the expense of repossessing your home.

Buying your policy

It is likely that when you are offered a loan or credit, you will also be offered insurance to go with it. However, with mortgage payment protection policies (see page 193) you can buy insurance from brokers and direct insurers as well as from lenders. In response to criticism that loan payment protection policies were being sold to people who would be unlikely to benefit from them, the Association of British Insurers★ (ABI) issued a Statement of Practice for the sale of, and treatment of, claims under all such policies issued after 1 July 1996. This states that insurers offering this sort of policy are obliged to make sure that prospective policyholders understand what they are buying; insurers are also supposed to:

- explain how the policy will benefit you if you are self-employed, on contract work or employed part-time, or have a pre-existing medical condition

- give details of the main features of the cover, and its main restrictions (i.e. the circumstances in which the policy will not pay out)
- provide written material that is clear and not misleading
- provide full details of cover after completion of the contract (i.e. send you a policy document after you have signed on the dotted line).

As well as ensuring that the person selling you this sort of insurance gives you information about the policy in accordance with the ABI guidelines above, you should also check:

- that you satisfy any qualifying criteria (e.g. the length of time you must have been in work for before you count as 'employed')
- how long you will have to wait before you are allowed to make a claim on the policy
- how long you will have to wait before payments are made
- how long payments will carry on for if you claim
- whether the insurer pays the lender (insurance worth having), or whether payments are made directly to you (to be avoided at all costs because your state benefits may be affected)
- whether doing temporary work will affect your claims
- what percentage of your outstanding balance will be paid off each month (for credit card and store card insurance)
- whether you will be able to cancel the insurance if you pay off the loan early
- whether the cost of the insurance is added to the loan (which means you will pay interest on it) or whether you pay for the insurance separately
- whether you will have to carry on paying the premium while you are claiming.

If, after taking into account the above considerations, you do decide that you need loan payment protection insurance, be very clear about its limitations. If you fail to get satisfactory answers to your questions, do not buy.

How to claim

The policy document should give details of how to claim, and should also list the evidence you will be expected to provide in sup-

Double trouble

Les bought loan payment protection insurance when he took out his mortgage. Having suffered from a chronic illness for several years, he realised that because of an exclusion for pre-existing illnesses the policy would be unlikely to pay out for any sickness claims relating to his condition. Subsequently Les was made redundant, at which point his policy paid his mortgage. Several months later, he had still not found a job but had to go into hospital for treatment for his condition. At this point, the insurer stopped his payments: Les was no longer registered as unemployed since he was unable to claim Jobseeker's Allowance, and the insurer would not pay a claim relating solely to his pre-existing illness.

port of your claim. If you are claiming because you are unemployed, you will usually have to show your insurer the letter from your former employer terminating your job; you may also have to prove that you are registered as unemployed, and that you are available for – and actively seeking – work. If you are offered temporary work while you are claiming, it may be a condition of the insurance that you let your insurer know before you accept the job. If you are claiming because of sickness or injury, you will need to supply proof of your medical condition from your doctor, and the insurer may ask you to attend a medical examination by a doctor of its choice.

Getting problems sorted out

If your claim is turned down and you think that the insurer is being unreasonable, you should complain – see Chapter 23. You should also tell the ABI if you are sold – or offered – this sort of insurance, and the salesperson has not followed the ABI guidelines concerning the information you should be given before you buy (see page 197).

Chapter 14

Long-term care insurance

Buying long-term care insurance should be the last thing on your mind if you haven't yet made provision for your retirement by paying into a pension of your own. However, if you have your pension sorted out but would not be able to cope financially if you had to pay for care in your old age, you could consider the option of long-term care insurance. You do not need this if you are happy to rely on the care that the state will provide – and prepared to use your savings and other assets such as your home to pay for care before you become eligible for state help (see opposite).

Once you have retired, you do not need to worry about replacing income if you fall ill because your pension will continue to be paid whatever your state of health. However, if you become very ill or disabled in some way, you may have to think about how you will pay the costs of long-term care, either in your own home or in a nursing or residential home. These can be considerable: in 1997, the average cost of a year's stay in a residential care home was over £12,000 (£16,276 in London), while the average cost of a year's care in a nursing home was over £17,000 (£22,776 in London).

In 1993, the responsibility for funding the care of elderly people of failing mental or physical health passed from central government to local authorities. The strengths and weaknesses of the current system as well as the future funding of long-term care for the elderly is currently the subject of a Royal Commission which is due to make its recommendations early in 1999. How the government translates these recommendations into legislation will not be known until the Commission has made its report. However, it is worth bearing in mind that if you are not likely to be eligible for state-funded care under the current regime (see below), it is very unlikely that you will qualify after the advent of any potential new legislation. The decisions you have to make as to whether or not to buy long-term care insurance therefore remain essentially the same.

What will the state provide?

Whereas healthcare provided through the NHS is free, long-term care provided by social services is not. If you want your local authority to help with long-term care, you will first have to go through an assessment of your care needs, followed by a means-tested assessment to determine how much you will have to contribute to the cost. This will involve assessing your capital, which includes your savings, investments and other assets. If you share your home with your spouse, a child or an elderly relative, your home will not count as part of your capital and those relatives will be able to continue living there. However, if you live alone your home will normally count as part of your capital and will usually have to be sold.

If the total value of your capital comes to less than £10,000 – which is unlikely if you live alone in a home that you own – you should receive the care you need free of charge. If your assets are worth between £10,000 and £16,000, you will have to pay something towards the cost of your care. If your assets are worth more than £16,000, you will have to foot the entire bill for care yourself until what you have paid has reduced the value of your assets to the limits given above – at which point the state will step in to help fund your care.

Warning

You may be tempted to try to reduce your assets by passing them on or using them up before you need care. However, if the local authority considers that you have deliberately deprived yourself of assets, it will assess you as if you still owned the assets you have chosen to give away or spend. Seek legal advice.

Paying for long-term care yourself

If you would not be eligible to have care costs paid for by your local authority, or are worried that legislative changes will affect your eligibility to state-funded care in the future, one – but by no means the only – solution is to take out a long-term care insurance policy. Buying long-term care insurance is a way of protecting your assets, including your home, so that they will not have to be used to pay for long-term professional care if you become too ill or disabled to look after yourself and do not qualify for state help.

It is not a foregone conclusion that you will need to pay for care in your old age: current figures indicate that 75 per cent of people over 65 do not need long-term care (although 25 per cent do). The problem with statistics like these is that they cannot predict which camp you will fall into, so your decision on whether or not to buy long-term care insurance centres on your attitude to risk. If you buy this type of insurance, you run the risk that you are paying for something you don't need, since – as with contents insurance, where you don't get your premiums back if you are not burgled – you don't get your money back if you don't need care. On the other hand, if you fail to buy this sort of insurance and subsequently join the minority of people who do need care, you run the risk of using up the wealth accumulated during your working life to pay for it.

If you are comfortable with the idea that you might not be able to leave your personal wealth to the next generation, then in strictly financial terms you don't need long-term care insurance. However, if you are anxious that your children or other heirs should inherit your home and/or other assets, and you could not meet the costs of care without eating into these potential legacies, 'pre-funded' long-

No heirs

Albert is 74 years old and recently widowed. He owns his house and has no children. Taking out a pre-funded policy (see page 205) is unlikely to be the best bet for Albert since he has no dependants and there is no one else to whom he particularly wants to leave his wealth. If he finds that he needs to pay for care, he is prepared to use his assets to meet the cost.

term care insurance (see page 205) – where you pay now to meet the cost of care in the future – could have a part to play in your financial planning.

The alternatives to insurance

Pre-funded long-term care insurance policies are not the only option if you want to plan ahead for long-term care, and you may prefer the alternatives if you do not want to tie your money up by paying for something you may never need. Since you are most likely to need long-term care after you have retired, consider taking steps before you retire to boost your income in retirement so that you will have more money available to pay for care if necessary. You can do this by paying additional voluntary contributions (AVCs) if you contribute to an employer's pension scheme, or by paying as much as the tax rules allow if you pay into a personal pension (see Chapter 18). Once your pension starts to pay out, the payments continue throughout your life, irrespective of your state of health.

With employer pension schemes and personal pensions you can usually take part of the proceeds as a tax-free lump sum at retirement. You could consider earmarking the lump sum to pay for long-term care when you need it. Another option is to build up a lump sum independently from your pension through other savings plans: the new Individual Savings Account (ISA) when it becomes available, for example – and possibly Personal Equity Plans (PEPs) in the meantime.

Planning ahead

Alison is 41 and married with one child. She is in good health and works full-time. The recent experience of having to arrange long-term care for her mother has left her concerned about meeting the possible future costs of her own care. Since Alison is only in her 40s and hasn't yet started paying into a pension of her own, any spare cash she has would be best spent on building up a pension to ensure that she has a reasonable income in retirement.

Immediate needs

Building up a lump sum means that you can adopt a wait-and-see approach to the possibility of having to pay for long-term care: if you don't need care, you have the lump sum; if you do need care, you can use the lump sum to pay for care directly or to buy an annuity (see Chapter 19) which pays out an income that can be used to pay for care until you die. The biggest problem with the annuity option is that the lump sum must be substantial if it is to meet care home fees. A man aged 85, for example, would need a lump sum of around £45,000 to pay care costs of £12,000 a year. A woman of the same age would need around £50,000. If you haven't built up this size of lump sum in savings, you may need to use the value of your home to raise the cash to buy an annuity. However, if you wait until you need care before buying the annuity, the terms are likely to be good because your poor state of health should reduce your life expectancy.

The alternative to buying an annuity which pays *you* an income is to buy an 'immediate care annuity' (these are offered by the same companies that sell pre-funded long-term care insurance – see page 205) in which case the income is paid directly to the residential or nursing home. The advantage of this is that the insurance company will usually have negotiated the level of fees that the home can charge, including future increases, and may be able to offer you a guarantee that the annuity proceeds will always be sufficient to meet the fees.

The disadvantage of buying an annuity is that you don't get the lump sum back once the income starts to be paid out. You can, however, arrange for the annuity to pay out for a 'guaranteed period' – of between six months and five years, for example – which ensures that if you die during the guaranteed period, the income will carry on being paid to your heirs for the period specified, unless they choose instead to take a lump sum totalling what they would have received in guaranteed payments. Alternatively, you can choose to have the 'capital' – i.e. the lump sum you used to buy the annuity – protected. You pay extra for this but it means that all or part of the lump sum can be repaid to your heirs when you die.

Tip

If you need long-term care now, or if you are already in care and need help paying for it – and have a lump sum available – it would be worth investigating the purchase of an annuity. If you buy from an insurer who also offers pre-funded long-term care insurance plans (see below), you may find that the cost of care will be cheaper because the insurer may have negotiated special rates with certain care homes.

A question of choice

The main non-financial question you need to ask when considering whether to buy long-term care insurance is: would you be happy to rely on your local authority to provide your care, even if you are prepared to start off paying for it yourself? The only way to answer this question satisfactorily is to investigate what is on offer and the choices available in your area. Age Concern* produces two very helpful fact sheets: *Finding residential and nursing home accommodation*; and *Local authority charging procedures for residential and nursing home care*. These look at both residential and home care options and are available from Age Concern (send an A4 SAE).

How long-term care insurance works

Pre-funded long-term care insurance provides a way of covering yourself against the possible future costs of long-term care. In exchange for either regular payments or a single lump-sum payment, you get an insurance policy that aims to cover the cost of personal care or nursing help when you need it – either in your own home or in a care home. Benefits will usually be paid either until your death, recovery or for a fixed number of years.

Warning

Policies which pay out only for a fixed number of years tend to be cheaper than those which continue to pay out until you die. However, with the former option you face the risk of running out of money to pay for care if you survive beyond the fixed term.

What is covered

When you come to claim, the insurance company will measure your state of health against a list of 'activities of daily living' (ADLs) in order to decide whether your claim is valid – and so whether the policy will pay out. Although these can vary from insurer to insurer, the activities of daily living generally include some or all of the following:

- washing yourself
- dressing yourself
- going to the lavatory
- continence
- moving from one room to another
- getting in and out of bed
- eating.

The policy will pay out – typically after a 90-day waiting period, although it could be as much as one year – if you are unable to perform two, three, or sometimes four of these activities without help from another person. The more you pay, the fewer the number of ADLs you have to fail before the policy will pay out. The policy should also compensate you for the costs of professional care if you can no longer look after yourself without the continual supervision and assistance of another person as a result of mental impairment due to an organic brain disease – such as Alzheimer's disease – or brain injury.

As well as paying out for professional care, either in your own home or in a residential home, some policies will also pay for the costs of adapting your home or providing devices to assist you in the activities of daily living with which you are having difficulty – fitting a stair lift, for example, or providing a wheelchair. (Leaflets providing information about mobility aids and adapting your home are available from the Research Institute for Consumer Affairs.*) You may also find that you can buy insurance which covers the cost of help with home and garden maintenance, including cleaning, shopping and laundry. But as you would expect, this level of cover costs more.

What is not covered

No long-term care insurance policy will cover you for the costs of going into a residential home because you choose to, but don't physically need to. Nor will policies usually cover you for assistance you require as a result of developing mental illness such as depression or schizophrenia. Policies are also likely to exclude certain types of condition: having the HIV virus or AIDS, self-inflicted injuries and disorders related to alcohol or drug abuse, for example. Some policies may refuse to pay a claim if you have failed to follow medical advice.

Choosing the right policy

Long-term care insurance is a relative newcomer to the UK insurance market and there are still only a handful of companies offering these products. However, with the uncertainty over the future of state funding of long-term care, these products are likely to become more extensively marketed and advertised. There are three main types of policy:

Pre-funded regular-premium policies As the name suggests, these policies allow you to pay premiums now – as regular monthly or yearly payments – for the possible costs of care in the future. You pay the premiums from the time you take out the policy until you need to claim, or reach a certain age (e.g. 85) – whichever comes first. As pre-funded policies are straight insurance, you do not get your premiums back if you do not need to make a claim – although if you stop paying premiums, a good policy should still pay a reduced amount towards the cost of care. However, if you do need to claim it is likely that what you have paid in premiums will amount to far less than meeting the costs of care out of your own resources.

Pre-funded lump-sum premium policies With this option, you pay for the insurance all in one go by paying over a lump sum. As with regular-premium policies, you won't get your money back if care is not required. The advantage of paying your premiums all at once is that you are likely to spend less in total than you would if you paid regular premiums for the same amount of time. A guarantee that you will not have to pay more in premiums (see 'Premium reviews', page 210) once you have reached a certain age – 70, say – may also be incorporated. The disadvantage is that you have to part with a large lump sum which won't be refundable if you change your mind after a few years.

Investment-linked policies With these policies, you pay a lump sum which buys an investment in the form of a single premium insurance bond (see Chapter 21), which is used to pay the premiums for a long-term care insurance policy. The apparent advantage of this sort of package is that you can get back some of what you have paid as a lump sum in the form of the cashed-in value of the bond. However, you don't get back the part of the investment used to pay the premiums for the insurance (or the commission paid to the salesperson) and you will probably find that if you do decide to cash the bond in, the insurance comes to an end as well. If you have decided to buy long-term care insurance because you are worried about paying for long-term care, concentrate on what is offered by the long-term care insurance part of the package – and compare it with policies that are not linked to an investment.

Warning

The selling point of investment-linked long-term care insurance policies is that you get the lump sum back – as you would expect from *any* investment. You are likely to be better off not mixing your insurance needs with an investment which may not be the most suitable for you. If you have a lump sum which can be invested to produce an income, consider instead *not* parting with it, and using the income to pay for a pre-funded regular-premium policy (see page 207). As well as preserving the lump sum, this option has the advantage that the insurance you buy won't necessarily come to an end if you decide to stop paying premiums – although it will pay a reduced amount.

How much cover?

As well as deciding how to pay for long-term care insurance, you need to consider how much cover you want. Before you can do this, you need to know the most expensive prediction of care costs (it could be anything from £8 per hour for home help, to £25,000 a year for nursing-home fees) and your probable retirement income. You then need to work out how much of your retirement income – or any savings and investments you have – could be allocated to pay for long-term care, either in full or in part. If you would be able to meet the costs of care out of your retirement income with enough left over to meet other financial commitments – household bills, for example, or income for your partner or other dependants – it is unlikely that you need long-term care insurance. However, if there is a shortfall between your retirement income and potential care costs, you should insure for the amount you would need to make up the difference. You should also take into account the effects of inflation (see below).

Tip

When working out the costs of care, be sure to use prices for the location where you would be most likely to enter a home (e.g. near your children). Care costs vary around the UK, so if you would be likely to move to a more expensive area you should make allowance for this.

Keeping your insurance up to date

Since you could be paying premiums for ten years or more – the average age for going into residential care is about 80 – it is very important that you make sure that the amount you insure for now will buy the equivalent level of care in the future. Given that the cost of care has risen above the rate of inflation over the past few years, a benefit of £1,000 per month in today's terms is not likely to buy as much in ten years' time because care costs will have risen quite substantially. One way to avoid finding out that your insurance pays out less than you need is to choose a policy which allows for automatic increases both in the level of cover – i.e. the amount you want the policy to pay out – and in the premiums. This can either be by a fixed percentage or in line with the Retail Prices Index (RPI) – plus say, 2 per cent to allow for the fact that increases in the cost of care typically exceed general inflation.

Warning

Watch out for insurance policies which make a virtue of keeping premiums fixed for a certain number of years: you could face a serious hike in your premiums if you find that the amount you are insured for will no longer meet your care costs.

As well as ensuring that the amount you are covered for will keep pace with rising care costs *before* you claim, you should also pursue the option of having the amount you are covered for – the 'benefit' – increased once you have started to claim. Policies which pay a level benefit are unlikely to keep pace with rising costs of care and so should be avoided, unless you want to find yourself having to make up any shortfall by using the assets that you hoped to protect by taking out this sort of insurance. You will pay more for the option of indexing your benefit but most policies offer it.

Premium reviews

As well as the likelihood that you will have to pay more in premiums to allow for increases before and after claiming, you should also be aware that premiums may go up when reviewed by the insurer – typically after five years. Because long-term care insurance is in its infancy in the UK, it is not clear how premiums might change in the long term. If insurers have under-estimated the number and cost of claims likely to be made under this sort of policy, premiums may go up. If, on the other hand, this sort of insurance becomes more popular, premiums may come down.

Calculating the cost

The higher the benefit you want, the more you will pay in premiums. The maximum payout with many policies is £36,000 per year, or

£3,000 per month. What you will pay for your policy depends on your sex, your age, your state of health and the type and level of benefits that you want. At any given age, premiums will be cheaper for men than for women. This is because men have a shorter life expectancy than women and are therefore less likely to make a claim, or to claim for as long. Regardless of when you take out a policy, your premiums will increase as you get older. Insurers may refuse your application if it is clear that you will need care in the near future. Alternatively, they may offer only a prohibitively high premium.

What you might pay for long-term care insurance

Sample monthly premiums for a monthly payout for care worth £1,000

Age when plan first started	Men	Women
40	£19.60–45.10	£23.60–52.18
50	£27.40–62.53	£33.50–67.78
60	£42.00–101.48	£51.80–95.98
70	£72.80–188.60	£91.10–151.70
80	£120.58–278.80	£162.30–230.74

Buying your policy

The biggest problem connected with long-term care insurance is that the sale of this sort of insurance is not regulated. Furthermore, it is unlikely that any new regulation of straight long-term care insurance will be introduced before the publication of the Royal Commission's report into the funding of long-term care (see page 200).

Owing to this hole in the regulatory framework, you should be extremely wary of anyone who tries to sell you long-term care insurance without carrying out a thorough review of your financial position – as it is now, and your projected status post-retirement. (If you are being sold investment-linked insurance – see page 208 – this should occur because the advice on the investment part is regulated under the Financial Services Act.) If you decide that long-term care insurance is something you want to consider, employ the services of an independent financial adviser who is registered with the Financial Services Authority* and make sure you understand exactly what you are buying.

What to check before you buy

Policies differ widely and can be difficult to compare. The following questions should help you choose between them:

- How many activities of daily living (see page 206) do you have to fail before the policy will pay out?
- Which illnesses or disabilities are *not* covered?
- Can you choose to be cared for in your own home?
- Is your choice of residential/nursing home restricted in any way?
- How long will you have to wait before the policy pays out?
- Is payment made to the carer or care institution, or to you?
- Can the benefit (see page 210) be increased in line with inflation in care costs or by a fixed percentage before you claim?
- If the amount you are insured for cannot be increased, how will any shortfall be dealt with?
- Can the benefit be increased once it has started to be paid out – i.e. are the benefits indexed or level (see page 209)?
- Are benefits paid until you die or for a limited period only?
- Is there a maximum amount that the policy will pay out?
- How often are premiums reviewed?
- For regular-premium policies (see page 207), at what age do you stop having to pay premiums?
- For lump-sum premium policies (see page 208), is there an age at which the benefit becomes guaranteed?
- What happens if you stop paying premiums – do you get a reduced benefit or will you get nothing?
- For investment-linked insurance, does the long-term care insurance come to an end if you cash in the investment part?
- What happens if the investment doesn't perform as well as expected and/or the premiums for the insurance have to go up?

How to claim

Make sure that someone you trust knows about your policy and is willing to deal with the insurer on your behalf in the event of a claim. If you are not able to perform two or three of the listed activities of daily living (see page 206), you might not be up to filling in a claim form either. To be on the safe side, inform your insurer in writing of the name of the person who will be acting on your behalf.

Part 4

Insurance for special cases

Chapter 15

Insurance and your work

If you occasionally do work for your employer at home rather than in the office, it is most unlikely that you need to make any changes to your insurance arrangements. However, if you become self-employed, your various insurers will need to know about it and – depending on the extent of your business activity – you may need to buy extra insurance. You may also need to review your insurance if you occasionally take on freelance work.

If you have recently become self-employed, and have not told your insurers, they may refuse to pay any claims you make under the insurance policies you already have. If you work from home in a small way – it is just you, your computer, a phone and a lot of paper, for example – your existing buildings and contents insurance should be enough to cover you, but check your policy and the amount you are insured for, especially if you have bought new equipment. If you are planning to use your car for business, you should tell your car insurer but be prepared to pay a slightly higher premium. If you have insurance against loss of income, such as loan payment protection insurance (see Chapter 13) or permanent health insurance (see Chapter 11), which pay out if you are made redundant or become ill, you should check that the cover is still appropriate to your new working circumstances. The insurer may also need to adjust the premium to reflect your new earning patterns.

Once you have dealt with your existing insurance, you need to consider whether you need any of the sorts of special business insurance outlined in this chapter. This will certainly be worthwhile if:

- the value of your business equipment is above a certain level and your normal contents policy will not cover it
- you use specialist tools and machinery in the work you do – very few contents policies will cover tools and machinery associated with a trade
- you will be working from separate business premises
- your work involves people visiting your home or business premises
- the type of work you do increases the risk of fire or theft (e.g. if you are a furniture restorer and you use and store flammable materials, or you provide a catering service from home)
- you will have to carry large amounts of cash (e.g. if you will be selling what you make at markets and fairs)
- you will be sending goods to customers (e.g. if you operate a mail order service)
- you will be rearing animals or growing plants or vegetables
- you will need to protect the data stored on your computer against loss or theft as well as insuring the computer itself
- you employ staff.

Tip

Any insurance you buy for your business is treated as a business expense for tax purposes, which means that you can deduct it from your earnings before working out your tax bill. This saves you tax.

Insurance for your business premises and equipment

If you operate separate business premises, you will need to insure both the property and the contents under policies that are separate from the insurance you already have for your home. If your home acts as your business premises, your existing buildings insurance (see Chapter 2) should cover damage to your home but your insurer may ask you to pay a higher premium if the work you will be doing increases the risk of damage from fire, theft, flood and so on. Your existing contents cover *may* cover some business equipment up to certain limits although it will not cover specialist tools and equipment. Wherever you carry out your work, you might also need to consider buying special business insurance for:

- business equipment, machinery, tools and other items necessary to your trade
- your stock – including supplies not yet used, and goods allocated to customers even if the customer has not yet paid for them
- goods in transit (e.g. on their way to a customer, or to a sub-contractor, in your own or someone else's vehicle, or sent by post)
- goods on a sub-contractor's premises (e.g. while the silk wedding dress you have made is at the house of the person who does your hand embroidery).

Insurance for consequential loss

You could also consider insuring against consequential loss, which means the losses that your business would suffer as a consequence of fire, theft or other disaster. Insurance for consequential loss is also known as 'business interruption' insurance and covers the possible loss of income and additional expenses as a result of your business being out of action. If your small factory was burned down, for example, not only would you need to rebuild and re-equip, but you would also have to pay your wage bill and some overheads while no money was coming in from the business. If your computer was stolen, not only would you have to replace the hardware, but you might also have to meet the cost of reinstating data such as a mailing list database.

Your home, your business

If you decide to take a lodger or paying guests, you will need to tell your insurers and get their agreement to continue your buildings and contents insurance. Your premiums may go up and theft and damage by your lodger and/or paying guests may be specifically excluded from your cover. You also need to pay attention to the public liability part of your contents policy, which is unlikely to cover you for injury to your paying guests or damage to their property. You will need special insurance for this. You may also need to consider employer's liability insurance if you employ someone to help you in your business (see page 219).

Insurance for money

If you want to be covered for loss of money and money substitutes (including cheques, postal orders, bankers drafts, stamps and so on) from your office, your home or while you are carrying it on your person (which you may do if you are banking your takings), you can include this sort of cover in your business contents policy. You can also buy insurance to compensate an employee who is injured while being robbed of your money.

If you hold money on behalf of your customers – if you are a travel agent or insurance agent, for example – you need an insurance bond to protect client money if your business fails.

Public liability insurance

Public liability insurance is not compulsory but it is advisable, especially if people visit your home or business premises. It covers you if a member of the public sues you for damages because they were injured at your business address or because you injured them or damaged their property in the course of your work – if you are a plumber and you flood someone's house, for example. If you use sub-contractors, you need to extend the cover to third-party public liability.

Product liability insurance

This sort of insurance covers you against claims arising out of faults in something you (or your employees) have designed, manufactured or serviced (if the stool you made collapsed under its purchaser, or the dishwasher you serviced gave its owner an electric shock, for example). You may be liable even if you were not negligent.

Professional indemnity insurance

If your work involves giving advice rather than making or designing something, professional indemnity insurance covers you for claims made against you where a client has incurred some financial loss as a result of your bad advice, fraud or negligence. This sort of insurance is therefore of most interest to people who advise or inform for a living, such as freelance consultants, translators and complementary health practitioners.

> **Warning**
>
> If you are an employee and you do occasional freelance consulting on your own account, do not assume that you will be covered by your employer's professional indemnity insurance. You will certainly be covered for the work you do for your employer but not necessarily for the freelance commissions you take on, so check with your employer. If your employer does not know about your freelance work, it is very likely that you will not be covered.

Employer's liability insurance

If you employ staff, you must have employer's liability insurance for everyone on the payroll (except for domestic servants and members of your family, who would be covered by your contents insurance) and you should display a current certificate at your place of work. Employer's liability insurance covers you for claims that might arise if an employee suffered physical injury or illness in the course of, or resulting from, his or her employment. This could be anything from a broken bone after tripping on the stairs to losing a limb. It would be necessary for the employee suing you for damages to show that the injury or illness was caused by your negligence or that of another employee.

Even though you do not *have* to include members of your family in this sort of insurance cover, it is sensible to do so. They may be your nearest and dearest but it does not mean that they cannot sue you for damages. If they were hurt (and had a valid case), the insurance would mean that they could claim financial compensation.

Insurance against loss of income

As soon as you move from being an employee to being self-employed, you lose the cushions that your employer may have provided against illness, accidents at work and your death. If you want to protect yourself (and your family) from loss of your income as a result of illness or death, consider topping up your life insurance (see Chapter 10), and taking out permanent health insurance (Chapter 11) and possibly critical illness insurance (Chapter 12).

You could also consider private medical insurance (Chapter 7), which would give you some control over the timing of an operation, so that you could either speed up the time it would take to get treated or organise it to coincide with a slack business period.

'Key person' insurance

If you are in business with a partner or you employ someone without whose expertise the business would lose money, you might want to consider 'key person' insurance. This pays out if the key person insured is out of action. You can organise life insurance, permanent health insurance or critical illness insurance for that person on this basis. It is also possible to buy insurance in case you or another key person are called for jury service.

You might want to think about taking out life insurance on the life of a business partner or the principal shareholder in your business for another reason: so that you would be in a position to buy his or her share of the business if his or her heirs decided to sell. If you will inherit your partner's share, you could take out a policy to cover any possible inheritance tax bill, although if your business partner is your spouse, this is unnecessary.

It's a lottery

There is no end to the things you can insure against if you are in business: had you, for example, thought what you would do if your five-person business lost four of its staff as a result of their syndicate winning the lottery? As well as wishing that you had joined the syndicate, you might kick yourself for not taking out insurance to cover the loss of business income while you found replacement staff. However, insuring against the loss of key personnel for other reasons is more normal.

Other insurance possibilities

A typical business insurance policy should cover your property, business interruption and your liability to both the public and/or your employees. However, you may need other more specialised insurance designed to cover your particular form of work:

- If your work involves a lot of driving and your business would suffer if you were unable to drive, it could be worth considering insuring against the loss of your driving licence. Insurance of this sort will not get your licence back but it can pay towards the cost of hiring a chauffeur.
- If you will be rearing animals or keeping kennels, you will need veterinary insurance and possibly extra public liability insurance.
- If you grow plants or vegetables, farming insurance could be worth considering.
- If you are in the entertainment business as a self-employed actor, comedian, disc jockey, clown, juggler, concert artist, musician, magician, escapologist or whatever, you could consider a specialist policy tailored to your particular needs, including loss of your equipment in public places, loss of fees, personal accident and public liability.
- Specialist insurance also exists to cover the particular requirements of self-employed professionals such as doctors, dentists and lawyers, for example.
- If you are in the building profession, you may want to investigate insurance aimed specifically at the construction industry.
- If you have intellectual property rights, you can take out insurance for the legal expenses involved in pursuing people who have infringed your patent, copyright, design, trademark, licence and so on and also for the legal costs of defending an action for your unintentional infringement of someone else's rights.
- You can also take out insurance against investigations by the tax authorities, which will pay the fees of an accountant if you are subject to an in-depth investigation or PAYE audit by the Inland Revenue and which may pay the legal expenses of appealing against a VAT assessment.

The list of other insurance possibilities is seemingly endless and it can be worth contacting your trade association, professional association or other national association for details of insurance packages specifically tailored to the kind of work you do. The particular advantage of doing this is that such associations may have negotiated a special deal for their members. However, check that the insurance covers everything you need it to: the special deal will be worthless if you find out that you cannot claim on the policy.

Chapter 16

Legal expenses insurance

If you would be happy to pay all the legal costs of bringing a civil action to court, you do not need legal expenses insurance. However, if you could not afford to go to court to settle a dispute, legal expenses insurance is worth considering – and may be your only option if you do not qualify for civil legal aid.

To qualify for civil legal aid to bring a civil case (as opposed to criminal law proceedings), there must be a reasonable chance that you will be successful and generally your disposable income (or that of you and your partner) must be less than £7,595 a year, and your total capital (excluding your house) must be less than £6,750. For personal injury cases the limits are £8,370 for disposable income and £8,560 for capital.

In late 1997, the government announced radical reforms to the civil justice system which included a thorough review of the legal aid scheme. The main proposals included the abolition of legal aid for some types of claims; the introduction of a stiffer test for gaining access to legal aid; and wider use of 'conditional fee agreements' backed by insurance.

Conditional fee agreements are already used for personal injury claims, and many solicitors are prepared to enter into this sort of arrangement – often called a 'no-win, no-fee agreement' – if you have a good chance of winning. If you lose your case, you do not have to pay your own legal costs (the no-fee part of the arrangement), although you will still be liable for your opponent's legal costs and perhaps for other expenses – which is where the insurance backing comes in. If you win, your solicitor gets up to double the normal fee.

The insurance option

Legal expenses insurance is not new and you may already have this sort of insurance as an add-on to your contents policy, or – for motor-related claims – as part of your car insurance. You can also buy stand-alone legal expenses insurance policies.

This sort of insurance aims to pay your legal expenses – including solicitors' fees and expenses, the cost of barristers and expert witnesses, court costs and possibly opponents' costs, if awarded against you – up to a certain limit. The limits for legal expenses that you buy as an add-on to other insurance tend to be lower than for stand-alone policies.

What is covered

Legal expenses insurance is primarily designed for cases that go to court, but it also covers the cost of legal bills if you settle out of court. It should cover you when you sue somebody else, and in some circumstances it will cover you if you are sued by somebody else. You may also find that certain criminal proceedings and appeals (mostly those connected with motoring offences) are covered, as well as hearings at industrial tribunals – if you have a claim for unfair dismissal, say.

If you lose your case, you may have to find the money yourself for any compensation, damages or fines, but the insurance should pay out for your own legal expenses bill as well as any of the other side's costs awarded against you. Most insurers will also include a free legal advice service as part of the package.

The types of cases that legal expenses policies will normally cover you for relate to:

- personal injury, where you are claiming compensation if you or a member of your family has been killed or injured in an accident caused by somebody else's negligence
- loss or damage to your property through somebody else's negligence
- disputes about contracts to buy or sell your house, or about house repairs and decoration (although you are unlikely to be covered for disputes relating to major building, restoration, alteration or demolition work)

- disputes about tenancy agreements or notice to quit, if you live in rented accommodation
- disputes with neighbours (e.g. about boundaries, noise and nuisance)
- disputes arising in connection with your contract of employment (e.g. about unfair dismissal or an industrial accident)
- infringement of your consumer rights over a contract to buy or hire goods and services
- defence costs, if you are charged with certain driving offences such as speeding; some policies will also cover you if you have a claim for uninsured losses (see page 89).

Before and after

At present, most legal insurance policies are 'before-the-event' policies – i.e. you have to take out the insurance *before* you know that you want to take legal proceedings against somebody and *before* the reason for your claim occurs. However, in response to the proposed changes to the legal aid system and the growing emphasis on conditional fee agreements (see page 222), the insurance industry is seeking to develop more 'after-the-event' policies, which would mean that you could take out insurance to cover your legal costs as the need arises. Only a very limited number of policies that aim to cover your legal expenses if you have already decided to sue someone currently exist. Some can be taken out in conjunction with a conditional fee agreement to cover the risk of your having to pay the other side's legal costs if you lose, and others exist independently. Your legal adviser will know about these policies.

What is not covered

You will find that the policy will not normally cover routine legal work such as conveyancing, making a will, standard probate work, and possibly divorce proceedings. A policy will also be unlikely to pay out if you have other insurance which could cover your legal costs: for example, contents insurance normally includes personal liability cover to pay your defence costs and damages in certain situations; car insurance should cover you if somebody else sues you after a road accident; and travel insurance covers personal accident and personal liability claims (both by and against you) if a case is brought outside the UK.

The insurance is also not likely to pay your legal expenses if:

- you have a poor chance of winning the case, or achieving a reasonable outcome
- you take your case to court without first consulting with your insurer
- you did not meet the insurer's time limit for informing it of your intention to claim (typically six months)
- your legal costs are likely to come to more than the amount you would get as a result of winning your case
- the dispute is directly connected to your work (e.g. about intellectual property rights – see page 221) – except for disputes with your employer over your contract of employment
- you are suing a member of your family (except for car accidents)
- you are suing a government department or local authority – although you would be covered if you lost money due to your case being unsuccessful
- you are in dispute with an insurer over the amount of an insurance claim (this does not apply only to the insurer with which you have your legal expenses policy).

How to claim

Because most policies currently on the market are before-the-event policies, you cannot go to law and then claim on the policy. Instead, you must first tell the insurer the full details of your case. If you contacted your solicitor before getting your insurer's agreement, you may find that the cost of your initial consultation with your solicitor will not be reimbursed – even if the insurer agrees to pay your later costs.

Before agreeing to meet your claim, the insurer may decide to act on your behalf by undertaking negotiations to settle the dispute. This is likely to happen if you are in dispute over a small amount of money (£1,000 or less), or your claim could be dealt with by the small claims court. If a reasonable settlement is offered, you will be expected to accept it. If you refuse, you may find that the insurer will refuse to cover your costs if you choose to pursue the matter in court.

If your insurer agrees that legal proceedings can go ahead, it may want to veto your choice of solicitor on the grounds that he or she is too expensive, or practises too far away from the location of the case. It will also want confirmation that your solicitor has the necessary expertise to fight the case. You will be expected to keep your insurer informed throughout the proceedings, and must also get its permission before you engage a barrister or an expert witness.

If it looks as though you will lose your case, the insurer may intervene to negotiate an out-of-court settlement rather than continue with the case. If you decide to call a halt to legal proceedings without the insurer's permission, it is very likely that the insurer will refuse to pay some – or all – of your legal expenses.

Most policies state that if you win and the other side has to pay your costs, these amounts go directly to the insurer, which may – if necessary – take on the responsibility for getting your opponents to pay up.

Special cases

Most legal expenses insurance provides cover for disputes which concern you, your family, your home and possessions. However, if you want other types of disputes to be covered, you may need to take out specialist legal expenses insurance. This could be the case if you run your own business and/or you employ other people (see Chapter 15), if you let property (see Chapters 2 and 3), if you own intellectual property rights (see page 221), or if you own a boat (see page 235).

Chapter 17

Specialist insurance

If you have out-of-the-ordinary or particularly valuable belongings; if you indulge in an unusual, expensive or dangerous pastime; or if you are arranging a one-off special event, you could consider taking out a specialist insurance policy. If there is nothing exceptional about your insurance requirements, it is unlikely that you will need to do this.

You can insure against practically anything happening to you or your property and even to other people, provided that you can put a figure on what your loss would be and that, broadly speaking, you cannot influence the outcome of what you are insuring against. Whether you need specially tailored insurance depends on what you want to insure and also on whether your current insurance could be extended to cover it: if you are insuring specialist sports equipment, for example, you may find that your current insurer is willing to extend your contents insurance to cover it (see page 48). You are most likely to need specialist insurance if your current insurance does not cover you or offer appropriate cover; your policy specifically excludes cover for what you want to insure; or you want insurance for a short time only. See other chapters in this book if:

- you own a home which is unusual in some way, or you let a property (see pages 27 and 34)
- you have particularly valuable or unusual belongings (see page 49)
- you own a vintage car or special number plates (see page 74)
- you intend to work abroad or take an extended holiday (see page 134)

- you run your own business or work as a freelance from home (see Chapter 15)
- you want to insure against possible legal costs (see Chapter 16).

This chapter contains information about specialist insurance which may apply to you if:

- you take part in sports which insurers generally regard as 'hazardous'
- you are going on an adventurous activity holiday
- you are organising a special event
- you have made expensive wedding arrangements
- you want insurance for your pets
- you own a horse or pony
- you own a small boat.

Sports insurance

If you belong to a sports club or are a member of a team, you may already have sports insurance as part of a group policy. Whether you need an individual policy of your own depends on what other insurance you have, and the type of sport you practise.

If your sports equipment is already covered by an all-risks extension on your contents insurance (see Chapter 3), and you would not be out of pocket if you could not work because of an injury – you already have permanent health insurance (see Chapter 11) for example, or your employer has a generous sick-pay scheme – it is unlikely that you need to buy specialist sports insurance. In addition, the 'personal liability' section of your contents policy should cover you if you are held legally liable after injuring someone else – but check with your insurer. If you have private medical insurance (see Chapter 7), you are probably already covered for any specialist medical treatment needed to aid recovery after an injury, such as physiotherapy; and if you have life insurance (see Chapter 10), you will be covered if you die while you are engaged in a sporting activity. But note that if the sport you play is considered to be particularly dangerous – rugby, for example (and see opposite) – any insurance connected with your well-being will cost more because there is a greater risk of the insurer having to pay out.

Sports insurance could be useful if the sport you have taken up is not already covered by your existing insurance. However, if your main concern is loss of income as a result of not being able to work because of injury, you should consider permanent health insurance instead (see Chapter 11).

Tip

If you have recently taken up a dangerous sport, you should tell your insurers – if you do not, they may refuse any claims relating to your sporting activities.

Insurance for activity holidays

Most standard travel insurance policies will not cover you if you take part in dangerous activities, so you will need to take out special insurance. Skiing insurance (see page 131) is a well-established example of a specialist policy: as well as providing the usual insurance you would expect from a travel policy, it also includes additional cover for the costs of mountain rescue and other eventualities linked to skiing and other winter sports – such as hiring skis if yours are delayed or stolen, and piste closure.

The growing popularity of activity holidays has resulted in an increasing number of specialist travel insurance policies which cater for the adventurous holidaymaker. You can now find policies which cover you for the extra risks associated with:

- scuba-diving
- parachuting
- hot-air ballooning
- ocean sailing
- motor sports
- mountaineering and abseiling
- bungee jumping
- hang-gliding and paragliding
- white-water rafting
- jet skiing
- bobsleighing.

It is very likely that if you buy an activity holiday as part of a package, the travel company will already have organised the relevant insurance; you should still check what is (and is not) covered very carefully. If you are going on a holiday that you have organised yourself, or are taking a package holiday to a resort where dangerous activities are on offer but not included in the price of the holiday, you should consider taking out specialist insurance instead of a standard travel policy.

As with standard travel insurance (see Chapter 9), you can take out this sort of policy to cover you for either a specific period of time, or for a whole year. If you regularly pursue any of the activities listed above, you should find that an annual policy will cover you for any holidays abroad as well as for taking part in your chosen activity in the UK.

Insurance for special events

If you are organising a garden party, fête, charity fair, cricket match, community pantomime or any other event which will be attended by members of the public, your first priority is to make sure that you, as organiser, have public liability insurance. You should also ensure that you have insurance against damage, loss or theft of any special equipment or cash. If you would lose money if the event had to be cancelled, you could consider cancellation insurance, which covers cancellation for reasons beyond your control. You could also consider insurance for more specific risks:

- **Rain insurance** pays out if a stipulated amount of rain falls within a certain number of hours (the stipulations vary according to the location and the season). You need to take out this sort of insurance at least 14 days in advance in summer (further ahead in winter). Make sure that the cover starts about three hours before the opening of the event.
- **Cricket insurance** pays out if rain stops play, if the pitch is waterlogged, or if the match has to be delayed, stopped or abandoned. If you are arranging a first-class match, you can extend the insurance to cover bad light.
- **Insurance for non-appearance** should pay out if the event has to be cancelled, or if you lose money because the celebrity you engaged does not turn up.

- **Insurance for prizes** broadly covers fund-raisers and events where the prizes on offer can be won purely by chance (e.g. hole-in-one, match-the-number-plate, 'crack the safe', dice-rolling contests). It covers you against contestants' winning streaks, and varies according to the type of event.

Weddings insurance

You cannot insure against the bridegroom or bride suddenly changing his or her mind at the last minute, but you can buy weddings insurance which usually covers:

- expenses incurred as a result of having to cancel or reschedule the wedding and/or reception for reasons beyond your control – this generally means the death, illness or injury of the key players (who is included depends on the policy) but may also cover jury service and redundancy
- the death, illness or injury of the bride or bridegroom and their parents (although as with all personal accident insurance – page 178 – the injuries for which you can claim are very specific and the payouts small)
- damage to, or theft of, the wedding dress or bridegroom's outfit
- loss of the rings
- loss of, or damage to, the wedding presents
- failure of suppliers (e.g. florists, caterers, wedding cars, photographers etc.) – but check the small print very carefully. It is very likely that the insurance will pay out only if your supplier fails to turn up as a result of having gone bust; if the supplier simply fails to meet the terms of your contract and is still in business, you can sue.
- your legal liability if someone is injured or his or her property damaged while at the wedding or reception. (If this is at a hotel or other venue which is not your home, or you have hired a marquee, it is likely that the owners will already have this insurance – but do check.)

Whether this sort of insurance is worthwhile depends on what you have already paid up-front for your wedding arrangements: if you have spent thousands of pounds, for example, you may feel that another £50 or so is just a drop in the ocean – and in this case, cover for cancellation could be useful (provided you understand its limitations).

Regardless of how much you have spent in preparation for the big day, you should first look at what your existing insurance will cover you for, or what it could be extended to cover. Your legal liability if a wedding guest is injured or has his or her property damaged while at your home should be covered by your contents policy (see Chapter 3), while buying an all-risks extension to this policy (see page 47) should cover clothes, rings and wedding presents. Meanwhile, the best insurance against failure of suppliers is to choose reputable firms and ensure that you have a clear written agreement, and – if possible – to avoid making full and final payment until after the delivery of goods and services.

You should also bear in mind that the wedding insurance will cover only a very limited period of time. Since you will have the rings – including the engagement ring – and wedding presents for a long time after the wedding, you may need to review the amount you are insured for (and any 'single article' limits, if your rings are particularly valuable – see page 46) under your contents policy, especially if you expect to receive gifts which will be expensive to replace.

Twins and multiple birth insurance

If you are pregnant and there are at least six months to go until the birth of your baby, you still have time to insure against the possibility of having twins (or any other multiple birth). You cannot weight the odds, however, so you will not be able to take out this sort of insurance – which pays a modest lump sum – if you already know that twins are on the way. You are also unlikely to be able to buy insurance if you have been receiving treatment for infertility. If there is a history of twins in your family or if you are an older mother, insurance for twins will cost more because there is a greater chance of the insurer having to pay out.

Insurance for pets

The main reason that you might want to take out insurance for your pets is to cover the cost of veterinary bills. Special pet insurance can also cover the death, loss or theft of your pets and your legal liability if they injure someone else, or their property – although you may find that you can extend your contents insurance to cover these eventualities (see page 43). Most policies will *not* offer legal liability cover if your dog is a dangerous breed as defined by the Dangerous Dogs Act.

Most pet insurance covers cats and dogs, although you can also find policies which cover rabbits, hamsters, birds, snakes and other exotic animals. No pet insurance policy will cover everything, but in general you will find that – within limits – the policy should pay out for:

- the cost of treatment if your pet is injured or becomes ill – including drugs, surgery, dressings and anaesthetics
- X-rays and laboratory tests
- specialist treatment such as physiotherapy, chemotherapy and radiotherapy
- overnight hospital expenses
- out-of-hours emergency treatment
- follow-up treatment and check-ups
- alternative medicine such as homeopathy, acupuncture and herbal medicine – provided treatment is administered (or supervised) by a qualified vet.

Some policies may also cover special dietary treatments if prescribed by a vet, but there may be a limit on the length of time the insurance will pay these costs – a month, for example. A handful of policies will cover boarding expenses for your pet if you have to go into hospital and there is no one whom you can rely on to look after your pet. Other policies cover the costs of having to cancel a holiday if your pet becomes ill enough to need surgery, or goes missing before or after you have gone on holiday.

Not all your pet's veterinary bills will be covered: typically, the insurance will not pay out for routine examinations, vaccinations, neutering, pregnancy (although complications arising from pregnancy may be covered), home visits or cremation costs. In some cases, you may not be able to claim for particular diseases or conditions for certain breeds – golden retrievers can be affected by hereditary eye disease, for example, while Cavalier King Charles spaniels are prone to heart problems.

If your pet is over a certain age, cover may be reduced or totally unavailable. All policies have limits on the amount you can claim. For some you can claim up to a certain amount each year but most set a limit per condition, which means that you will probably have to pay for all treatment costs for any persistent or recurring problems once you have reached that limit.

Horses and ponies

You can insure the horses and ponies you keep for riding, hunting and show events (as an amateur) using either the policy you have for other pets or animals (see above), for which you will pay more, or using a separate equestrian policy. If you ride professionally, cover is more expensive. The amount you pay is based on the amount you have the pony or horse insured for and the type of riding you do – if you use the horse for point-to-points or hunter trials, for example, your premiums may be more expensive. If your horse is over a certain age – usually 12 years – there may be a limit on the amount you can insure it for, and you will usually have to supply a vet's certificate when you apply for the insurance.

The policy aims firstly to cover you for the animal's death, whether from natural causes or from being destroyed (for which it should pay you the lower of the market value or the amount you have insured it for) and for any damage the animal does to other people or their property. In addition, the policy may cover (or could be extended to cover):

- vet's fees – although there will be a maximum that can be paid out
- theft or straying – which may include the costs of advertising or offering a reward, as well as guaranteeing you the lower of the animal's market value and the amount it is insured for if you do not get it back
- loss or damage to riding tack and saddlery (up to a specified limit)
- a percentage of the amount you are insured for – or the animal's market value – if it is too old to be ridden (or unable to fulfil the

function for which it is kept) and you have decided to put it out to pasture rather than have it destroyed.

Insurance for small boats

Some contents policies (see Chapter 3) can be extended to cover small boats. These should include cover for the boat when it is out of the water – while it is kept in your garage, for example. Alternatively, you can take out separate 'small craft' insurance. If you belong to a sailing club or are a member of a class association, you may find that you are offered a discount if your club has arranged a package deal.

A small craft is defined as a boat 'not more than five metres long with a maximum speed of 17 knots, if power driven'. The insurance should cover you against:

- loss of, or damage to, your boat and its equipment from external causes, including stress of weather, stranding, sinking, collision or vandalism
- theft of the boat and its equipment
- damage caused by fire, lightning and explosion
- breaking of the propeller shaft
- the outboard motor dropping overboard
- reasonable salvage charges (the costs charged by professionals for pulling vessels off rocks and getting wrecks out of the way of other vessels)
- your legal liability for injuries to other people or damage to their property – including damage to piers, docks and jetties.

As with most insurance for property, you will not be covered for damage due to wear and tear; and you may find that cover is limited if you use the boat for racing.

Buying specialist insurance

There are two ways of buying specialist insurance: you can either buy an off-the-peg (or package) policy, or you can have insurance tailor-made to your own specific requirements. If you are following the first course of action, contact a broker or other insurance intermediary who will be able to tell you if a specialist off-the-peg policy exists for your particular requirements, and find the policy that best meets your needs. Off-the-peg policies exist for all the situations described in this chapter and for the 'Special cases' described in other chapters.

Tip

If you want to find out more about the range of off-the-peg specialist insurance policies available, you should consult *The Insurance Buyer's Guide to Schemes, Packages and Unusual Risks*,* which is published annually by Kluwer Publishing. Try your nearest large public library.

Tailor-made insurance

If your requirements are particularly unusual and you cannot find a policy to cover you, you could ask a broker to arrange a tailor-made policy. Provided the broker can find an insurer willing to accept your risk, you should be able to get some form of insurance cover – at a price. What you pay will be determined by the insurer's assessment both of the probability of having to pay out and the costs of setting up the insurance.

Insuring the unusual

Most unusual insurance is arranged at Lloyd's, which is why you have to go through a broker – members of the public cannot approach Lloyd's directly.

Celebrities often favour this sort of policy to protect their assets, a famous example being the Hollywood star Betty Grable who insured her legs for $1 million at Lloyd's, while singer Bruce Springsteen has his voice insured for $3.5 million. But you don't have to be a film or rock star to get insurance to protect your livelihood, hence the move by a whisky distiller to insure his nose and the food critic who took out a policy to insure his taste buds.

Part 5

Insurance as an investment

Chapter 18

Personal pension plans

If the only provision you have made towards your retirement income is paying National Insurance, you should give serious thought to paying into a pension scheme. If you do not already belong to an employer's scheme or you are self-employed, you can take out a personal pension plan.

The scandal generated by the mis-selling of personal pensions and the subsequent naming, shaming, and (in some cases) fining of rogue advisers has done little to promote confidence in what can be an extremely efficient way of saving for retirement. The main advantage of taking out a personal pension plan is tax: in common with pension schemes run by employers, you get tax relief on what you pay into the

---

Changes in the offing

The government wants more people to make their own provision for retirement and has proposed that the main vehicle for encouraging people to do so will be a second-tier 'stakeholder' pension. Consultation is underway as to how this might work, whether or not it will be compulsory and what effect it will have on the current second-tier state pension: the State Earnings-Related Pension Scheme (SERPS).

Despite these proposed changes, employer pension schemes and personal pension plans will continue to co-exist with the state schemes (or their proposed substitutes) as a means of making provision for a more substantial income in retirement.

---

plan (within limits – see page 242). In addition, the capital growth of the fund is not taxed and you may be able to take part of the proceeds as a tax-free lump sum. However, since these tax advantages exist to encourage you to save for your retirement, the main disadvantage is that you cannot get at your money until you retire.

How personal pension plans work

Personal pension plans work on what is called a 'money purchase basis' which means that until you retire, the money you pay into your personal pension plan is invested to build up a lump sum. How the money is invested depends on who you buy the pension plan from; the plans offered by insurers are typically with-profits (see Chapter 20), unit-linked (see Chapter 21) or a combination of the two. Other pension providers offer unit trust plans, deposit administration schemes (which work like cash savings accounts), or self-invested or self-administered personal pensions (SIPPs and SAPPs) where your contributions are invested in a broad range of investments of your own choosing.

When you decide that you want a pension income to start being paid, you use the lump sum you have accumulated to buy an annuity (see Chapter 19), which is what pays your pension. Depending on the type of pension you pay into, you may be able to take some of your fund as a tax-free lump sum (see page 244). The amount of pension you end up with depends on how much you contribute, how long you contribute for, how well your investments perform and annuity rates at the time you decide to convert your pension fund into an income.

The personal pension arrangements on offer from insurers come in several guises. They all work in the same way in terms of what happens to your contributions, but there are important differences between the amount you can contribute and what you get out at the end. The main types are:

- **Personal pension plans** for self-employed people and employees who can't (or don't want to) join an employer's scheme.

- **Group personal pension plans** which are personal pension plans arranged for a group of employees by an employer – they work in exactly the same way as a personal pension plan you organise for yourself (although your employer may have negotiated better terms).
- **'Appropriate' or 'rebate-only' plans** for certain employees who can contract out of SERPS (see page 245).
- **AVC and FSAVC plans** for boosting your employer's pension scheme.

How much can you pay into a personal pension?

Because of the generous tax breaks – you currently get tax relief at your highest rate on contributions you make to a personal pension plan – the amount you can pay in is limited by the Inland Revenue. The maximum you can contribute each year is expressed as a percentage of your 'net relevant earnings'. These are your taxable profits if you are self-employed (broadly, your business income less expenses and capital allowances and some losses), or, if you are an employee, your salary plus the taxable value of fringe benefits (perks) less any allowable expenses. The older you are, the higher the percentage of net relevant earnings that you can contribute. If you are an employee, any contributions your employer makes to your personal pension plan count towards the overall percentage limit. However, as well as a percentage limit there is also an overall limit on the amount of earnings which can be taken into account. In the 1998-9 tax year, this limit is £87,600.

The amount you can pay in also depends on when you took out your personal pension plan. The types of personal pension plan discussed in this chapter have been available since 1 July 1988. Before that date, personal pension plans were called 'retirement annuity contracts': although these work in a broadly similar fashion to current personal pension plans, the limits on what you can pay in are different (as shown in the table, overleaf).

Making up for lost time
If you have been earning for the past seven years or less but have not been paying into a pension plan during that time, you can make use of unused tax relief from those years either by backdating your con-

Inland Revenue limits on contributions to a personal pension plan

	Contribution limits as a percentage of your net relevant earnings	
Your age at the start of the tax year (6 April)	Retirement annuity contract taken out before 1 July 1988	Personal pension plan taken out since 1 July 1988[1]
up to 35	17.5%	17.5%
36–45	17.5%	20%
46–50	17.5%	25%
51–55	20%	30%
56–60	22.5%	35%
61–74	27.5%	40%
75 or over	You can no longer contribute	

[1] Earnings over the fixed limit of £87,600 in the 1998-9 tax year should not be included when calculating the maximum percentage contributions

tributions to an earlier tax year (called 'carrying back' your contributions – see Tip, below) and/or adding unused relief from another six years to the amount you are allowed to contribute in the current tax year (called 'carry forward' relief). The easiest way to claim the relief is to fill in your tax return following the guidance given in Inland Revenue Help Sheet IR330 (available from the Self-Assessment Orderline★), which also contains working sheets to help you calculate how much unused relief you may have.

If you do not have a tax return to fill in, ask your tax office for form PP43 for carrying back relief and/or form PP42 for carrying forward relief. You will also find a detailed explanation of the tax rules in *Which? Way to Save Tax 1998-9*, published by Which? Books.★

Tip

If you want to backdate any payments into a personal pension that you make in the 1998-9 tax year to the 1997-8 tax year – and you have not yet sent back your tax return – you can do this by filling in the relevant boxes on your tax return. Any tax relief you are owed will be set against tax due on 31 January 1999, thus reducing the amount you have to pay. If you do not owe any tax, you can claim a rebate.

Tax relief on life insurance

Part of your personal pension plan contributions – up to 5 per cent of your net relevant earnings – can be used to buy life insurance (see Chapter 10). This must pay out a lump sum if you die before retirement. If you take out this sort of insurance, you get tax relief at your top rate on the life-insurance premiums; the downside is that the amount you contribute towards paying for the life insurance reduces the maximum you can contribute to your pension.

Making a transfer

If you have any pensions left behind in a previous employer's scheme – if you have changed jobs or become self-employed, for example – you are allowed to switch them into a personal pension plan by taking a transfer value which is treated as a lump-sum contribution to your plan (without affecting the other limits). Whether or not this is worth pursuing depends on the sort of scheme in which you left your pension. Broadly speaking, you will be better off leaving your old pension where it is if:

- you have pension rights in a public-sector scheme (e.g. you were a teacher, or worked for the NHS or local government)
- your scheme was part of an industry-wide arrangement and you still work (or may return to work) in that industry
- your ex-employer's scheme offered particularly good benefits (e.g. an inflation-proofed pension after retirement).

Even if none of the above apply to you, it may still be better to leave your old pension well alone if the invested transfer value will not match the benefits you would get from the old pension. The sums involved are complicated and you should get independent professional advice before making any sort of transfer – which includes swapping your current employer's scheme for a personal pension plan. You can get specialist advice from an actuary (contact the Association of Consulting Actuaries★) or from an independent financial adviser (IFA), who must be specially authorised to deal with pension transfer business – contact the Society of Pension

Consultants★ (SPC), which can put you in touch with actuaries and specialist IFAs. It is worth remembering that the bulk of mis-sold personal pensions in the 1980s were sold to people who were wrongly advised to leave an employer's scheme.

How much can you take out of a personal pension?

You can decide to buy a pension with the lump-sum investment you have built up by paying your own contributions (but not any National Insurance rebate – see opposite) as early as age 50; the earliest you can buy a pension with a retirement annuity contract taken out before 1 July 1988 is age 60 (unless you switch to a personal pension). However, you can also defer buying your pension until you are 75. Bear in mind that the longer you leave your contributions invested, the bigger the fund should be and so the more you will have available to buy your pension income. For more on annuities, see Chapter 19.

Although most of your invested contributions will have to be used to buy an annuity (which is why these are referred to as 'compulsory-purchase' annuities), you can take part of your fund as a tax-free lump sum at the time you decide to buy your pension. Again, the amount is limited by Inland Revenue rules and will depend on when you took out your pension plan – see the table below.

How much tax-free lump sum?

Date you started paying into your personal pension	Maximum amount of tax-free cash you can take at retirement after taking a tax-free lump sum
Retirement annuity contract taken out before 17 March 1987	Three times the remaining pension: e.g. if, after taking a cash lump sum, you would have a pension of £6,000, the maximum lump sum would be £18,000 (3 × £6,000)
Retirement annuity contract taken out on or after 17 March 1987 and before 1 July 1988	Three times the remaining pension up to an overall maximum of £150,000 per plan[1]
Personal pension plan started on or after 1 July 1988 and before 27 July 1989	25% of your fund, after deducting amounts to be used to provide dependants' pensions up to a maximum of £150,000 per plan[1]
Personal pension plan taken out on or after 27 July 1989	25% of your fund, excluding 'protected rights' if the plan has partly been used to contract out of SERPS – see page 245

[1] In practice, the £150,000 limit is easily avoided

How much can you pay into an appropriate or rebate-only plan?

If you are an employee and you do not already belong to an employer's scheme which is 'contracted-out' of the State Earnings-Related Pension Scheme (SERPS), you can choose to redirect some of your National Insurance contributions into a personal pension plan specially set up for the purpose. Contracting out of SERPS (see below) means that the government gives you a rebate on what you and your employer pay in National Insurance. If you are contracted-out through an employer's scheme, you get the rebate by paying a lower rate of National Insurance. If you use an 'appropriate' or 'rebate-only' personal pension to contract out of SERPS, the amount of National Insurance taken from your pay does not change. Instead, the Department of Social Security (DSS) pays the rebate into your personal pension plan after the end of the tax year. In the 1997-8 tax year, the rebate ranged from to 3.4 per cent (3.8 per cent from 6 April 1999) of earnings on which National Insurance is paid for a 16-year old, through to a maximum of 9 per cent for older people. The DSS also pays tax relief on the rebate.

How much can you take out of an appropriate or rebate-only plan?

The money paid by the DSS into your personal pension plan constitutes your 'protected rights' which act as a substitute for the part of the SERPS pension that you will no longer receive. Your protected rights can be used only to buy a pension from normal state retirement age (currently 65, or 60 for women born before 6 April 1950) and they cannot be taken as a lump sum. Once the pension you have bought starts being paid, it must increase in line with price inflation up to 5 per cent a year. It must also provide a widow's or widower's pension if your spouse is 45 or over at the time you die (younger if she or he is caring for a dependent child).

Should you contract out of SERPS?

If you are not already using an appropriate or rebate-only pension plan to contract out of SERPS, think very carefully before contracting out, especially if there is a chance that you might stop being eligible for the National Insurance rebate (see above) in future: for example, if you become self-employed, join a contracted-out employer's scheme, or give up work altogether.

You should be aware that charges can eat heavily into what are relatively small investments, and may wipe them out altogether if you stop paying anything into the plan. (If you are already contracted-out through an appropriate or rebate-only plan, it may be better to stay contracted-out because of these charges.) You may also want to wait and see what happens with the proposed stakeholder pension (see page 239) before making a decision to contract out. This might well turn out to be simpler and less expensive than a personal pension.

How much can you pay to boost your employer's pension scheme?

If you are currently contributing to an employer's pension, you cannot take out a personal pension plan unless you are not already contracted-out of SERPS (see page 245), or you have earnings from self-employment. You can however top up your employer's pension by making 'additional voluntary contributions' (AVCs) – either into a plan run by your employer or a plan you take out yourself called a 'free-standing additional voluntary contribution plan' (FSAVC plan). Most AVC – and all FSAVC – schemes run by insurers work on a money purchase basis (see page 240).

The amount you can contribute depends on Inland Revenue limits and on the amount you are already contributing to your main pension. You will get tax relief at your highest rate on a maximum of 15 per cent of your pensionable earnings (the earnings your employer uses to calculate your pension). So if you have pensionable earnings of £20,000, the most you can contribute to your main employer's scheme together with an AVC plan is £3,000 (i.e. 15 per cent of £20,000). To find out what you can pay into an AVC or FSAVC, multiply your earnings by 15 per cent then deduct what you are already paying into your employer's main scheme.

What can you get out of a boosted employer's scheme?

You cannot take a cash lump sum from an AVC or FSAVC scheme into which you started making payments after 8 April 1987. Instead, your accumulated fund is used to buy pension benefits, which must not (when added to those from your main scheme) take you over the other pension tax limit of two-thirds of your final salary after a minimum of 20 years' service. If you find that your AVC or FSAVC contributions have taken you over the limit when you decide to buy your pension, you will get back the excess funds after tax at 33 per cent (in the 1998-9 tax year) has been deducted.

Choosing the right personal pension plan

If you are in the market for a personal pension plan – in whatever form – there are four main points to consider:

- the type of investment
- its performance
- charges
- the flexibility of the investment.

Which type of investment?

If you decide to buy a personal pension from an insurer, your contributions will typically be invested in a with-profits fund (see Chapter 20), a unit-linked fund (see Chapter 21), or in a combination of the two types. Which sort you choose will depend on your attitude to risk. In general, the longer you have to go until retirement, the more risk you should be prepared to take; while the nearer you are to retirement the more wary you should be. If you choose a plan which combines both with-profits and unit-linked investments, you can balance the risk by splitting your contributions between the two types.

There are no hard-and-fast rules about which type of investment is best, but if more than 15 years are likely to elapse before you will want your pension, a unit-linked plan is probably the better choice; although with-profits and unitised with-profits plans have performed better over the past 10 to 15 years, over the longer term (20 to 30 years, say) unit-linked plans should provide higher returns. However, if you are taking out a pension with fewer than 15 years to go until retirement, you are probably better off taking out a less risky with-profits plan, which should be less susceptible to the vagaries of the stock market. If you already have a unit-linked fund, consider switching your investments into a cash-deposit plan (or the cash fund of a unit-linked plan) when you are about five years away from retirement so that the value of your accumulated investment fund is protected. For more information on financial planning and investment strategies (including risk assessment), consult *Be Your Own Financial Adviser*, published by Which? Books.*

Performance

The two main factors affecting the success of your investments are performance and charges. When you take out a personal pension plan, a fund manager invests your money in a range of assets such as shares and government bonds. The investment growth that the fund manager achieves will have a major influence on the value of your pension. Sadly, there is no way of knowing how well your investments will grow in the future. Past performance is not a guaranteed guide to future performance but it is all you have to go on. However, plans which have shown *consistently* good investment performance in the past make a good starting point. For information on how to find out more about pension plans, see page 251.

Charges

It does not matter how well the plan performs if charges eat into your investment. When you pay into a personal pension, the pension provider takes some of your payments to cover the costs of administering and managing the fund. Depending on which insurer you buy your pension from, some of your payments will also be used to pay commission to the people who sold it to you: the problem is that most providers of personal pensions levy the bulk of the charges in the first few years. However, since January 1995 you have been in a better position to see how charges affect your investments because pension plan providers are now obliged to include charges in any illustration of potential benefits. You can see how costs can affect pension plans by comparing projections from different providers for the same contributions and length of investment (see page 252).

Flexibility

As well as performance and charges, you also need to make sure that the plan will suit your personal circumstances and that it will be sufficiently flexible to meet your changing requirements – which means that you should consider the following:

- **What you can afford to invest?** Most plans set a minimum amount that you can pay in of around £250 a year or £25 a month for regular-premium plans, and typically £500 to £1,000 for lump-sum contributions. The maximum amount you can contribute depends on your earnings and Inland Revenue rules (see page 242).

- **How do you want to pay?** You need to decide whether you want to make regular monthly or yearly payments, or whether you would prefer to make lump-sum payments of irregular size and frequency – the most flexible plans will allow you to do both. If you are an employee, the discipline of saving a regular monthly amount corresponds with being paid monthly; however, regular-premium plans can cost more than single-premium plans and you may be charged extra if you cannot keep your payments up. If you are self-employed or your earnings fluctuate, it would be better to choose a plan which accepts lump-sum payments whenever you choose to make them (e.g. after you have calculated your net relevant earnings at the end of your accounting period). If you want to combine regular monthly payments with the option of paying lump sums as well (e.g. you want to take advantage of carry-back and carry-forward rules – see page 242), look for a plan which accepts both sorts of payments without penalty.

- **Do you want to allow for increases?** If you have decided that you want to make regular payments, check that you can increase them and find out whether this can be done automatically in line with inflation or by a fixed percentage.

- **Is the retirement date flexible?** Most plans will ask you to set a date for retirement when you take the plan out. If you don't know when you want to retire or think you might change your mind, try to ensure that you are either not obliged to set a retirement date, or will not face a penalty for changing the date. Note that you can usually change to a later retirement date without penalty, but changing to an earlier date can cause problems.

- **What happens if you stop making payments?** Make sure that you are not penalised if you stop paying into the plan. A good plan will let you stop and restart payments without penalty or charges. Alternatively, consider the premium waiver option, for which you pay extra. This comes into play if you cannot keep up payments because you become ill, provided you have the necessary net relevant earnings (see page 241). Your contributions are treated as though they are still being paid, so your pension continues to build up.

- **How long do you have to pay in for?** With some plans, you have to pay in for a certain amount of time before the plan will be worth anything to you – which is why it is so important to study any illustrations you are given very carefully (see pages 252–3). Other plans may reward you with a loyalty bonus if you pay in for a certain amount of time (e.g. ten years).

Tip

If you don't want to commit yourself to long-term regular payments into a personal pension plan – your earnings vary from year to year, for example, or your earnings future is uncertain – but you want the discipline of regular saving, consider making regular payments into a savings account to build up a lump sum to pay into the pension plan once or twice a year.

Buying a personal pension

You can buy a personal pension direct from an insurer that sells personal pensions or through an independent financial adviser – see Chapter 22 for general information about getting advice and buying insurance as an investment. You would be wise to seek help if you do not feel completely confident about evaluating your own pension requirements, and this is also advisable if you are considering:

- switching from an employer's pension scheme into a personal pension plan (see page 243)
- transferring an ex-employer's pension scheme into a personal pension plan (see page 243)
- moving an existing personal pension to a new provider.

Before you approach an insurer or adviser, you should be clear about the features you want (see 'Choosing the right personal pension plan', page 247). You should also have a good idea of how much you can afford to contribute, how much you are *allowed* to contribute (see table, page 242) and the form in which you want to contribute (see page 249). It is also sensible to do some preliminary research in order to find out which personal pensions offer the features you want and have a good performance record – even if you intend to use an adviser. You can do this by looking at the regular reports published in *Which?*★ magazine and the personal finance pages of other publications. It is also worthwhile consulting the performance tables published in specialist magazines used by independent financial advisers, such as *Money Management,*★ *Pensions Management*★ and *Planned Savings.*★

> **Tip**
>
> Even if you have already decided to approach a financial adviser, it is worth doing some preliminary investigations into what is on the market so that you are in a better position to evaluate the advice you are given and ask for more details if necessary.

If you are using an adviser, he or she should draw up a shortlist of options based on the information you have given about your requirements and financial circumstances. The next step will be to provide you with a 'key features' document for each plan as well as an 'illustration of benefits'. If you have drawn up your own shortlist, you will need to get this information directly from the insurers (provided that they are prepared to deal with you directly). You may also want to get this information yourself if your preliminary research highlighted a successfully performing company which did not appear on your adviser's shortlist. Whoever you are getting information from, make sure that all the illustrations use the same assumptions about the amount you will contribute and your projected retirement age – otherwise you will not be able to compare them properly.

How to compare pension plans

For each plan you are considering, you will find that the illustration of benefits follows a standard format set by the Personal Investment Authority (see Chapter 22). Projections such as these do not tell you about definite future performance but provide a very useful way of comparing charges. You may find it helpful to fill in the table, opposite, to make it easier to compare plans – all the details should appear on the illustration of benefits. The table includes the cost of the advice, which is also given in the illustration. The lower the projected fund or the transfer value of the pension, the higher the charges will be.

You should also compare the key features documents to make sure that all the plans meet your requirements in terms of flexibility – see 'Choosing the right personal pension plan', page 247. For details of what a key features document should tell you, see Chapter 22.

What happens next

Once you have made your comparisons of both key features documents and illustrations, it is up to you to decide which plan best meets your needs and/or to ask more questions if you are still unclear about anything. All is not lost if you sign on the dotted line and then change your mind because you are allowed what is called a 'cooling-off' period (typically 14 days) to think about the commitment you have just made. Note that if you acted on an execution-only basis (i.e. you did not receive advice – see page 277), there is no cooling-off period. If you feel that the advice you have been given – either by your adviser or by a company representative – was not up to scratch, you should complain (see Chapter 23).

How to compare personal pension plan illustrations

	Example	Plan A	Plan B	Plan C
Name of plan	–			
Pension age for illustration	65			
Proposed contribution (gross)	£5,000			

Projected fund if future rate of return is:

	Example	Plan A	Plan B	Plan C
6% per annum	£18,800			
9% per annum	£38,600			
12% per annum	£77,400			

Projected monthly pension payable if future rate of return is:

	Example	Plan A	Plan B	Plan C
6% per annum	£109			
9% per annum	£268			
12% per annum	£628			

Projected transfer value at end of year (assuming 9% return on the investment):

	Example	Plan A	Plan B	Plan C
year 1	£5,230			
year 2	£5,670			
year 3	£6,160			
year 4	£6,680			
year 5	£7,250			
year 10	£10,900			
year 15	£16,400			
year 20	£24,600			
year 25	£37,000			
Full term	£38,600			

How much will the advice cost?

	Example	Plan A	Plan B	Plan C
Cost of advice	£152			

Source: The Equitable Life Assurance Society

Chapter 19

Annuities

An annuity is a way of buying an income. You do this by handing over a lump sum to an insurer, which agrees to pay you an income in exchange. If you have a personal pension plan or belong to an employer's pension scheme which is not linked to your final salary, you will eventually *have* to buy an annuity because this is what pays your retirement income. If you are over 70, you could choose to buy an annuity if you have a lump sum and you want it to pay you a guaranteed income. If you are younger than 70, you are likely to get better rates of return from other investments.

Annuities that you have to buy with at least 75 per cent of the accumulated lump sum from a personal pension or from an employer's money purchase scheme are called 'compulsory purchase' annuities; those you choose to buy yourself – to fund long-term care, for example (see Chapter 14) – are called 'purchased life' annuities. They work in exactly the same way except in how the income from them is taxed. The whole of the income you get from a compulsory purchase annuity is taxable. With a purchased life annuity, part of the income you get is tax-free (because this part is treated as if it were a return of the lump sum you handed over when you bought it).

How annuities work

You hand over a lump sum to an insurer and the insurer pays you an income, the size and frequency of which are agreed at the time you buy. A lifetime annuity will carry on paying the income until you die, while a temporary annuity will pay out for a fixed number of years. In neither case do you get the lump sum back. The income you get from the annuity depends on your age when you bought it, your sex (the income paid to women tends to be lower than that paid to men of the same age because women live longer), and the level of annuity rates at the time of purchase (which depends on long-term interest rates, and, in turn, on general economic conditions). Your health and habits (for example, whether you are a long-term smoker) may also be relevant.

Choosing the right annuity

The type of annuity you choose depends on how you want the income to be paid and on whether you need to provide a pension for your partner after your death. The more you want to have in the future, the lower the starting pension will be.

Standard annuities (also called 'level' annuities) pay a fixed amount of income which never changes, so these are not a good idea if you want your income to keep pace with inflation.

Escalating annuities pay an income which increases each year, either by a fixed percentage (which you agree at the outset) or in line with inflation (so these are sometimes referred to as 'index-linked' annuities). Compared with a standard annuity, the income you get in the first few years will be lower but in later years it will be higher. If you want a better chance that your retirement earnings will keep pace with inflation, choose this type.

Guaranteed annuities guarantee to pay the income for a minimum fixed period – typically five years, but it can be ten – which means that even if you die during this 'guaranteed' period the income will carry on being paid to your dependants or they will receive a lump sum. This type is a good choice if you want to know that some of your lump sum will be paid back if you die; however, if you are concerned about providing an income for your partner in the event of your death, a joint life annuity (see below) is a better choice.

Joint life annuities pay you income while you live and then continue paying out that income – or a proportion of it, typically a half or two thirds – to your surviving partner until his or her death.

Impaired life annuities pay out a higher income to people who have a shorter life expectancy than average, such as smokers or people with a serious illness.

Investment-linked annuities are linked either to a with-profits fund (see Chapter 20) or a unit-linked fund (see Chapter 21). The income paid is not guaranteed and fluctuates according to how well (or how badly) the investment fund performs.

When and how the income is paid

The income you get from an annuity is also influenced by how and when the income is paid to you. Payments are usually made half-yearly in arrears, which means that you have to wait six months after buying your annuity before receiving the first payment. You can arrange for different payment terms but these may affect the income you get: if you ask for more frequent payments or for immediate payment on buying the annuity, you will get a lower income; if you wait longer for the first payment to be made, the income should be higher.

Protected rights

If part of your pension pot is made up of National Insurance rebates from contracting out of SERPS, you do not have a choice in the type of annuity you can buy – it must pay an escalating income and it must provide a dependant's pension (if appropriate) – see Chapter 18 for more details.

How much income?

Once you have decided on the type of annuity you want and how you want the income to be paid, the most important factor is finding the annuity that will pay the biggest income for the lump sum you have available (see table, opposite). Timing is also an important factor, since if annuity rates are low when you retire, you may get a better deal by waiting (see page 258).

If you have a fund from a personal pension, your pension provider has to let you exercise the 'open-market' option, which means that you can take your fund to any insurer that sells annuities to get the best rate on offer. However, for the purposes of comparison with rates on offer elsewhere, it is worth finding out what your

Why you should exercise the open-market option

The table below shows the yearly income that a lump sum of £100,000 would have bought in March 1998, with the income being paid monthly in arrears. The escalating annuities allow for the income to increase by 5 per cent each year (except for the annuities for 70-year-olds where the income increases by 3 per cent each year). The joint life annuities assume that the income will continue to be paid at the same rate after the first death.

Yearly income from a standard annuity bought with a lump sum of £100,000:

	Top rate	Lower rate	Yearly income you could miss out on by not exercising the open-market option
man aged 60	£8,800	£8,340	£460
man aged 70	£12,022	£10,708	£1,314
woman aged 60	£8,093	£6,152	£1,941
woman aged 70	£10,302	£9,157	£1,145

Yearly income from an escalating annuity bought with a lump sum of £100,000:

man aged 60	£5,492	£4,927	£565
man aged 70	£9,922	£8,287	£1,635
woman aged 60	£4,794	£4,129	£665
woman aged 70	£8,271	£7,001	£1,270

Yearly income from an escalating joint life annuity bought with a lump sum of £100,000:

man aged 60, woman aged 57	£4,002	£3,588	£414
man aged 65, woman aged 63	£4,737	£4,210	£527

Yearly income from a standard joint life annuity bought with a lump sum of £100,000:

man aged 60, woman aged 57	£7,244	£6,667	£577
man aged 65, woman aged 63	£7,885	£7,290	£595

*Source: March 1998 figures from the Annuity Bureau**

pension provider could offer since some will pay better annuity rates to people who built up their pensions with them.

Warning

As well as not necessarily offering you the best annuity *rate*, your pension provider may not be able to provide the *type* of annuity you want: all the more reason for comparing its annuities with what is on offer elsewhere.

If you have a retirement annuity contract (the name for personal pensions taken out before 1 July 1988), your pension provider does not have to let you exercise the open-market option but in practice most do. Exercising the open-market option converts your retirement annuity contract into a personal pension plan. If you have a fund from an employer's scheme, the trustees of the scheme may buy an annuity on your behalf.

Playing the waiting game

If you are using the accumulated fund from a pension fund to buy an annuity, you do not have to buy the annuity on the day you retire – you can put off doing so until you are 75. If your pension provider offers an 'annuity deferral' or 'income draw-down' option, you can leave your fund invested but withdraw an income from it within limits set by the Inland Revenue. (Broadly the income you take cannot be more than what you would have got if you had bought an annuity.) You are still allowed to take up to 25 per cent of your fund at retirement as a tax-free cash lump sum but you must decide to do this when you start drawing the income – you cannot change your mind later. The risks you take if you choose the income draw-down option are that annuity rates will fall still further and that the fund you leave invested will fall in value.

This option may also be available only to people who have at least £100,000 in their personal pension fund. You should also be aware that commission and charges for income draw-down schemes are higher than those for buying an annuity. The Personal Investment

Authority,★ which regulates these sorts of investments, has expressed concern about this and has launched an investigation into how income draw-down schemes are being sold.

Buying an annuity

You can buy an annuity direct from an insurer or through a financial adviser. If you are considering deferring taking your pension, you should definitely get independent advice – see Chapter 22.

Before you buy, find out what rate your own pension provider will give you, then see if you can better it. You can find information on annuity rates in a wide range of personal finance publications and specialist magazines such as *Money Management,*★ *Pensions Management,*★ *Planned Savings*★ and *Moneyfacts Life & Pensions.*★ There are also fax services★ which give up-to-date rates. Alternatively, you could approach an adviser such as the Annuity Bureau★ and Annuity Direct★ which specialise in annuities and keep up-to-date databases on the whole market.

Chapter 20

With-profits policies

If the insurance industry gets its way, with-profits policies in some form or another will have a large part to play in the new Individual Savings Account (ISA), which will become available in April 1999. However, do not let the apparent new tax-free status of with-profits policies that you buy as part of an ISA blind you to the fact that they are long-term investments, and could be a very poor buy if you cash in early. With-profits policies require commitment: you should be willing to save regularly for at least ten years – or keep a lump sum untouched for at least five years. In return for your commitment, the insurer will guarantee at least part of the payout (see below). If you cannot commit yourself to long-term saving, do not buy a with-profits policy. If you are looking for life insurance to protect your dependants, see Chapter 10.

How with-profits policies work

With-profits policies are life insurance and investment rolled into one. 'With-profits' refers to the fact that as well as getting life insurance, you share in the profits of the insurer's with-profits investment fund – typically a mix of shares, gilts, company loans and property. The return you get is in the form of 'reversionary' bonuses (added annually), which are guaranteed to be paid when the policy comes to an end ('matures') or when you die. Annual bonuses are calculated on the basis of the performance of the with-profits fund over time, which has the effect of smoothing the ups and downs of the investments within the fund and of producing steady growth.

As well as the bonuses added during the life of the policy, you may also get a 'terminal' bonus when the policy matures. There is no way of knowing how big (or small) this will be, although the terminal bonus can account for up to 60 per cent of the final payout. Insurers that pay higher annual bonuses tend to place less reliance on the terminal bonus, which means that more of your return is guaranteed. By contrast, insurers that pay low annual bonuses tend to place greater emphasis on the terminal bonus, which means that the return you get will be a mixture of guarantee and gamble.

Lack of commitment costs

With-profits policies are usually designed to last for a minimum of ten years (for tax reasons). If you pull out before the policy comes to an end – or 'surrender' early – you may get a nasty shock, particularly in the early years when the policy could be worth a lot less than what you have paid in. In general, charges – and any commission paid to the person who sold you the policy – are taken from your premiums in the first few years. However, a handful of companies stagger commission payments over the life of the policy, which means that the surrender value of the policy may come as less of a shock if you decide to cash in early. Low surrender values can be less of a problem with policies from life offices (insurers that sell life insurance) which do not pay commission, such as Equitable Life.

Warning

As with any investment, you should not buy a with-profits policy without first considering other investments which may be more suitable for your personal situation. For more information on the investment options open to you, consult *Which? Way to Save and Invest*; for guidance on financial planning and strategic investing see *Be Your Own Financial Adviser*, both published by Which? Books.*

Choosing the right policy

If you buy with-profits insurance, your money is invested in the same way. However, with-profits policies are different in terms of how the bonuses are added, when you get your money and how it is taxed. The type of products sold by insurers on a with-profits basis include:

- conventional with-profits endowment policies
- unitised with-profits savings (endowment) plans
- low-cost with-profits endowment policies linked to an interest-only mortgage
- with-profits bonds
- with-profits whole-of-life policies
- with-profits personal pension plans
- investment-linked with-profits annuities
- school fee plans.

No-bonus policies

In the past insurers also sold 'non-profit' policies: savings plans that paid out a guaranteed amount at the end of the term or on death. 'Non-profit' referred to the fact that you did not share in the insurer's profits and so no bonuses were added to the guaranteed amount. This made these policies a very poor investment.

Conventional with-profits endowment policies

These policies base the annual bonuses you get on a 'sum assured', the amount of which is decided when you take out the policy. When the policy comes to an end (or you die), you are guaranteed to get the sum assured plus any bonuses which have been added to it – and in the case of some policies, bonuses added to the annual bonuses. There is no guarantee that bonuses will be declared but once they have been added to the sum assured, they cannot be taken away. You may also get a terminal bonus (see page 260).

The minimum ten-year term together with the life insurance element (among other things) makes these policies 'qualifying' – which means that there is no further tax to pay when you receive the proceeds at the end of the term. However, if you cash in early you may have to pay tax if you are a higher-rate taxpayer.

Unitised with-profits savings plans

These are a cross between with-profits plans and unit-linked plans (see Chapter 21). An increasing number of insurers are offering this type instead of the conventional with-profits endowment policies. Instead of basing the bonuses on a sum assured (see opposite), your premiums buy units in the with-profits fund after charges have been deducted. Bonuses are added at regular intervals, either by increasing the value of your units or by adding bonus units. You may also get a terminal bonus. The amount that will be paid out at maturity (or on your death) is based on the value of your units, which increases as you buy more units and as bonuses are added. Once added, bonuses cannot be taken away – apart from in very exceptional circumstances when the bonus rate announced at the beginning of the year has to be revised downwards by the insurer. You will also lose out if you cash in early. The tax position is the same as for a conventional with-profits endowment policy.

Totally tax-free savings plans

When you get the proceeds of a with-profits policy, tax has already been paid by the insurer – which is why there is no further tax to pay when you get the proceeds. This is not the case with a tax-exempt savings plan or baby bond from a friendly society where the proceeds are genuinely tax-free; however, they are not charge-free, so the relatively small amount that you are allowed to invest (£270 a year in 1997-8) can easily become a very small amount.

Low-cost with-profits endowment policies linked to a mortgage

If you already have an endowment mortgage, then you will almost certainly have a low-cost endowment policy to go with it. These work, and are taxed, in the same way as conventional with-profits endowment policies and unitised with-profits savings plans, except that straight life insurance is included in the package at the insistence of your lender, which has an interest in knowing that the loan will be paid off if you die (as you do, if you have dependants). You pay interest only to your mortgage lender and premiums for the insurance policy, which aims to build up a sufficiently large lump sum to pay off the loan at the end of the mortgage term.

'Low-cost' refers to the fact that the sum assured (see page 262) is usually much less than you would need to pay off the loan when the policy starts (see the bonus statement below). It is assumed that the addition of bonuses over the life of the policy (and possibly at the end) will more than cover the loan. People who took out this sort of mortgage-linked insurance when the product was first introduced in the early seventies have found that their payouts have been more than enough to cover the loan. However, when they were first introduced, insurers made very conservative estimates about growth rates. More recently, some people have found that they are being asked to pay extra premiums to make up for a shortfall as a result of over-optimistic projections of growth in the late eighties and a general downward trend in annual bonus rates.

Bonus statement for a low-cost £40,000 endowment mortgage ending in 2010

Life insured	Smith A and Jones B	
Policy number	A-B 123789 W	
With-profits sum insured	£13,760	The guaranteed sum assured to which the bonus is added
Existing annual bonus	£9,104.80	The bonus that has been added in previous years
New bonus added at 31.12.97	£708.20	The bonus being added this year. (The bonus rate is 2.5% on the with-profits sum insured and 4% on the existing bonus)
Total annual bonus	£9,813.00	Amount guaranteed to be paid in full as long as all contributions are paid and the policy is not altered or cashed in early
Year policy first participated in bonus	1985	

The total payment on death is guaranteed to be no less than £40,000

Source: Norwich Union

The attraction of a low-cost endowment mortgage for lenders is the commission that they receive for selling you the insurance policy. They do not get commission for selling you a repayment mortgage (where you pay both interest and capital so that the amount of your loan gradually goes down), even though this is a cheaper and better option for most people. However, if you plan to move a lot, an interest-only mortgage backed by an investment can be worth considering – although the investment does not have to be an insurance policy.

With-profits bonds

Most with-profits policies are regular-savings products, but to invest in a with-profits bond you need a lump sum of £1,000 or more that you can afford to tie up for at least five years. Your lump sum buys units in a with-profits fund and grows by having bonuses added to it in the same way as a unitised with-profits savings plan (see page 263). Most insurers allow you to cash in part of the bond each year to take as an 'income'. Whenever you cash in the bond, there is no further tax to pay on the proceeds unless you are a higher-rate taxpayer. However, there are special rules if the proceeds from your bond take you into the higher-rate tax band; special rules also allow higher-rate taxpayers to put off paying tax on the proceeds by cashing in parts of the bond. These special rules make all insurance bonds particularly attractive to higher-rate taxpayers. For more details on how investment-type life insurance is taxed, see *Which? Way to Save Tax 1998-9* published by Which? Books.*

With-profits whole-of-life policies

This is essentially life insurance in the form of a with-profits savings plan which pays out a lump sum on your death. Once you start paying premiums, you carry on doing so for the whole of your life (hence the name), although in practice you stop having to pay premiums once you reach a certain age (e.g. 80 or 85). The main reason for buying this sort of life insurance rather than straight term insurance (see Chapter 10) is to cover possible future inheritance tax bills which may arise on your death. Although these policies do build up a cash-in value, it is likely to be fairly low, and by cashing in you lose the life cover. Certain forms of unit-linked whole-of-life policies could be a better choice (see Chapter 21).

With-profits personal pension plans

If you take out a regular-premium with-profits personal pension, your contributions are invested in the same way as a conventional or unitised with-profits savings plan, so you need to be prepared to commit yourself to making contributions over the long term. Alternatively, you can invest a lump sum in a single-premium with-profits plan or buy units in one of the range of funds available with a unit-linked plan – both options work like a with-profits bond (see page 265). Buying with-profits benefits means that this part of your pension fund will be guaranteed at retirement (see the statement below). For more on personal pensions and their different tax treatment, see Chapter 18.

Statement of with-profits retirement benefits

	Guaranteed value which will be paid at retirement	Non-guaranteed final bonus (the actual amount payable will be determined at retirement)	Total value
Value of benefits as at 31 December 1996	£13,801.58	£477.60	£14,279.18
Benefits purchased during 1997 (allowing for initial charge)	£1,816.89	n/a	£1,816.89
Enhancements of benefits purchased in 1997 as a result of reduced charge	£19.03	n/a	£19.03
Guaranteed interest and bonus declared in 1997	£981.75	n/a	£981.75
Change in final bonus in 1997	n/a	£1,013.39	£1,013.39
Value of benefits as at 31 December 1997	£16,619.25	£1,490.99	£18,110.24

Source: The Equitable Life Assurance Society

Investment-linked with-profits annuities

This type of annuity is linked to a with-profits fund which pays an income in the form of the bonuses. The initial income can be high compared with a non-investment type annuity, but the bonuses are not guaranteed and so neither is the income. For more on how annuities work, see Chapter 19.

School fee plans

These are simply with-profits savings plans and/or bonds dressed up as a way of saving up to pay school fees, but you need to start paying in at least ten years before your child is ready to start school.

Buying your policy

If you have decided that a with-profits policy is definitely what you are looking for and you are prepared to commit yourself to paying premiums over the long term, the key factors to consider when buying a policy are performance, commission and charges. You can get hold of performance data by consulting specialist magazines such as *Money Management*★ and *Planned Savings*★ or by using one of the fax services★ available. Anyone who sells this type of policy should be authorised under the Financial Services Act (see Chapter 22) and so should provide information on charges and commission in the key features document they are required to give you. In addition, they should give you an illustration of what the policy will be worth if you surrender it early. You can also ask for a with-profits guide explaining how the company sets bonus levels among other things.

Your options if you stop paying premiums

To get the best from a with-profits policy, you have to keep paying the premiums for the length of time agreed when you took it out. However, if you find that you cannot keep to your original commitment, there are steps that you can take to make sure that the money you have paid out is not completely wasted. The obvious option is to cash in the policy but this is rarely a good idea because you may not get back what you have paid in premiums; if you surrender in the early years, you may get nothing back. (Note that cashing in is not an option for with-profits pensions and annuities.)

There are alternatives, but whether they are viable options depends on how long you have been paying into your policy and whether your insurer will agree to offer them. Note that none of the following alternatives apply if your policy is only a couple of years old.

- **Partial surrender** You cash in the bonuses you have built up so far but you continue to pay premiums. This way you get cash, but the future growth of the policy is based on a smaller amount.
- **Make the policy paid up** You stop paying premiums but keep the policy, which continues to grow to the end of the term. You do not get cash straightaway and you will get a smaller payout at the end than you would have if you had carried on paying premiums. With personal pension plans, this is your only option.
- **Borrow** You get a loan secured against the cash-in value of the policy but continue to pay the premiums. This is a flexible and cheap way of raising cash while maximising the policy benefits, but it will not help if you cannot afford the premiums – unless you use the cash from the loan.
- **Sell the policy** If your policy has been running for at least seven years and has a cash-in value of at least £1,500, you may be able to sell the policy on the traded endowment market (the buyer takes over payment of the premiums and gets the benefits on maturity or when you die). You will get a better price than if you cash in the policy. You can sell your policy at auction, to a market maker or through an intermediary. Auctioneers (look out for advertisements in the press) charge a fee based on the cash-in value of the policy or on the difference between this and the price realised. Market makers will provide a free valuation of your policy and charge no fee if you decide to sell – contact the Association for Policy Market Makers★ for a fact sheet and list of its members. Intermediaries (known as 'trawlers') charge a fee but cover the market to get the best deal from market makers. Contact the Association of Policy Traders★ for a list of trawlers. Using a trawler or market maker is convenient but you are likely to get the best price at auction – you can set a minimum reserve price which should be no less than the cash-in value you can get from the insurer.

Chapter 21

Unit-linked policies

From April 1999 you will be able to use part of your savings in an Individual Savings Account (ISA) to buy investment-type life insurance, so unit-linked policies will start to look more attractive than they have in the past. If you are a higher-rate taxpayer – or a very active investor – this sort of investment-type life insurance has always been worth considering. However, if you cannot afford to take a risk with your money, do not invest in a unit-linked policy. If you just want life insurance, look elsewhere.

How unit-linked policies work

Unit-linked policies give you a combination of life insurance and a unit-trust-type investment. Your premiums (less charges) buy units in one or more of the insurer's investment funds of which there is usually a choice. The most common types of funds are:

- **equity funds** which invest in shares both in the UK and abroad, either directly or through a unit trust
- **fixed-interest funds** which invest in British Government Stocks (gilts), company loan stocks and other investments which pay out a fixed income
- **property funds** which invest in office blocks, factories, shops and so on
- **cash funds** which invest in bank deposit accounts and other investments where the return varies in line with interest rates in general
- **managed funds** which invest in a wide range of assets, which might include gilts, shares and property

- **unitised with-profits funds** where your units increase in value by having bonuses added – see Chapter 20 for more details.

The value of your policy is directly linked to the price of the units in the fund, which can go up and down in line with the underlying investments – so these policies tend to be riskier than with-profits policies. You can usually spread your invested premium over several funds and you can also switch your money from one fund to another. If you die before the policy comes to an end, the insurer pays out the amount of the life insurance or the value of the units if this is higher. The life cover is paid for either by deducting an amount from your premium before it is used to buy units or by cashing in units to generate the money needed to pay for the life insurance.

Warning

You should not buy a unit-linked policy without first considering other investments that may be more suitable for your personal situation. For more information on the investment options open to you, see *Which? Way to Save and Invest*; for guidance on financial planning and strategic investing, see *Be Your Own Financial Adviser*; for more detail on the taxation of investment-type life insurance, see *Which? Way to Save Tax 1998–9*, all published by Which? Books.*

Choosing the right policy

Unit-linked life insurance comes in several different forms, although the way in which your money is invested is the same whichever sort of policy is on offer. Where the products differ is broadly in the way in which you pay your premiums, the length of time you are expected to invest for, and the amount of life insurance built into the policy. The types of unit-linked insurance on offer include:

- unit-linked savings plans (the same as unit-linked endowment policies)

- low-cost unit-linked endowment policies linked to a mortgage
- flexible whole-of-life policies
- single-premium bonds
- unit-linked personal pension plans
- unit-linked annuities
- school fee plans.

Unit-linked savings plans

This is the generic term given to regular-premium unit-linked savings plans where you agree to pay premiums at regular intervals for a minimum of ten years (for tax reasons). Pulling out early is costly because you may get less than you have paid in premiums. The amount of life cover you get depends on the type of unit-linked savings plan you buy:

- **maximum investment plans** give you just enough life cover to make the policy 'qualifying' for tax purposes so they are primarily an investment vehicle
- **endowment plans** give you more life cover and tend to last for up to 25 years.

If you need to stop paying premiums after a couple of years or so, you can make the policy 'paid up', which means that you stop paying premiums but your investment continues to grow (provided the unit price rises) until the end of the term.

Unit-linked endowment policies linked to a mortgage

This is a riskier version of the low-cost with-profits endowment mortgage. Because the value of the lump sum that you are building up over the term of the mortgage can fall as well as rise, you take the risk that you will not have a sufficiently large lump sum to pay off the loan. For more on how low-cost endowment mortgages work, see Chapter 20.

Flexible whole-of-life policies

Whole-of-life policies are investment-type life insurance which has no fixed term so that it pays out whenever you die (provided you have paid your premiums). 'Flexible whole-of-life' is the name given to unit-linked whole-of-life insurance, which allows you to choose how much of your premium will be used to provide life insurance and how much will be used for investment. 'Flexible' refers to the fact that the balance between protection and investment can be varied throughout your life. These can be worth considering as an alternative to straight term insurance (see Chapter 10) if you choose 'maximum protection' – i.e. the highest level of life cover. This is because they can work out cheaper in the early years but premiums may have to rise if the investment part does not do sufficiently well to fund the high level of life cover (units are cashed in to pay for this). The alternative to a possible increase in premiums is a reduction in the amount of life cover. If you choose minimum protection, most of your premiums are invested and you get very little life cover.

Single-premium bonds

If you want to invest in a single-premium bond, you need a lump sum which you are prepared to tie up for several years. Single-premium bonds (which are a form of whole-of-life insurance) provide very little life cover and so should be viewed primarily as an investment akin to a unit trust – although switching between funds in a single-premium bond tends to be cheaper than switching between different sorts of unit trust. Most insurers allow you to cash in part of the bond each year to take as an 'income'. Whenever you cash in the bond, there is no further tax to pay on the proceeds unless you are a higher-rate taxpayer. However, there are special rules if the proceeds from your bond take you into the higher-rate tax band and also special rules which allow higher-rate taxpayers to put off paying tax on the proceeds from cashing in parts of the bond. These special rules make all insurance bonds particularly attractive to higher-rate taxpayers. For more details on how investment-type life insurance is taxed, see *Which? Way to Save Tax 1998-9* published by Which? Books.*

Unit-linked personal pension plans

A unit-linked personal pension plan works exactly like other unit-linked policies except that you cannot get at your investment until you choose to take your pension. A unit-linked personal pension is riskier than the with-profits version (unless you can buy units in a with-profits fund) but provides greater scope for growth if you have a long time to go until retirement. For more on personal pension plans, see Chapter 18.

Unit-linked annuities

This type of annuity is tied to a unit-linked investment and so the income you get from it depends on the performance of the investment fund. The income can vary from year to year and might be very low in some years. For more on how annuities work, see Chapter 19.

School fee plans

This is the name given to ten-year unit-linked savings plans (see page 271) used to plan ahead for the potential cost of school fees. Other investments can do this job equally well.

Buying your policy

The main factors you need to consider when buying a policy are consistently good performance in the past, commission and charges. You can get hold of performance data by consulting specialist magazines such as *Money Management*,* *Planned Savings*,* and by using the available fax services.* Anyone who sells this type of policy must be authorised under the Financial Services Act (see Chapter 22) and so must provide information on charges and commission in the 'key features' document they are required to give you.

Chapter 22

Buying insurance as an investment

If you are sold insurance as an investment – which includes personal pensions – the person selling to you must be authorised to do so and must follow certain procedures when giving you advice. This does not mean that you are protected from financial loss if your investment does not perform as well as you had hoped, but it does mean that you can seek redress if you lose money as a result of bad advice, dishonesty or negligence. You will also have access to compensation if the business you buy from goes bust.

By the end of 1999, a new super-regulator in the form of a streamlined and more efficient Financial Services Authority (FSA)* with more extensive powers should have emerged, a reformed Financial Services Act will have been drafted and a new system for consumer complaints and compensation will have been put into place. In the meantime, you will see an increased emphasis on consumer awareness (for example, as we go to press television advertisements are planned, to encourage pension mis-selling victims to come forward) and gradual changes in the way complaints and compensation are dealt with. However, the rules for what should happen at point of sale – which is what this chapter deals with – look set to remain largely unchanged. Note that the rules for non-insurance-based investments (for example, shares) are slightly different and are not discussed here.

Making the rules work for you

Everyone selling insurance as an investment must follow a set of rules when doing business with you. If they fail to follow those rules, they can be fined or closed down. Knowing what those rules are can help you to avoid bad advice. In practical terms it means getting answers to the following questions (the importance of which is explained in more detail, below):

- is your adviser authorised?
- what is he or she authorised to do?
- is he or she competent?
- who does your adviser represent?
- how will you pay your adviser?
- is the person giving you advice?
- has he or she asked the right questions?
- has he or she given you detailed information about the product(s) recommended?
- can you change your mind?
- has your adviser given you reasons for recommending a particular product?

Is your adviser authorised?

Anyone selling you – or advising you on – a pension or other investment-type insurance must be authorised under the Financial Services Act, which includes business conducted over the Internet. The Financial Services Authority is responsible for authorisation but currently delegates these powers to the Personal Investment Authority★ (PIA) for full-time investment advisers and to Recognised Professional Bodies★ (RPBs) for people who give advice as an adjunct to their main business (accountants and actuaries, for example). (The RPBs are: the Association of Chartered Certified Accountants, the Institute of Actuaries, the three Institutes of Chartered Accountants in England and Wales, Ireland, and Scotland, the Insurance Brokers Registration Council, and the three Law Societies.) If you deal with an adviser who is not authorised, you lose access to the Investors Compensation Scheme★ if he or she runs off with your money or goes bust. You can check whether an insurer or adviser is authorised by contacting the FSA Central Register.★

> **Warning**
>
> Authorisation is not for life. As part of its regulatory duties, the PIA monitors compliance with its rules and has the power – which it uses – to withdraw or refuse authorisation. It is therefore important to check a firm's *current* authorisation status. If you have been approached by a firm which is not authorised, report it to the PIA.

What is your adviser authorised to do?

Advisers are supposed to tell you what types of investment they are authorised to sell and also whether they are authorised to handle your money when you start to do business with them (this will be set out in a 'terms of business' letter which you should receive). The FSA Central Register also has these details.

Is your adviser competent?

Anyone who advises on or sells investments must pass parts 1, 2 and 3 of the Financial Planning Certificate as a minimum. Experienced advisers may demonstrate their competence by taking further examinations – the Advanced Financial Planning Certificate, for example – and/or undergoing regular assessments. All advisers must undertake appropriate Continuing Development. Advisers who want to specialise in pensions can also take the pensions examination of the Advanced Financial Planning Certificate or can obtain one of the following qualifications (look for the letters in brackets after their name):

- Associate of the Pensions Management Institute (APMI)
- Fellow of the Pensions Management Institute (FPMI)
- Associate of the Chartered Insurance Institute (ACII)
- Fellow of the Chartered Insurance Institute (FCII).

Who does your adviser represent?

An adviser must tell you whether he or she is an independent financial adviser (IFA) who is able to advise on the products of any company or whether he or she is a tied agent or company representative who can advise only on the products of one particular company. For more on choosing an adviser and getting good advice, see *Be Your Own Financial Adviser*, published by Which? Books.★

How will you pay your adviser?

Advisers – whether tied or independent – must tell you how you will pay them, which can either be on a commission basis (i.e. their commission is taken from your money before it is invested) or by paying a fee, or a combination of both.

Is the person giving you advice?

It is important to establish whether the person you are dealing with is giving you *advice* on a product or whether he or she is dealing on an 'execution-only' basis. If the latter, the adviser is not required to find out as much information about you or to make sure that the product is suitable for you, because he or she will simply be following your orders. If you act on an execution-only basis, you give up some of the protection you get by taking advice.

Has the person asked the right questions?

The 'know your customer' rule is key. The way in which your adviser gets to know you is by conducting a 'fact find', which should cover full personal details such as your age, your income, your tax position and your existing financial commitments. In the case of pensions advice, the fact find should also ask about the benefits you have already built up under the state scheme, past and present employers' and personal pension schemes and when you are hoping to start drawing your pension. Without this information, the adviser is unlikely to be able to give you 'best advice' which means recommending products only which are suitable for you given what the adviser knows from the fact find. An independent adviser must also look for the most suitable providers. Both types of adviser should tell you if the products they are authorised to advise on (or sell) are *not* suitable for you.

You should also feel free to volunteer or emphasise information that you think is relevant, or that you feel particularly strongly about, such as not wanting to commit yourself to regular saving, not wanting to tie your money up for more than a certain number of years or not wanting to invest in certain sorts of companies for ethical reasons. Make sure your wishes are reflected in the fact find.

Has the adviser given you detailed information about the product(s) recommended?

Before you make a decision about buying a personal pension or other insurance as an investment, you should receive detailed information in the form of a 'key features' document, which should also contain an 'illustration' of projected benefits taking into account the provider's charges and using standard growth rates laid down by the PIA. These are 5 and 10 per cent for most policies and 6 and 12 per cent for pensions. This means that you can compare the costs of similar products. If you are recommended a product which is invested on a with-profits basis, you can also ask for a 'with-profits guide'. What these two documents contain is described in more detail below.

Key features document   This should have in it details of the key features of the policy or pension including:

- the nature and aim of the product
- the risks involved
- the commitment required by you
- description of the main terms of the product set out in a question-and-answer format
- a warning about the effects of cashing in early
- a statement telling you about the effect of charges on the growth rate and what the charges are for
- details of the amount of commission that will be paid to your adviser
- an illustration using PIA standard growth rates (see above), your age, sex, the premiums you want to pay, and proposed retirement age (for pensions). The illustration should also show what you could expect to get back in the first five years, every fifth year after that and the final year. Illustrations for pension products will also take inflation into account so that you get an idea of what the projected benefits mean in today's money.

The key features document and the illustration contain useful information which you should read very carefully before buying. The illustration is particularly useful if you want to compare one product with another.

With-profits guide   If you buy a policy or pension which is invested on a with-profits basis (see Chapter 20), you can also ask for a copy of the with-profits guide. The kind of information you can expect to find in this includes details of:

- what the with-profits fund invests in
- how bonuses are set and the reasons why
- how expenses affect investment returns
- recent payouts on with-profits policies just ended
- the insurer's status (i.e. mutual or owned by shareholders) and financial solvency.

Can you change your mind?

If you decide to go ahead and invest, the person advising you should tell you that you have the right to change your mind within 14 days. After you have sent your money to the provider of the product – or have handed it over to your adviser if he or she is authorised to handle clients' money – you should receive a 'cancellation notice' to enable you to do this. Note that you must cancel within 14 days of receiving this notice if you are to get your money back in full.

Has your adviser given reasons for recommending a particular product?

After you have paid your money over, you should receive a 'reason why' letter in which the person who sold you the product sets out the reasons for recommending it to you and the basis for the advice given.

Getting problems sorted out

If you think you have been given bad advice or you think that the person advising you has not followed the rules for giving you advice, you should complain. First write to the firm that gave you the advice. It is obliged, by law, to investigate and assess your complaint. If you are unhappy with how your complaint is handled or you reach deadlock, contact the firm's regulatory body – the firm should have told you which this is but if it doesn't, contact FSA Public Enquiries★ which can point you in the right direction (currently most likely to be the PIA Ombudsman★).

Chapter 23

How to complain

If you make a valid claim and it is reduced or rejected, or if you think your insurer is taking too long to deal with your claim, complain to your insurer or broker. If you are not satisfied with the response you get – or you fail to get a response at all – take the matter further (see below for how to do this).

If you are not happy with the advice you get when buying insurance as an investment, do not simply take your business elsewhere – make use of the complaints mechanism that the insurer is legally obliged to have in place and tell the regulator (by contacting the Personal Investment Authority or FSA Public Enquiries*) if you are not satisfied with the way in which your complaint has been handled.

As part of the streamlining of the regulation of the financial services industry, consultation is taking place about making the system for dealing with unresolved consumer complaints more efficient. It has been proposed that all complaints and redress procedures should be brought under the authority of a single financial services ombudsman, but how this will work in practice will not been known until well into 1999. In the meantime, the systems described in this chapter will continue to apply.

Complaints procedures

If you have a complaint about insurance, your first stop should always be the insurer from which you bought your policy or investment (even if you bought it through an intermediary or adviser) or your broker if you have a Lloyd's policy. Insurers that sell pensions or investments are legally obliged to have in place a mechanism for dealing with complaints. Insurers that sell general insurance (see

Chapters 2 to 17) are not – although in practice they do operate complaints procedures (you should either be given details when you take out the insurance, or you will find the information in the policy document).

Making your complaint

Your insurer should tell you which department to complain to. If it does not, write to the claims manager stating that you wish to make a complaint. Your complaint is likely to be more successful if you follow these steps:

- Act quickly: complain as soon as you can, while the details are still fresh in your mind.
- Gather supporting evidence (e.g. photographs of damage).
- Complain in writing, including key information such as the number of your policy.
- State clearly what you want – if you are seeking compensation or you want the amount you have been offered in settlement of a claim increased, say by how much and why. If appropriate, itemise your out-of-pocket expenses.
- Ask for your letter to be acknowledged and for the insurer to tell you by what date it intends to resolve the matter. If you do not already know, ask if the insurer belongs to an ombudsman scheme.
- Keep all documents and copies of your letters and make a record of any telephone calls noting the date, time, name of the person you spoke to and details of what was said.
- If you have not heard anything after two weeks, write again.
- If you have not heard anything after four weeks, refer your complaint to a higher level of the insurer's complaints procedure. If your complaint is about the time it has taken for a claim to be dealt with, and your insurer is a member of the Insurance Ombudsman scheme, see the box opposite.
- If the insurer makes you an offer in 'full and final settlement', remember that if you accept it, you are unlikely to be able to ask for more later.
- If you reach deadlock at the highest level of the insurer's complaints procedure, take your complaint further – see opposite.

Taking the matter further

Once you have reached deadlock with the insurer (but see box, below), you can still take the matter further. Who you turn to depends on the type of insurance that you have a problem with.

Unresolved complaints about general insurance

There are currently two schemes set up to deal with deadlocked complaints about general (i.e. non-investment-type) insurance: the Insurance Ombudsman Bureau★ (IOB), to which most general insurers belong; and the Personal Insurance Arbitration Service★ (PIAS), to which a handful of insurers belong. The Insurance Ombudsman Bureau can make awards of up to £100,000 (£20,000 a year for awards relating to permanent health insurance) which are binding on the company, provided that you bring a complaint within six months of reaching deadlock. The Personal Insurance Arbitration Service can also make binding awards of up to £100,000. If you are not happy with the decision of either scheme, you can take the matter to court. Note that neither scheme can deal with a complaint you have about an intermediary who sold you a policy.

No more shilly-shallying

Since April 1998, if your insurer is a member of the Insurance Ombudsman's scheme, the Ombudsman will intervene on your behalf if your insurer is taking too long to process an insurance claim. If you do not get a reply to your claim within four weeks or so, contact the Insurance Ombudsman Bureau.* The Ombudsman will then inform your insurer that it has eight weeks to deal with your claim. If your claim has not been settled to your satisfaction within that time, the Ombudsman will automatically investigate your case as a complaint against the insurer. Since this costs the insurer £500, it is likely to respond to earlier chivvying.

Unresolved complaints about Lloyd's policies

If you have a problem with a Lloyd's policy and your broker has been unable to resolve your complaint, you can take the matter further by writing to the Complaints Department at Lloyd's.* The department will undertake a full investigation and make a recommendation as to how the problem should be solved. If you are not happy with the recommendation, you can take your complaint to the Insurance Ombudsman Bureau.

Unresolved complaints about investment-type insurance

Complaints about investment-type insurance (i.e. those products regulated by the Financial Services Act) are dealt with by the Personal Investment Authority (PIA) Ombudsman,* membership of which is compulsory for insurers selling personal pensions and other investment-type insurance. There is also a voluntary part which members can choose to join for some forms of insurance. The compulsory part currently has a limit on awards of £100,000 (plus up to £1,500 for distress and inconvenience); the voluntary part also has a limit of £100,000 and no restrictions on the awards for distress. You must make your complaint within six months of reaching deadlock with your insurer.

When things go horribly wrong

If your insurer goes out of business, you should be covered by the Policyholders' Protection Act. In the case of general insurance, this means that you are guaranteed to receive 90 per cent of any valid claim which your insurer is unable to meet (100 per cent in the case of car insurance). In the case of life insurance (including investment-type life insurance), the Policyholders' Protection Board will find another insurer to take you on. The Act guarantees that, provided you carry on paying premiums, at the end of the policy term you will get 90 per cent of the guaranteed sum at the time your original insurer went out of business.

If an insurer from which you bought investment-type insurance – including personal pensions – goes out of business and you lose money as a result, the Investors Compensation Scheme* will normally step in. It can compensate you fully for the first £30,000 of your loss and for 90 per cent of the next £20,000 lost – a total of £48,000.

Glossary

ABI Abbreviation for Association of British Insurers (see below).

Accident insurance Insurance which pays out a lump sum if you suffer certain specified injuries, such as loss of a limb or loss of sight.

Accident-sickness-unemployment insurance See Loan payment protection insurance.

Activity of daily living Description of certain basic human functions (e.g. eating, washing and dressing) used as a measure to assess the validity of claims, particularly in the context of long-term care insurance but also some other health-linked insurance.

Actuary A specialist in statistics who calculates insurance risks and premiums.

Additional Voluntary Contributions Extra pension contributions you make to boost the pension you will get from an employer's pension scheme.

ADL Abbreviation for Activity of daily living (see above).

All-risks Insurance which covers any loss or damage (except for exclusions), as opposed to that caused by specific occurrences.

Annuitant Person to whom the income from an annuity is paid.

Annuity A lump sum investment which buys you an income for a fixed number of years or for life; you do not get the lump sum back.

Appliance insurance Mechanical breakdown insurance you can take out against the cost of repairs to domestic appliances and other electrical goods.

Appropriate personal pension Type of personal pension used to contract out of the State Earnings-Related Pension Scheme (SERPS).

Association of British Insurers Body which represents insurance companies.

Assurance Term used for insurance which will pay out for something that *will* happen (e.g. death) as opposed to something that *may* happen (e.g. fire). These days, life assurance and life insurance are used interchangeably.

AVCs Abbreviation for Additional Voluntary Contributions (see page 285).

Averaging Reducing a claim in proportion to any under-insurance.

Bedroom-rated policy Buildings or contents insurance which bases the sum insured on the number of bedrooms in your home.

Benefit The money paid when a claim is made under insurance related to your health (e.g. permanent health insurance and life insurance).

Betterment Term used when a claim makes you better off than you were before loss or damage occurred; your claim will either be reduced or you will have to repay some of what you received in settlement of your claim.

BIIBA Abbreviation for British Insurance and Investment Brokers' Association (see below).

British Insurance and Investment Brokers' Association Body which represents insurance brokers.

Broker See Insurance broker.

Buildings insurance Insurance which covers the fabric of your home.

Car insurance Compulsory insurance if you want to drive a car on a public road.

Certificate of motor insurance Document issued by insurers to confirm that insurance has been taken out in accordance with the requirements of the Road Traffic Act.

Claim What you have to do in order to get payment under an insurance policy.

Claims and Underwriting Exchange Register Database of information taken from insurance application and claim forms, and used by insurers to combat fraud.

Commission Money taken from your premiums by an insurer to pay the intermediary who sold their policy.

Company agent In the context of general insurance, an insurance company employee who sells only his or her employer's policies, or an agent selling the policies of a maximum of six insurance companies. See also Tied agent.

Company representative In the context of investment-type insurance, a salesperson authorised only to advise on, or sell, the products of the company that he or she works for.

Compulsory excess The amount of money which the insurer requires you to pay towards a claim.

Compulsory purchase annuity An annuity that you buy with the fund you have built up in a personal pension plan or employer's scheme.

Condition Requirement of a policy that you must meet for any claim under the insurance to be valid (e.g. to take reasonable care of your belongings, or to claim within a certain number of days).

Contents insurance Insurance against loss or damage of your possessions.

Convertible term insurance Term insurance that carries the option (for which you pay extra) to convert to investment-type life insurance.

Cover The protection your policy gives you.

Cover note In the context of car insurance, a temporary document confirming cover until the policy or certificate of insurance is issued.

Credit insurance Another name for loan payment protection insurance.

Creditor insurance Another name for loan payment protection insurance.

Critical illness insurance Insurance which pays out a lump sum if you are diagnosed with, or suffer from, any of a specified list of life-threatening conditions.

Decreasing term insurance Term insurance where the amount that will be paid out on death during the term reduces by a fixed amount each year.

Deferment period See Deferred period.

Deferred period In the context of insurance to protect income, an agreed period of time during which payment is not made on a claim. Generally, the longer the deferred period, the cheaper the premiums.

Dental insurance Insurance which aims to cover the cost of private dental treatment, either as a stand-alone policy or as part of a private medical insurance policy.

Direct insurer Insurance company which sells its policies directly to the public (i.e. not through insurance intermediaries).

Disclosure A person's obligation to tell his or her insurer everything that might influence its assessment of the risk it is taking on.

Endorsement An amendment or addition to an insurance policy that becomes part of the policy.

Endowment mortgage Interest-only mortgage linked to an investment-type life insurance policy.

Endowment policy Investment-type life insurance which provides for payment of a certain sum following a specified number of years, or on death (whichever comes first).

Excess The first part of a claim paid by the policyholder. If the amount of the loss is less than the excess, there is no point in claiming.

Exclusion Something which is not covered by the policy.

***Ex gratia* payment** Any payment an insurer makes which is not strictly required under the terms of the policy.

Extension An addition to an existing policy that extends the cover without the need to take out an extra policy (e.g. an 'all-risks' extension to a contents policy to cover belongings outside the home).

Family income benefit policy Term insurance which pays out a series of lump sums until the end of a specified term.

Financial Services Act 1986 The legislation under which investment-type insurance and its advisors and sellers are authorised.

Financial Services Authority The regulator responsible for implementing the Financial Services Act.

Flexible whole-of-life insurance A whole-of-life insurance policy invested on a unit-linked basis which can be used for insurance and/or investment purposes. It is 'flexible' because you can vary the amount of life cover.

Free-standing Additional Voluntary Contributions Additional voluntary contributions you make to a scheme that you take out independently to boost your pension from an employer's pension scheme.

Friendly society Similar to a mutual insurance company in that a friendly society is owned by (and set up for) the benefit of its members, to whom it offers life insurance and sickness insurance.

FSA Abbreviation for Financial Services Authority.

FS Act Abbreviation used by the FSA to refer to the Financial Services Act.

FSAVCs Abbreviation for Free-standing Additional Voluntary Contributions (see page 288).

Green card A document issued to policyholders who intend to drive abroad as evidence of minimum insurance legally required in the country visited (not necessary in Europe since UK policies include minimum legal cover).

Hazardous activity Any activity you take part in which – in the insurer's view – makes you a higher-than-average risk.

Holiday insurance The popular name for travel insurance.

Hospital cash plan Insurance which pays out a modest cash sum in specified circumstances (e.g. if you have to go into hospital, you need dental treatment, or you become pregnant).

IBRC Abbreviation for Insurance Brokers Registration Council (see page 290).

IFA Abbreviation for independent financial adviser (see below).

Illustration An example showing the proceeds you might get from an investment-type life insurance policy or pension plan.

Immediate annuity An annuity where the income starts being paid immediately, or shortly, after purchase.

Impaired life annuity An annuity paying better-than-normal rates to someone whose life expectancy is shorter than average.

Impaired Lives Register Record kept by insurers of people who have been refused life insurance or who have had their premiums loaded on medical grounds.

Income protection insurance See Permanent health insurance.

Increasable term insurance Term insurance where the amount of cover (and the premium) can be increased – either at certain times or on given events, such as the birth of a child.

Increasing term insurance Term insurance where the amount of cover and the premium automatically increase during the term, either by a set percentage each year or in line with inflation.

Indemnity The basic principle of insurance, which means that insurance puts you back to the same financial position you were in before you suffered loss or damage.

Independent financial adviser Insurance intermediary authorised under the Financial Services Act to advise on, and sell, investment-type insurance and personal pensions from any company.

Index-linking Increasing the amount you are insured for to keep pace with inflation.

Insurable interest A principle of insurance whereby you can take out insurance against something happening only if you stand to lose financially. Everyone has an unlimited insurable interest in their own life.

Insurance adviser Another name for an insurance intermediary (in the context of general insurance, as opposed to investment-type insurance).

Insurance broker An insurance intermediary registered with the Insurance Brokers Registration Council under the Insurance Brokers (Registration) Act 1977.

Insurance Brokers Registration Council Body responsible for insurance brokers.

Insurance consultant See Insurance intermediary.

Insurance intermediary Generic term for someone who sells insurance policies (but does not underwrite them).

Insurance Ombudsman Bureau Independent arbitrator which runs a scheme set up by the insurance industry to deal with consumer complaints about insurers which are members of the scheme.

Insurance premium tax A purchase tax imposed on most non-life insurance premiums.

Insured, the Person or people covered by a policy.

Insurer Insurance company or Lloyd's underwriter which accepts insurance risks (i.e. issues the policy and pays claims).

Investment-type life insurance Life insurance policies which pay out either at the end of a fixed term or on death (whichever comes first).

IPT Abbreviation for insurance premium tax (see above).

Key features document Written information that must be given to an investor about an investment-type life insurance policy or pension plan.

Knock-for-knock An agreement between insurers whereby each pays its own policyholder's claim, regardless of who was to blame for a motoring accident.

Legal expenses insurance Insurance which aims to meet the legal costs of bringing a civil action.

Liability Legal responsibility for injury to another person or damage to another person's property.

Life insurance Insurance which pays out on death (also called life assurance).

Life office Another name for an insurance company which sells life insurance and/or annuities.

Lifetime annuity An annuity which pays you an income for life.

Limit of indemnity The highest amount an insurer can be called on to pay under any policy or section of a policy (separate sections of a policy may each have separate limits).

Lloyd's The London insurance market.

Lloyd's broker Insurance broker entitled to do business at Lloyd's.

Lloyd's underwriter Person or company which issues insurance policies at Lloyd's.

Loan payment protection insurance Insurance which aims to cover loan repayments in the event of sickness and/or unemployment.

Long-term care insurance Insurance which aims to meet the cost of personal or nursing care, either at home or in a residential home.

Long-term disability insurance See Permanent health insurance.

Loss adjuster Person appointed by the insurer to investigate insurance claims.

Loss assessor Person who specialises in negotiating claims on behalf of the policyholder.

Low-cost endowment mortgage A low-cost version of an endowment mortgage.

Material fact Anything that may affect the insurer's view of the risks involved in insuring you (see Disclosure).

Major medical expenses insurance Health insurance which pays out a lump sum if you undergo specified surgery.

Maturity The agreed date when an investment-type life insurance policy will come to an end, or 'mature'.

Maximum protection Option within a flexible whole-of-life insurance policy which gives more life insurance than investment.

Mechanical breakdown insurance Insurance which aims to meet the cost of certain repairs needed to your car, appliances or other electrical goods.

Mortgage indemnity insurance Insurance that some mortgage lenders insist you buy in order to cover them against the risk of your defaulting on the loan.

Mortgage payment protection insurance Loan payment protection insurance which aims to cover mortgage repayments in the event of sickness and/or unemployment.

Mortgage protection insurance Life insurance designed to pay off your mortgage if you die before the mortgage comes to an end.

Motor insurance General term covering insurance for motor vehicles – cars, motorbikes, vans and so on.

Mutual insurance company Insurer set up for the benefit of its policyholders rather than owned by shareholders.

New-for-old Cover that pays for a new replacement for lost or destroyed property (it ignores the principle of betterment).

No-claims discount Traditionally, a reduction in your premium for car insurance as a reward for not claiming; increasingly found with other forms of insurance.

Over-insurance Paying for more cover than you need.

Paid-up policy The name given to an investment-type life insurance policy when premiums stop being paid before the policy comes to maturity.

Payment protection insurance See Loan payment protection insurance.

Payment protection plan See Loan payment protection insurance.

Peril Technical term for the occurrences covered by a policy (e.g. fire).

Permanent health insurance Insurance that replaces part of your income if you are unable to work because of illness or disability.

Personal Investment Authority Body responsible for policing most investment businesses and independent financial advisers (including insurance companies which sell investment-type insurance) that deal with the general public.

Personal pension plan A pension where your contributions are invested in a fund that is used to buy an annuity when you retire.

PHI Abbreviation for permanent health insurance (see above).

PIA Abbreviation for Personal Investment Authority (see above).

PMI Abbreviation for private medical insurance (see opposite).

Policy The document containing the terms of the contract which you and the insurer enter into when you buy insurance.

Policyholder Person to whom the policy is issued.

Policyholders' Protection Act 1975 Legislation providing for a compensation scheme for people who lose money because their insurer has gone out of business.

Pre-existing condition A health problem which you have at the time you apply for insurance.

Premium The price you pay for insurance, or the amount you invest in an investment-type insurance.

Premium loading When the insurer increases your premium to take account of the fact that you are a higher-than-average risk.

Private health insurance See Private medical insurance.

Private medical insurance Insurance which aims to meet the cost of private medical treatment.

Professional indemnity insurance Insurance that insurance intermediaries not tied to a particular company must have in order to meet any liability claims as a result of negligence.

Proposal form The application form you may fill in when buying insurance.

Protection-only life insurance See Term insurance.

Purchased life annuity An annuity which you *choose* to buy, as opposed to a compulsory-purchase annuity.

Rebate-only personal pension See Appropriate personal pension.

Reinsurance Insurance that insurers buy to cover themselves against having to pay out more in claims than they have collected in premiums.

Renewable term insurance Term insurance which guarantees that you can take out a further term insurance policy at the end of the original term.

Renewal notice Document you should receive shortly before an insurance policy is due for renewal.

Replacement as new See New-for-old.

Reversionary bonus Regular bonus added to the sum assured of a with-profits policy.

Risk The name given to the item which is insured (e.g. your house is the risk with a buildings policy).

Schedule Section of a policy setting out details of the insured, what is to be insured, any special terms and the premium to be paid.

SERPS Abbreviation for State Earnings-Related Pension Scheme (see below).

Sickness and accident insurance A combination of accident insurance and sickness insurance which pays a weekly cash lump sum for a limited amount of time if you are unable to work due to short-term illness.

Single-premium bond Investment-type life insurance where you invest a lump sum.

State Earnings-Related Pension Scheme State pension scheme which pays an earnings-related pension on top of the basic state pension to employees who earn enough money to pay National Insurance.

Sum assured The amount that will be paid out from a life insurance (assurance) policy.

Sum insured The maximum that a policy will pay out.

Surrender value The amount you get if you cash in a whole-of-life or regular-premium savings plan early.

Syndicate Group of underwriters at Lloyd's.

Term insurance Life insurance which pays out if you die within a specified period (the 'term').

Terminal bonus Bonus which may or may not be paid when a with-profits policy matures.

Tied agent Intermediary who sells the products of one company or a limited number of companies.

Travel insurance Insurance you buy when travelling abroad.

Under-insurance Buying less insurance cover than you need, with the result that your claims can be reduced in line with the amount of the under-insurance.

Underwriter Company or person that takes on the risk of insuring you and pays your claims.

Uninsured losses Costs which are not covered by your policy, even though they may relate directly to an insurance claim.

Unit-linked policy Investment-type life insurance where the premium you pay is invested in units in various investment funds.

Utmost good faith Translation of the Latin *uberrima fides*, meaning that you and the insurer are supposed to deal fairly and honestly with each other when entering into an insurance contract; you deal honestly with your insurer by disclosing all material facts.

Voluntary excess The amount of money which you agree voluntarily to pay towards any claim in exchange for a reduction in the premium.

Waiver of premium An optional extra you can buy when you take out certain forms of insurance to protect yourself against not being able to pay premiums during a period of prolonged illness.

Warranty insurance See Mechanical breakdown insurance.

Whole-of-life insurance Investment-type life insurance which pays out on death.

With-profits guide Document you can ask for when considering with-profits insurance.

With-profits policy Investment-type life insurance where bonuses are added to the sum assured (or to units in a with-profits fund) and paid out at maturity or on death.

Addresses

Age Concern England
Astral House
1268 London Road
London SW16 4ER
Tel: 0181-679 8000
Fax: 0181-679 6069
Email: infodep@ace.org.uk
Web site: www.ace.org.uk

Age Concern Northern Ireland
3 Lower Crescent
Belfast BT7 1NR
Tel: (01232) 245729
Fax: (01232) 235497

Age Concern Scotland
113 Rose Street
Edinburgh EH2 3DT
Tel: 0131-220 3345
Fax: 0131-220 2779
Email: acs@ccis.org.uk

Age Concern Wales
4th Floor
1 Cathedral Road
Cardiff CF1 9SD
Tel: (01222) 371566
Fax: (01222) 399562
Email: accymru@ace.org.uk

The Annuity Bureau
Enterprise House
59–65 Upper Ground
London SE1 9PQ
Tel: 0171-620 4090
Fax: 0171-261 1888
Email: peter@annuity-bureau.co.uk
Independent financial adviser specialising in annuities

Annuity Direct
32 Scrutton Street
London EC2A 4SS
Tel: 0171-684 5000
Fax: 0171-684 5001
Independent financial adviser specialising in annuities

Association of British Insurers (ABI)
51 Gresham Street
London EC2V 7HQ
Tel: 0171-600 3333
Fax: 0171-696 8996
Web site: www.abi.org.uk
Written enquiries preferred. If checking whether intermediaries have professional indemnity insurance, you must quote their postcode

Association of Chartered Certified Accountants
29 Lincoln's Inn Fields
London WC2A 3EE
Tel: 0171-242 6855
Fax: 0171-831 8054
Email: services.enquiries@acca.co.uk
Web site: www.acca.co.uk
A Recognised Professional Body – see page 275

Association of Consulting Actuaries
1 Wardrobe Place
London EC4V 5AH
Tel: 0171-248 3163
Fax: 0171-236 1889
Email: acahelp@aca.org.uk
Web site: www.aca.org.uk

Association for Policy Market Makers
Holywell Centre
1 Phipp Street
London EC2A 4PS
Tel: 0171-739 3949
Fax: 0171-613 2990
Email: apmm@dircon.co.uk

Association of Policy Traders
Skipton Chambers
12 Market Street
Bury BL9 0AJ
Tel: (0345) 191919
Fax: 0161-797 1919
Email: polreg@cix.co.uk

Belfast Climate Office
32 College Street
Belfast BT1 6BQ
Tel: (01232) 312353
Fax: (01232) 313981
Web site: www.met-office.gov.uk
Call for proof of severe weather relating to claims on buildings insurance in Northern Ireland. A small charge may be made for supplying information

British Diabetic Association
10 Queen Anne Street
London W1M OBD
Tel: 0171-323 1531
Fax: 0171-637 3644
Email: katal@diabetes.org.uk
Web site: www.diabetes.org.uk

British Epilepsy Association
Anstey House
40 Hanover Square
Leeds LS3 1BE
Tel: (0800) 309030 *(helpline)*
Web site: www.epilepsy.org.uk

British Geological Survey
Global Seismology and Geomagnetism Group
Murchison House
West Mains Road
Edinburgh EH9 3LA
Tel: 0131-667 1000
Fax: 0131-667 1877
Email: ukeqs@bgs.ac.uk
Web site: www.gsrg.nmh.ac.uk
For information on earthquakes and earth tremors in support of a buildings or contents insurance claim

British Insurance and Investment Brokers' Association (BIIBA)
14 Bevis Marks
London EC3A 7NT
Tel: 0171-623 9043
Fax: 0171-626 9676
Email: enquiries@biiba.org.uk
Web site: www.biiba.org.uk

Fax services
See page 301

Financial Services Authority (FSA)
Web site: www.fsa.gov.uk
The FSA was in the process of relocating as we went to press but should be fully installed in its new premises by the end of 1998. To contact it, call the FSA Public Enquiries number (see page 298)

FSA Central Register Enquiries
Tel: 0171-929 3652
*To check that your adviser is authorised, give the
name (or trading name), address and telephone
number of the firm's main place of business*

FSA Public Enquiries
Tel: (0845) 6061234
For any enquiries. Calls charged at local rate

**Incorporated Society of Valuers and
Auctioneers**
3 Cadogan Gate
London SW1X 0AS
Tel: 0171-235 2282
Fax: 0171-235 4390
Email: hq@isva.co.uk
Web site: www.isva.co.uk
For insurance valuations

**Independent Financial Advisers'
Association**
12–13 Henrietta Street
London WC2E 8LH
Tel: 0171-240 7878
Fax: 0171-240 7979
Email: webcontrol@ifaa.org.uk

Institute of Actuaries
Staple Inn Hall
High Holborn
London WC1V 7QJ
Tel: 0171-242 0106
Fax: 0171-405 2482
Email: institute@actuaries.org.uk
Web site: www.actuaries.org.uk
A Recognised Professional Body – see page 275

**Institute of Chartered Accountants in
England and Wales**
PO Box 433
Chartered Accountants' Hall
Moorgate Place
London EC2P 2BJ
Tel: 0171-920 8100
Fax: 0171-920 0547
Email: comms@icaew.co.uk
Web site: www.icaew.co.uk
A Recognised Professional Body – see page 275

**Institute of Chartered Accountants in
Ireland**
Chartered Accountants' House
87–89 Pembroke Road
Ballsbridge
Dublin 4
Republic of Ireland
Tel: (00 353) 1 668 0400
Fax: (00 353) 1 668 0842
Email: ca@icai.ie
Web site: www.icai.ie
A Recognised Professional Body – see page 275

**Institute of Chartered Accountants of
Scotland**
27 Queen Street
Edinburgh EH2 1LA
Tel: 0131-225 5673
Fax: 0131-225 3813
Web site: www.icas.org.uk
A Recognised Professional Body – see page 275

Institute of Public Loss Assessors
14 Red Lion Street
Chesham HP5 1HB
Tel: (01494) 782342
Fax: (01494) 774928

**Insurance Brokers Registration Council
(IBRC)**
63 St Mary Axe
London EC3A 8NB
Tel: 0171-621 1061
Fax 0171-621 0840
A Recognised Professional Body – see page 275

Insurance Ombudsman Bureau
City Gate One
135 Park Street
London SE1 9EA
Tel: (0845) 6006666
Fax: 0171-902 8197
Email: complaint@theiob.org.uk
Web site: www.theiob.org.uk

Investors Compensation Scheme
Gavrelle House
2–14 Bunhill Row
London EC1Y 8RA
Tel: 0171-628 8820
Fax: 0171-477 1814

The Law Society
113 Chancery Lane
London WC2A 1PL
Tel: 0171-242 1222
Call for relevant fax number
Web site: www.lawsociety.org.uk
A Recognised Professional Body – see page 275

The Law Society of Northern Ireland
Law Society House
98 Victoria Street
Belfast BT1 3JZ
Tel: (01232) 231614
Fax: (01232) 232606
A Recognised Professional Body – see page 275

The Law Society of Scotland
Law Society Hall
26 Drumsheugh Gardens
Edinburgh EH3 7YR
Tel: 0131-226 7411
Fax: 0131-225 2934
Email: lawscot@lawscot.org.uk
Web site: www.lawscot.org.uk
A Recognised Professional Body – see page 275

Lloyd's of London
Complaints Department
One Lime Street
London EC3M 7HA
Tel: 0171-327 6385
Fax: 0171-327 6975/5225
Web site:
www.lloydsoflondon.co.uk
For complaints relating to policies or insurances underwritten at Lloyd's which your broker has been unable to resolve

Met Office Insurance Consultancy
Johnson House
London Road
Bracknell
Berkshire RG12 2SY
Tel: (01344) 854565
Web site: www.met-office.gov.uk
For proof of severe weather relating to claims on buildings insurance in England and Wales. A small charge may be made for supplying information

Motor Insurers Bureau
152 Silbury Boulevard
Central Milton Keynes
MK9 1NB
Tel: (01908) 240000
Fax: (01908) 671681

Personal Insurance Arbitration Service (PIAS)
Chartered Institute of Arbitrators
24 Angel Gate
City Road
London EC1V 2RS
Tel: 0171-837 4483
Fax: 0171-837 4185
Email: 71411.2735@compuserve.com
Web site: www.arbitrators.org

Personal Investment Authority (PIA)
7th Floor
1 Canada Square
Canary Wharf
London E14 5AZ
Tel: 0171-538 8860
Fax: 0171-418 9300
Ask for the consumer helpline

PIA Ombudsman
Hertsmere House
Hertsmere Road
London E14 4AB
Tel: 0171-216 0016
Fax: 0171-895 8579

Recognised Professional Bodies (RPBs)
See separate entries for:
- **Association of Chartered Certified Accountants**
- **Institute of Actuaries**
- **the three Institutes of Chartered Accountants**
- **Insurance Brokers Registration Council**
- the three **Law Societies**

Research Institute for Consumer Affairs (RICA)
24 Highbury Crescent
London N5 1RX
Tel: 0171-704 5200
Fax: 0171-704 5208

Royal Institution of Chartered Surveyors (RICS)
12 Great George Street
Parliament Square
London SW1P 3AD
Tel: 0171-222 7000
Fax: 0171-695 1505
Web site: www.rics.org.uk
For house rebuilding cost valuations (ask for the Information Centre)

Scottish Climate Office
Wallace House
220 St Vincent Street
Glasgow G2 5QD
Tel: 0141-303 0110
For proof of severe weather relating to claims on buildings insurance in Scotland and bordering parts of England. A small charge will be made for supplying information

Self-Assessment Orderline
PO Box 37
St Austell
Cornwall PL25 5YN
Tel: (0645) 000404 *(daily, 8am–10pm)*
Fax: (0645) 000604
E-mail: saorderline.ir@gtnet.gov.uk
Web site: www.open.gov.uk/inrev/sa
For Inland Revenue help sheets and leaflets

Society of Pension Consultants (SPC)
St Bartholomew House
92 Fleet Street
London EC4Y 1DH
Written enquiries only

PUBLICATIONS
Inclusion in this list of publications and fax services in no way constitutes an endorsement by Consumers' Association or Which?, except in relation to its own publications

The Insurance Buyer's Guide to Schemes, Packages and Unusual Risks
Kluwer Publishing
Croner House
London Road
Kingston-upon-Thames KT2 6SR
Tel: 0181- 547 3333
Fax: 0181-547 2637
Email: info@croner.co.uk

Moneyfacts Life & Pensions
Subscriptions Department
66–70 Thorpe Road
Norwich NR1 1BA
Tel: (01603) 476476
Fax: (01603) 476477

Money Management
FT Finance
PO Box 387
Haywards Heath
West Sussex RH16 3GS
Tel: (01444) 445520
Fax: (01444) 445599
For subscriptions and back issues

Pensions Management
FT Finance
PO Box 387
Haywards Heath
West Sussex RH16 3GS
Tel: (01444) 445520
Fax: (01444) 445599
For subscriptions and back issues

Planned Savings
33–39 Bowling Green Lane
London EC1R 0DA
Tel: 0171-505 8000
Fax: 0171-505 8186
Email: juliad@finance.emap.co.uk

Which? and Which? Books
FREEPOST
PO Box 44
Hertford X, SG14 1YB
Tel: (0800) 252100
Fax: (0800) 533053
Web site: www.which.net

FAX SERVICES

If you have access to a fax machine, you can obtain information by faxing the numbers given below and pressing START at the prompt. Calls are charged at premium rate. The number of pages you may receive is for guidance only and is subject to change. Inclusion in this list of fax services in no way constitutes an endorsement by Consumers' Association or Which?

Moneyfacts
Term insurance premiums (6 pages)
(0336) 400853
Purchased life annuities (5 pages)
(0336) 400235
Compulsory purchase annuities (5 pages)
(0336) 400236
Full-cost with-profits endowment
policies (6 pages)
(0336) 400851
With-profits bonds (8 pages)
(0336) 400857
Low-cost with-profits endowments (6
pages)
(0336) 400850
Unit-linked endowments (5 pages)
(0336) 400852
Calls are charged at 50p per minute

Financial Adviser
Compulsory purchase annuities for men
(0897) 439401
Compulsory purchase annuities for
women
(0897) 439402
Compulsory purchase annuities for joint
lives
(0897) 439403
Purchased life annuities for men
(0897) 439404
Purchased life annuities for women
(0897) 439405
Purchased life annuities for joint lives
(0897) 439406
Calls are charged at around £1.50 per minute

Index

Page references in **bold type** indicate an entry in the Glossary

Which? Way to Save and Invest

Whether you've got £50 or £5,000 to play with, it pays to pick the right investment. Many more people are shareholders as a result of privatisations and building society conversions. But deciding what to do with your spare cash can be a daunting task. You want to make sure that your dependants are protected and that you are prepared for the future, for retirement and for any emergency.

This book helps you to work out an overall investment strategy to suit your financial circumstances and ensure that you make the most of your savings. Written in straightforward language, it covers all the important areas of saving and investing from the traditional choices such as National Savings and banks, to unit trusts, investment trusts and commodities.

Paperback   210 x 120mm   416 pages   £14.99

Available from bookshops, and by post from
Which?, Dept TAZM, Castlemead,
Gascoyne Way, Hertford X, SG14 1LH

You can also order using your credit card
by phoning FREE on (0800) 252100
(quoting Dept TAZM)

Which? Way to
Save Tax 1998-9

With self-assessment in place and a new tax regime in operation, the tax-payer now, more than ever, needs guiding through the complexities of the British tax system. *Which? Way to Save Tax*, fully updated to reflect the changes brought about by the 1998 Budget, helps you to ensure that you are paying the right amount of tax.

Written for the non-specialist, this book helps you to understand and make the most of the new tax rules. It guides investors through the overhaul of capital gains tax – essential reading for the millions of new shareholders created by the conversion of building societies to banks – and explains the biggest shake-up in tax-free investment for over a decade. It offers reliable and independent advice on tax as it affects employment, families, homes, investments, inheritance, pensions and the self-assessment regime.

Which? Way to Save Tax contains the answers to common tax questions, and should also help you work out whether some of the estimated billions of pounds of overpaid tax belong to you.

Paperback   210 x 120mm   352 pages   £14.99

Available from bookshops, and by post from
Which?, Dept TAZM, Castlemead,
Gascoyne Way, Hertford X, SG14 1LH

You can also order using your credit card
by phoning FREE on (0800) 252100
(quoting Dept TAZM)

The Which? Guide to Giving and Inheriting

Giving is easy, but it takes planning to make sure that those to whom you're giving receive as much as possible. Gifts are often wrapped in an unnecessary tax bill or miss out on available tax relief. Even if your means are fairly modest, you may be unwittingly – and needlessly – storing up a tax bill for your heirs.

With the use of handy calculators and over 40 examples of typical situations, *The Which? Guide to Giving and Inheriting* shows you how a knowledge of the tax rules, and taking simple steps such as making a will, can help you to:

- use the tax system to increase the value of your giving
- exercise some control over the way your gifts may be used
- ensure that you pass on your home and possessions intact
- make tax-efficient donations to charities.

Paperback   216 x 135mm   224 pages   £9.99

Available from bookshops, and by post from
Which?, Dept TAZM, Castlemead,
Gascoyne Way, Hertford X, SG14 1LH

You can also order using your credit card
by phoning FREE on (0800) 252100
(quoting Dept TAZM)

Be Your Own Financial Adviser

Financial advice, like any other advice, can be good, bad or indifferent. But armed with the right facts, and some basic techniques, you can be your own financial adviser. This guide shows you how to clarify your financial needs and create a financial plan to meet them, just as a personal adviser would do for you.

Be Your Own Financial Adviser profiles the different products (investments, savings, insurance, loans) available, shows you how they can fit into your financial plan, how to choose the type best suited to you and where to get current information about them. It alerts you to any areas where you could be losing out, such as having savings in uncompetitive accounts, or where you are taking unnecessary risks with investments.

The book also lists the points to check out when you're talking to providers of financial products or financial advisers and how to interpret the information you're given. Simply written and full of useful tips and warnings, the book puts you in charge of your financial destiny.

Paperback   216 x 135mm   352 pages   £9.99

Available from bookshops, and by post from
Which?, Dept TAZM, Castlemead,
Gascoyne Way, Hertford X, SG14 1LH

You can also order using your credit card
by phoning FREE on (0800) 252100
(quoting Dept TAZM)